DID I REMEMBER TO TELL YOU...?

A Pastor's Last Words to His Congregation Before He Retires

THOMAS P. WILLIAMSEN

FOREWORD BY THE REV ROY OSWALD

Did I Remember to Tell You...?
ISBN: 1493552775
ISBN-13: 9781493552771

Thomas P. Williamsen
2013
All Rights Reserved
tomwilliamsen@aol.com

Available through Amazon.com

Scripture are from the New Revised Standard Version
and the New International Version, or are translations by the author

Did I Remember To Tell You...?

A Pastor's Last Words to His Congregation Before He Retires

Thomas P. Williamsen

Foreword by The Rev Roy Oswald

DEDICATION

To my family who supported me,
My friends who encouraged me,
And the members of Gloria Dei! who loved me.

If I took away everything in my life, except for the time I spent at Gloria Dei!, my life would be rich beyond description.

As I look back on our thirty three years together, I realize that all I ever wanted, was to be your pastor.

TABLE OF CONTENTS

FOREWORD

December, 2013

W‌HAT A TREAT to be able to write this foreword to the book by colleague, fellow pilgrim, and friend, Tom Williamsen. This book was a nice surprise in allowing me to see another side of someone I thought I knew fairly well.

I've know Tom for well over 30 years. We are both ordained ELCA clergy but didn't travel in the same circles. I'd always thought of him as rough and tumble, hard working, and slightly overweight. We never had enough extended time together for me to encounter his rich spiritual side and the kind of compassion he had for everyone, especially the ones down on the luck and in trouble with the law. For a parole officer to assign delinquent teen ages to Tom says a lot about how he extended his time with troubled young people. I knew a little about his workaholic behavior when early in his ministry it slipped out that he sometimes stays up most of the night working and then just sleep at the church.

A life changing experience for Tom came some 35 years ago when he attended an Alban Institute workshop I was leading on "Holistic Health and Parish Ministry. Prior to participants having an afternoon off I invited those interested to come outside and do a simple physical conditioning test to ascertain the kind of physical shape they were in. It consisted of stepping on and off a chair 30 times in one minute.

People were to take their pulse prior to the test, then immediately after doing the exercise plus taking it one minute later. One's physical condition is determined by how quickly one's pulse rate drops in one minute after the exercise. Tom did not test well in this exercise which disappointed him. At the end of that session out of doors I indicated that I was going on my daily hour long run and invited anyone who wanted to join me. Tom was the only one who tried. After about a mile he was way behind me but something changed in him during that short run. Somehow, I know he had gotten hooked. Following that workshop, he became an addicted runner, much like me.

Most people do not understand what it means to be an addicted runner. Over the course of 35 years I could not <u>not</u> run everyday. When running strenuously for an hour one often attains a runner's high. The body in physical stress begins producing endorphins in the brain and a euphoric feeling ensues. It is really moving into an altered state of consciousness, and one is able to view oneself, one's life and work from a whole new perspective. In truth it is a chemical additions produced inside one's brain. Most of the 14 books I've written are filled with insights I've had during a run.

Tom also became an addicted runner. He's run marathons. He even completed one 50 mile race in Washington County, Maryland. As he developed into a daily runner he began peeling off excess weight. People in his congregation at the time became real concerned about him as he got thinner and thinner. They thought he might be dying. They kept bringing him cakes and cookies to fatten him back up.

His other addiction was golf. He loves playing on different golf courses around the country. Whenever he would be given an honorarium for doing someone's wedding or funeral, he would save that money to be able to play in another famous golf course in the country or in several other countries. In his home he had huge pictures of his golf idol, Arnold Palmer. In 1985 he played with Palmer in a Pro-am on Hilton Head Island. After 9 holes Tom was one shot behind. Then Tom shot 40 and Palmer shot 31. So much for dreams.

All of this says something of Tom's drive and his determination to be the best he could be. Tom's real passion, as you will come to see, is his complete dedication to be an instrument of God's love to others. He appeared to have incredible stamina for this single minded focus. It comes as no surprise that he started a congregation from scratch and built it up to an average attendance of 300. Total membership now stands at 1100. How many pastors have the kind of winsome personality that can go knocking on people's doors as a complete stranger and entice them to consider becoming part of a new congregation.

As he continued through the years to worm his way into the hearts of his people, he may have missed how these same people where worming their way into his heart. These days in the middle of worship opportunity, he looks out on the congregation and he sees someone in tears. As he admitted to me several months ago, saying good-bye to this congregation is one of the hardest things he's ever undertaken. Right now, this task is tearing him apart. He claims his identity is completely tied up being a pastor of Gloria Dei Lutheran Church and being intimately connected with its members. Without this congregation he doesn't know who he is. I know this too will pass, if it doesn't kill him and it is clear to me that this great lover of God will always find someone in need of a listening ear and a compassionate heart, but in the meantime he has to face into the agony of saying good bye to the people he has nurtured in the faith. For many, Tom is the only pastor they have known. He is going to be a hard act to follow.

What I find most impressive in this book is the depth of spirituality flowing through Tom. Tom is the incarnation of some central parts of scripture. If he preaches the way he writes, Gloria Dei has been feasting on solid spiritual food for years.

A symbol of his spirituality has been his commitment for years to take sabbatical time in a monastery. He doesn't just go stay there to get away, he is a full participant in the monastic community, getting up for all daily offices of prayer, seven plus mass to be exact, including Vigils at 4:00 am, Lauds at 6:00 am, Eucharist at 8:30, Tierce at 9:00, Sext at 9: 50, Sext at 11:4 5, Midday prayer at 1:45, Vespers at 5:20 and Compline at 8:15. There have been weeks of retreat that I have also escaped a Catholic monastery, longing for the time and space for introspection, including eating meals in silence, but I stayed on the periphery of the monastic community. Tom's stay at a monastery is completely different. He became part of the monastic community, attending all seven plus times of prayer in the chapel with the brothers. This says so much about him. The majority of clergy when getting away for sabbatical time want to study at the feet to some biblical or theological scholar as a way of being spiritually revitalized. Tom's way of spiritual renewal is to go to prayer. Deep down he knows that divine wisdom will come to him if he just attends to prayer.

Personally, the surprise for me in this book was how it moved me spiritually. I fell in love with God again. It reminded me what mission in all about—namely to an agents of God's love to a broken and hurting world. It allowed me to see a side of Tom I had never known. I'm envious of his congregation for being able to be touched by his simple, down to earth preaching style on such a regular basis for all these year. What a gift.

As with all good communicators, you tell people what you are going to say to them, then you says it, then you remind them of what you just said to them. This book is nice reminded of what he has been saying to his people for years.

Thanks, brother, for asking me to do this.

Roy M. Oswald

INTRODUCTION

If there is a theme to this book, the following might state it succinctly:
The nearer we are to the heart of God,
the more we long to make a difference to the heart of the world.

THIS LITTLE BOOK dances around that theme. It does so, not in a systematic way, but with little thoughts and devotions. Consequently, the book should not be read in one sitting, but in bits and pieces, and dribs and drabs, allowing some of the thoughts to ruminate and digest in your heart and mind.

Our Lord calls us into an intimate and loving relationship with God, self, and neighbor. Jesus simply said, "'Love the Lord your God with all your heart and with all your soul and with all your strength and with all your mind'; and, 'Love your neighbor as yourself.'" (Luke 10:27)

This book does not pretend to be deep or cover a lot of new ground. The thoughts contained are merely the musings of a retiring pastor, who wants to share some spiritual and theological thoughts with the parishioners he has served loved. I pray that from this petite tome, you might draw some small inspiration for your walk with the Lord.

Thank you to the monks of Bolton Abbey who welcomed me into their community while I finished this book.

Thank you to Paul Stillwell and Donald Smith for editing the manuscript, and to Heather McHugh, for preparing it for publication.

May you rest in God's embrace,
Pastor Tom

Preface

My retreat to Bolton Abbey Monastery

in Ireland

Three months prior to my retirement

November 14-December 7, 2013

Pastors are a most blest people. We preach the Good News that God is present and active in the lives of every person. We teach about cross and resurrection. But, for me, I think the greatest blessing is that I was invited into parishioner's lives and families. We are with families in their most joyous of times. We share weddings, baptisms, births, graduations, confirmations, and the myriad of joys that families celebrate. We do this, not only with members, but, with their extended families. I know so many families: mothers and fathers, sons and daughters, cousins, aunts and uncles. It is an honor to be part of their lives.

We are also invited to be present at some of their most difficult times. Times of great sorrow and distress. We counsel when marriages are in trouble. We meet with young people who just do not know what direction they should go. We see some through addiction problems.

We hold their hands when they die and preside at their funerals. How blest I am. There are some things I would have changed about my ministry, but the time I spent visiting folks in the hospital or their homes, or my office, I cherish. I treasure the relationships. And they brought to me my greatest joys. What an honor.

I made the retreat to assess my life as an ordained Lutheran Pastor, deepen my relationship with God, and become prepared to lead my congregation to a healthy conclusion of our ministry. How we say good-bye will impact how Gloria Dei! says hello to the next Pastor. What follows on these next pages is a small part of the journal I kept on my retreat. It comes with grammatical errors and incomplete sentences. It is just as I wrote it, warts and all. Some of it is pretty personal, but for the sake of honesty I wrote of some painful times.

Retiring was more difficult than I imagined it would be. In very many ways, my work has defined me. I wonder who I will be without it. My identity is intertwined with my call as pastor of Gloria Dei! I feel I was born to be Gloria Dei!'s pastor. To be certain that I was spiritually prepared to lead the congregation to a healthy goodbye, I made a three-week retreat to Bolton Abbey, about sixty miles southwest of Dublin, in County Kildare. I had made four previous retreats there. My first retreat was in 1996. Bolton Abbey is small community, at present only seven monks, and is a working cattle farm. The living space is big farm house and part of a twelfth century tower castle.

I made a two-month retreat at Bolton Abbey during May and June 1996. I wanted to spend some time in prayer and solitude, and finish a book I was writing for The Alban Institute. I went to deepen my relationship with God and tend my call as pastor. I received more than I hoped. I was blessed by the monks' warm and heartfelt reception, and was given a glimpse of who God intended me to be. Bolton Abbey is a contemplative community, meaning the monks do not work outside the monastery. Their work is prayer and study. They pray for the world and deepen their spiritual life. The monastic life fosters prayer and study. Most monasteries have extensive libraries. Consequently, monks have written some of the greatest spiritual classics.

In 1996, I was the first Lutheran any of these monks had ever met. They were a tad worried about how I would fit in to their community. After all, I was to be there for a considerable time. They fessed up later that they were not worried because I was Lutheran; it was because I was Norwegian! Evidently, Norwegians have a reputation for being a bit grim. I was glad I could change their opinion.

Cistercians, also called Trappists, are a twelfth century reform movement of the Benedictine Order, begun at Citeaux (Latin Cistercium) and La Trapp in France—hence the names. The rule of St. Benedict (ca 600), which they follow, demands hospitality to the stranger and traveler. Hospitable they are, especially to one devilishly handsome Norwegian Lutheran preacher.

The book of Acts was written to Theophilus. Theophilus means "lover of God." It is not clear if Luke was writing to a person or to those who love God. My journal is the same. I wrote is as if to Theophilus, a love of God.

1. O Theophilus, I am so glad to be here. It feels like home. It has felt that way from the first time I made a retreat here. As soon as I saw Brother Francis in the car to pick me up, I knew I was where I should be. I am welcomed into and embraced by the entire community. Being able to live within the enclosure helps give me a monastic and prayerful rhythm to my day.

2. It is 11:00 a.m. and it feels as if I have been up forever. We are awakened at 4:00 a.m. for Vigils (the night prayers) at 4:15 a.m. When I say we are awakened, I mean bells ring over the loudspeaker so loudly that the dead could be roused. The bells make it clear; "Get up!" The bells call us to the Divine Office, the name of the seven worship services (plus Mass) a monk performs every day. Vigils, is sometimes a said office (worship

service). That means there is no singing. Psalms and prayers are read for forty minutes. Sometimes, Psalms are chanted, but only on one note. Because we are tired, our minds are sluggish and are capable of focusing on the liturgy better. They don't wander off into other thoughts. Consequently, for me, Vigils is one of my favorite offices. Vigils, envelops a sleeping world in the embrace of God. We pray for a world at rest.

After vigils we eat breakfast- cereal, fruit, and coffee. By now it is 5:00 a.m. and we go back to our rooms to pray, or study, or write.

At 6:00 a.m. the bells call us to private prayer in the chapel until Lauds at 6:15 a.m. At 8:30, we celebrate the Eucharist. They permit me to receive the sacrament here. I did not ask, the abbot just offered it to me in 1996. After Mass, the Grand Silence ends. The Grand Silence runs from 8:00 p.m. to 9:00 a.m. There is no speaking except in emergencies, etc.

There is no need for a clock or a watch. The bells tell us what to do and where to go. They call us back for Tierce at 9:50 a.m., and 11:45 for Sext. In the intervals we do some work. I think I will be the designated cleaner and dish washer. After Sext, we eat the large meal (dinner) of the day. Meals here are in silence. At dinner, however, someone reads while we eat. Today Brother Francis read from The Vatican Chronicles and a chapter from the Rule of St, Benedict. I get very hungry by noon with only cereal for breakfast. At 1:45 p.m. is midday prayer followed by free time. There is always hot water for tea and coffee, and a table in the kitchen for light talk, conversation, and very enjoyable banter.

Vespers is at 5:20, and "tea" (supper) at 6:00 p.m. Compline is at 8:15, and sleep after Compline. To an outsider this life seems easy. It is not. It is hard to fake prayer here for very long. If the monk does not have a deep spiritual life, he can't make it. That is why there is a 90% attrition rate. Those who remain, those who long to love God and serve in the monastery, reap the rewards of joy and laughter, love and friendship, faith and trust, and an ever-deepening spiritual life.

3. It is only the second day here and I have already fallen into the monastic rhythm. It is a grand rhythm of prayer, study, solitude, work, and rest. In prayer, we stand before God. In solitude, God makes God's self, known, in work, we share service to each other, and in rest, we quiet our busy minds.

4. Prayer unites people of every race and religion. Never do we feel God's presence more than when we pray together. The Psalmist wrote, "Seven times a day I go to the Lord." The seven offices and Mass draw the community together, and fill us with love for each other. I love prayer. It is my very lifeblood.

5. In an environment surrounded by prayer and in the company of warm and gracious men, it is impossible not to see love in the universe. How I wish this for everyone.

6. At Gloria Dei! we use a book of letters compiled by Brother Alberic, a monk at Bolton. His spiritual director Tony McHugh wrote the letters. They are wonderful letters, full of insight and inspiration. Today Alberic told me of a conversation he had with Tony. Tony told him, "The greatest commentary on Christ you will ever read is yourself." It is one of those little sentences that both challenges and comforts. And one upon which we need meditate and let simmer on the burners of our hearts. The full truth of the statement comes slowly, I think.

7. Brother Antony may be one of the gentlest men I have ever met. He is totally without guile and almost unaware of any slight he may experience. What ever is, he just accepts. I

would like to package him up and take his spirit with me. It is a shame the world cannot experience him, but I do not think the world will ever be ready for such innocence and purity.

8. I have been remembering my years as pastor. Just when I feel that I draw closer to wisdom, I retire. Kierkegaard wrote, "We live our lives forward but we understand by looking back." I hope and pray that I was faithful in my work and ministry. In so many ways, I do not want to retire. But it is time. A new and younger pastor can bring vigor and vitality. I feel confident that I am leaving a healthy congregation for my successor. For that I am thankful.

9. When I was ordained in 1972, the world was exploding. The war in Viet Nam was raging and civil rights was a national cause. I was in the midst of it. I knew that it was not possible to sit on the sidelines. To do so would be cowardice. At my first parish, Christ Church, involvement was difficult because Carl (the senior pastor) was leery of creating controversy in the congregation. It was not until I got to my second call at Augustana in north east Baltimore, that I felt free to pursue some kind of social ministry.

10. Early in my ministry, I was an angry person. I didn't want to be angry and wished I weren't, but so often when I would speak with someone on a controversial topic I would respond unkindly. I think it was the coupling of two disparate traits: insecurity and arrogance. I just couldn't believe someone could not see how smart my argument was. I didn't like that part of me, but time and time again my anger would rise and I found it difficult to control. It wasn't like a wild beast, it was more like an untamed horse that bucked off his rider.

Nevertheless, there was more to me than anger. I could also be tender and gentle. Oddly enough, I was gentle with some whom others found to be unsavory. I felt called to speak for those on the fringes of society. For a while, Faye and I worked at a Methadone maintenance center with drug addicts. We also volunteered at a center for the homeless and exploited. Both places in Baltimore. We would, periodically get a call to house someone, which we gladly did.

11. I guess today is the day I reflect on my forty-plus years in the ministry. If I count the time I was in seminary, I have been working in the church for forty-six years. In seminary, I served in three different churches. I was youth director at a church in Minneapolis and one in Eden Prairie. The summer after my first year in seminary, I took over for a pastor in Zahl, North Dakota. I was responsible for five little churches. I think it was one of most enjoyable and rewarding times in seminary. I loved the people. Zahl was way up in the north western corner of North Dakota. I remember telling one lady in Minneapolis where I was going, and she replied, Oh, you'll love it there. Every 4th of July they have a picnic under the tree." She wasn't kidding: only one tree in Zahl.

12. The longer I was at Gloria Dei! the more protective and vigilant I became about what was preached and taught. It was essential that the congregation knows God's love. Anything that detracted from that knowledge was anathema. Sundays became increasingly difficult because of the pressure I placed on myself. I wanted to be certain what I preached was edifying for the congregation, consistent with Lutheran theology, yet reflect what I believed. Sometimes it was difficult to reconcile what I believed with what the church has historically taught. For instance, I no longer believe in original sin, at least the way St, Augustine taught it. Yet, when I preach, it is incumbent on me, as an ordained Lutheran pastor, to be consistent with church doctrine. How do I do that? I did not feel free to preach "Tommy's doctrine." On some issues, I had to

be silent. It got so bad the last few years that the anxiety of Sunday began on Monday. By Saturday, I was a basket case.

13. I loved preaching at Augustana, but I was not very good yet. When I look back at those sermons, I cringe. It was not that there were necessarily bad, they just didn't hold together and were boring. It is a good thing I could sing. The congregation said they loved my sermons. I am not sure I believed them. I think they just loved me. They were pretty special people.

14. Music has been so central to my ministry, I don't know what it would have looked like had I not sung, written music, and played the guitar. I composed *Alive on the Vine* at Augustana, and have used it since 1974. It still is the best musical piece I have written. The baptism song I wrote for my niece's baptism in 1976 has become a tradition at every baptism. I sang a different song once at Gloria Dei! The couple, whose baby I baptized, were disappointed that I did not sing the song. They made me sing it for the family after worship. I have sung it at every baptism since then.

15. At Gloria Dei!, my music took on an even greater importance, especially when Debbie Greene joined the music staff. Together, we make a wonderful music team. She makes me better than I am. We have been singing together for over twenty-five years. You can't create a symbiosis. Either it is there or it is not. Funerals would not be the same without the music we provide. Our music adds a great deal to Sunday morning worship. After a few years of singing and playing together, we were able to anticipate each other's musical actions, and respond accordingly. All I have to do is look at her, and she knows that I am to change something in the service, cut out a verse of a hymn, or add a song. I will treasure the three albums we made. They will be a continual reminder of the music we made. I know it touched the hearts of the congregation.

16. I have known a few holy people in my life. They are holy
not because of some intrinsic quality they possess on their
own. They are holy because they all have been people of
prayer. God fully possessed them. Their influence on me
has helped me become a better person and pastor.

My Dad was the greatest influence in my life. His model for
life and ministry was invaluable for my growth as person
and pastor. While he was alive, I would call and say, "Dad, I
have a problem." He would always listen. Once, when I was
a young pastor at Christ Church, I called and began to moan
about this thing in the church or that person who was on my
case. He listened for a while and then responded, "Tommy, I
don't ever want to hear you complain about your congregation
ever again. You are not there to be their judge. You are their
servant called to love and care for their souls. I don't want
you to complain about them to anyone, not even God!" With
that, he hung up. It seemed pretty harsh, but I have tried to
live up to that standard. How I viewed my congregations
turned around 180 degrees. It may seem harsh but it isn't.
I was called to love and serve. Judging does no good.

My intern supervisor, Dr. Ed Goetz, was one such holy
man. He had a great impact on me and his influence
is chronicled in other chapters, so I don't feel the need
to include him here. Let it suffice to say, he helped me
learn to love parish ministry and regard the calling as
one of service to God by loving God's people.

Roy Oswald has been a great friend for almost forty years.
We don't see as much of each other as we used to but
he changed my life. When I was at Augustana, I had a
depressive episode. He said, "Tom I am going to change
your life." I was overweight and overworked. I had a desk
drawer full of Twinkies and a bed in my office where I

slept when I had late nights and early mornings. He started me running and taught me to meditate. I am convinced that both those things helped save my ministry.

Somewhere in the late 80's, Roy ran the Marine Corps Marathon. He invited a number of us to celebrate at his apartment in DC. I knew that Tilden Edwards was going to be there. I had known Tilden for about ten years and just loved being in his presence. Tilden is a man of few words. Tilden had facilitated my spiritual growth and taught me to pray in a deep and meaningful way, and make it an integral part of my day. His presence spoke more than words could. I brought Faye to party, to congratulate Roy, but also to meet Tilden. I told her of his special presence. When anyone came through the door, Faye would ask, "Is that he?" I kept saying, "When he comes you will know it. Stop asking." Finally, after we had been there about an hour, Tilden showed up. "That is Tilden. I just know it," she blurted. Of course, she was right. There is something about holy people that is ineffable but noticeable. The numinous surrounds them and they shine like the sun.

Two monks have blessed me with their presence and knowledge. Father William from Holy Cross Abbey in Berryville was my spiritual director for many years and Father Albert from Bolton Abbey who lived in the room next to mine when I made a two month retreat there in 1996. It is not possible to relate their impact on my life. Sometimes I would just want to be silent with them. At first you think to yourself, "These a simple and loving men and I just relish being around them." After a while though I thought, "These men must be pleasing to God," and your focus shifts from them to God and God's presence surrounds and embraces your time together. I can think of no greater accolade to pay to someone.

I have been fortunate to have many mentors. There is an old saying, "When the pupil is ready the teacher will come." I think it is true. We can only be taught when we are teachable.

17. I think, overall, I did a pretty good job at Augustana. The church grew and was vital by the time I left.

One of my prouder moments came my last week at Augustana. Baltimore Mayor William Donald Schaefer, the MD health officer, and representatives from the Robert Wood Johnson Foundation (who gave us $1,000,000), and I dedicated The Brehms Lane Medical Center. It is housed at the church. It took two long years to pull all the resources together and get permission from the city to proceed with the project. We had three doctors, a social worker, a mental health practitioner, and complete nursing staff. The Maryland Health Officer and I had visited Granger Westburg in Chicago, where we saw two holistic health centers. Our medical center learned from that experience. Included in the medical center was someone who taught good physical health and mental practices. The pastor was available to nurture spiritual health when a patient so desired. Medical care in the community was poor, and we helped get them good care. The medical center is still going strong.

18. As I look back, one of the saddest moments in my ministry was when Augustana closed. I heard through the grapevine that it might close. I offered to take a year's leave of absence from Gloria Dei! to see if we could pump new life into the church. They turned me down. My final visit was the concluding day of the senior group from the church. Susan Coale was with me. We were on our way to make a hospital call at Good Samaritan Hospital. I wanted to show her the church. We walked in on the party. Fred Altman was there as was Lucille

Upperco, my old secretary. It was such a blessing to see them all but it was bitter sweet. It did not have to die. I might not have been able to save her, but I would like to have tried.

19. Brother Antony comes from a family of gentle and kind people. His father was imprisoned for two years during the struggle for Irish independence. When he came out he told Antony, "Do not be bitter. Do not hate. There are good people on both sides and there are bad people on both sides." What an astonishingly beautiful way to see the world. He must have had some part that was gay. After all Jesus was like us in every respect."

20. Last summer he visited his sister in Devon, England. During his visit, a speaker came to town. He maintained that Jesus was gay. A crowd gathered were the man was to speak to protest his thesis. Antony asked is 96 year old sister if she would like to join the protest. "No, absolutely not. What difference would it make if Jesus was gay. My goodness, what am enlightened Christology.

21. Towards the end of 1980, I knew my time at Augustana was ending. City ministry had taken a toll and I needed a change for my own mental and emotional heath. Mental health has always been a problem for me. It seemed that I was ok for about seven years. Then my health would plummet. Depression is an Olympic sport for Norwegians. I may not have been a gold medalist but I stood on the podium. I looked for a new call.

The bishop's office wanted me to begin a congregation on the Broadneck Peninsula. I resisted. I felt that I deserved a bigger church. After all, I had been "faithful in a little." I could be faithful in a bigger church. I kept turning the call down. Three times they offered the job. Three times, I said, "NO." Finally, Faye said, "Tommy, I think God wants you to go there." I made a weeklong retreat at Holy Cross Abbey in Berryville,

Virginia to discern what I needed to do. In the prayer and
solitude of their guesthouse, I knew I needed to accept the call.

22. After Lauds this morning, as we were sitting around the
    kitchen table, Alberic mentioned that it was better to have
    false gods than to have a false image of the true God. Boy
    does that resonate with me. My entire ministry focused on
    helping folks experiences the God of love. Too many have an
    image of an angry and vengeful God. Changing your image
    of God is painfully slow work and the old image is like a bad
    tape that keeps playing in the back of your head and seems
    to get louder in stressful times. I pray that my ministry has
    helped my folks develop a deep relationship with a God who
    loves them more than the one who loves them most. If I have
    done that, then everything else is just frosting on the cake.

23. *I thought long and hard about whether or not to share this next
    section with you. Honest and genuine reflection, and my personal
    integrity, however, demand that I include this journal entry.*

    Certain moments in everyone's life haunt them and surround
    them like a shroud. In the middle of the night or at an
    unexpected moment they come like a thief in the dark. They
    call to mind a time that was particularly difficult and painful.

    That time, for me, was in the middle of the first decade
    of the new millennium. My depression was deepening.
    Depression is so insidious and its effects happen so slowly
    that it took time for me to realize what was happening. By
    then, I was a mess. I needed hospitalization. What a blow. A
    month before my hospitalization I had lectured at Oxford
    University in England. I literally had stood in the footsteps
    of Lloyd George, Albert Einstein, Albert Schweitzer, and
    other luminaries. Here I was a pastor, with few credentials,
    lecturing to some of the best minds in the country. Now that

did not matter at all. I was in a psych ward with others who were having similar problems. It was a bitter pill to swallow. Over the years, I had learned to hide what was going on inside. I am a private person and do not like to share much of my personal life. My Dad had told me that I was there to do ministry not receive it. I'm not sure that is the best way to go but it is how I did my ministry. Not many at church, except for Faye, and those few who knew me well and from whom I could not hide, understood I was struggling. I did my best, but for a couple of years but I couldn't keep it up. After I returned from the hospital, I knew I needed to get away and heal. I had no idea how long I would need to be gone. I spoke with Faye, my doctor, some close friends I respected, and the church council. In January, I left to convalesce. I knew I would heal. I knew that God was with me. I knew that God would walk with me though the dark night. That was my salvation. I knew that the congregation would be ok and I trusted them. I went to our home in the Virginia Mountains. My time in the monastery had prepared me to be alone. I sang the offices (worship), just as I did in the monastery. I wrapped my day in prayer. I also saw a counselor and took medication. I was gone three months. While I was gone, the staff did a wonderful job ministering to the congregation.

They were wise, diligent, and loyal. The church council was supportive, took an exceptional leadership role, and really kept the congregation moving forward. Nonetheless, my illness and absence took its toll on the congregation. We lost about thirty families. The next couple of years were difficult, but the members who remained, were faithful, supportive, loving, and determined to continue our ministry together. In some ways these were blest years because God was walking with us, leading us. I thought about leaving, but did not want to run away because things were difficult. That would have been unfaithful. Besides, I did not want my successor to inherit a congregation that was having a difficult time.

Prayer and time help heal the deepest of wounds. I
pray that my time here at Bolton Abbey will bring more
healing. I know that if I lay it at the feet of our Lord,
God will redeem it and heal my memory of it. I am
God's blessed child and God has loved me forever. Those
words were with me through the healing process.

In this special place of silence and prayer, I am ready to let it
go. I have carried it far too long. Its weight is too heavy and
its burden too great. I offer it to God who can redeem it. God
takes crosses and turns them into empty tombs. God takes
the worst times in our lives transforms and hallows them. I
am stronger for having gone through that deep valley. I am
a better pastor because of it and Gloria Dei! is healthy. God,
working through us has blessed our work and our ministry.

Thanks be to God who gives us victory through our Lord
Jesus Christ. Amen

Two days later
In the prophet Joel, the locust came and destroyed the
crop, leaving nothing. It was sheer devastation. The Lord
replied, "I will restore to you those lost years." The truth
is a lot of good happened during those years. They were
not all eaten by the locust. We got though those years. I
got through those years. I am the better for it. I forget
who said it, maybe Hemmingway. The gist of it is, "That
which does not break you makes you stronger."

LORD, I give you those years and my memories. You
have the power to heal the memories and redeem them.
You can emancipate us from remembrances that enslave
us. Bless our congregation. Fill them with joy and
gladness. Remind us all that your blessings never fail. Be
with those who, for one reason or another, left Gloria

Dei! May their walk with you fill them with joy and may their faith in you continue to fill them with hope.

24. Two events released me from fear that Gloria Dei! would not be successful. The second week of "door knocking" was in the community of Ulmstead. I knocked on the door of Betsy Moran. Betsy was a member of Woods Presbyterian Church in neighboring Severna Park. I told her that I had met her pastor and that it was a wonderful church. She replied, "Thanks, but I would really like to help you get the church off the ground." She assured me that she was not going to leave Woods, but she knew that the area on the peninsula needed a new church. I was stunned. I took her up on her offer, and the next six months she worked diligently to help us.

Two days later, I knocked on the door of Suzanne Forthofer. When I was knocking on doors during the day, I tried not to go in the homes. I made appointments to visit with them later. It did two things. First, it allowed me to knock on more doors and second it gave us more time to visit, not only with the person who was home, but also with the rest of the family. Suzanne, however, would hear nothing of it. So, in I went. Katie was about two or three, Brian was still crawling, and Morgan, the dog, was in a playpen. We then realized that we had a Christ Lutheran Church connection. It was a grand visit. She also said, "Let me know what I can do." I did and, like Betsy, she was an enormous help. I left knowing that there was a community of people who would help make Gloria Dei! a reality. She joined and still is active in the church's ministry.

God has blessed Gloria Dei! with members who are faithful, conscientious, committed, and love the Lord.

25. I finally feel as though I can begin the process of preparing myself to lead the congregation these last three months and celebrate our time together. It really has been an extraordinary

ride. Our first worship service was All Saints Sunday in November of 1981. We worshipped at the community college. You don't realize how much goes into a worship service until you have to start from scratch. I thought, "I'll need to find a couple of kids to be acolytes." But they will need two candlelighters with which to light the candles. Oops, we need candles and candlesticks to hold the candles. Then we will need an altar for the candlesticks. We probably should have ushers, who will need bulletins that need to be typed (yes, this is pre-computer age) and copied. We will need a piano and probably someone to play it. We will need hymnals for the congregations and chairs set up. And, oh, I know I forgot something. Oh, maybe a nursery, and someone to staff it. The first service went off without a hitch. I spent hours and hours writing the sermon. I still remember it and could preach it on a moments notice. We had over 200 people show up for the first service. We were hoping to get about 125. What a day that was. I still get goose bumps thinking about it.

26. After two months of being at the community college, Don Smith, the principal of Belvedere Elementary school, offered us the use of the school for Sunday School and worship. Faye was the first Sunday School superintendent and organized the Sunday School. In fact, before we left the community college, she prepared our first Sunday School Christmas Pageant. It was wonderful. I have no idea how she pulled it off. We had costumes and everything. That program told folks that we were really serious about the business of beginning a community of faith.

27. Belvedere Elementary School had "Bucky the Beaver" as a mascot. A huge twelve foot high image of Bucky is painted on the wall of the all purpose room where we worshipped. The first Sunday at the school I had Bucky to my back and the congregation faced him. After worship, one fellow

suggested that we turn the congregation around 180 degrees. He said it felt as though they were worshipping Bucky.

For the next four years, I stared at Bucky every Sunday.

28. I don't know how single pastors can do it. The pressure of beginning a new church is significant, especially for someone as competitive as I am and for whom failure is not possible. Through those first years, Faye was indispensable. My supervisor told me that he did not want Faye working those first few years. It put us in a financial bind, but we made it. And he was wise suggesting that Faye not work. I needed her too much. When I was worried she brought me hope. When I wondered what to do next, she had wise counsel. Child care was mostly her responsibility. The first five years or so at Gloria Dei! kept me busy 24/7. During the day, I still knocked on doors, and met with key members. In the evenings were meetings about social ministry, Sunday School, worship, articles of incorporation, constitution, the list was endless. Two nights a week and once during the day I taught, either a Bible study or a class on prayer. As time progressed, we appointed a building committee. The pace was hectic, my golf game was a disaster, but the results were worth the effort.

29. Every day the kids would ask, "Dad are people coming over tonight?" My first office was in our home and our first meeting room was in our basement. If there was to be a meeting, the kids had to pick up their stuff so the house was presentable. At the time, Kaaren was in third grade and Erik in kindergarten. Those first years were hard on the kids as well. We didn't really have a normal home life, and a lot was expected of them.

30. Today Father Ambrose and I visited the cemetery. All the monks who had been at Bolton are buried there. As we looked he quietly said, "Here lay all the monks who were indispensable to the monastery." All right, Ambrose, point taken!!

31. This monastery is the keeper of the solitude. Gloria Dei! can be the same. It can provide a place and environment where people can touch the most secret and sensitive places of their hearts. It can provide a place and environment where God can bring the divine touch to the most secret and wounded places of our heart. It is essential ministry.

32. Well it is Thanksgiving. I haven't written much in my journal the last few days. I have been quiet. A joy has come over me. I am so blessed that it is difficult to put into words. What a career, I've had. I don't like to call it a career, because ministry isn't a job. It is a blessing. I have served three congregations that allowed me to grow and mature. Each congregation has given me a different blessing.

    At Christ Church I was untried and untested. Carl Folkemer (my intern supervisor and senior pastor when I was called as assistant pastor) gave me enough freedom to spread my wings, so to speak.

    He was, though, a tough taskmaster. One Sunday I didn't arrive for the 8:45 service until 8:40. Traffic was bad because of an accident. He told me that I was unprepared spiritually to lead the congregation and to go to my office and get ready for 11:00. Never was late again.

    One Monday he asked, "Don't you have any black shoes? I don't want you wearing brown shoes on Sunday." I did have a pair of black shoes—wooden clogs. I clopped down the marble aisle in them. He never said a word about it. I loved working for, yes "for" not with, him. He taught me a lot. The best advice about preaching I ever received came from him. He said, "Preach in such a way that, if the congregation has a disagreement with the sermon, that there quarrel is with Jesus not you." It made sense. I was not there to preach what

Tommy thought but what Scripture and our Lord taught. It was because of Carl that I was able to pull off the medical center at Augustana. While I was at Christ Church, we built an apartment building for elderly and the John L Deaton Medical Center. It wasn't an acute care hospital or a nursing home but something in the middle. It was staffed by University of Maryland Hospital and health insurance policies paid for people's stay. I was the first chaplain. It was during this time that I became friends with Mayor Schaefer. It was through that relationship that we were able to get a $1,000,000 grant from the Robert Wood Johnson Foundation and money from both state and city. It was an exciting time for me. At Augustana, we had a special day to celebrate our relationship with Mayor Schaeffer. He was a good friend to Augustana. In 1977 we got word that the local fire station was to close. I went to city hall, spoke with the mayor, and outlined the dangers of not having a fire station in the immediate area. Ten minutes later, he had called and told the powers that be that the station would stay. When I accepted the call to Gloria Dei! he wrote a letter to the bishop asking that I stay in the city.

33. Jim Shelton and Murel Beatty were on my mind today. I loved those guys and when Murel died it broke my heart. For ten years we were together at least three days a week. We did a TV show for WBAL, called Children's Chapel. Jim was the leader and did the puppets. I was the music director and Murel helped with the music. He had a deep baritone voice that made you weep with joy. We taped two show every other week and were on 52 weeks a year for five years. Each week a different church would bring their Sunday School. The folks at the station called us the God Squad. Their was TV cop show at the time called the Mod Squad. I really enjoyed doing the show and TV stations in DC and Philadelphia picked up the show for a few years. The audience, however, was not kids, it was older people.

I couldn't go into a nursing home without someone recognizing me. The folks tuned in to see the kids. They were the stars.

34. Today I am overcome with joy. It is interesting, sadness, sorrow, and grief descend like a shroud, but joy bubbles up from within. I makes me think that there is always joy inside us I just can't always access it.

35. One of the monks here asked what my parishioners call me. Romans called priests Father and Church of Ireland calls then Vicar. I told him pastor. He asked if I liked the title pastor. I told him I didn't think of it as a title but a job description. Pastor means shepherd. I like it when someone calls me "Pastor Tom." It honors and defines the sacred relationship. That is why I always called the other pastors, Pastor Anna or Pastor Hoda. I do not particularly need it from folks who are not members.

36. One of the harder things pastors do is preside at funerals of friends. It happens all of the time. It is important to be a comforting consoling presence for the family and friends, but sometimes it is hard. There have been many times I just finish, go into my office and sob. It has to come out sometime.

37. The more I think about Gloria Dei!'s future the more excited I am. Becci Ropp said that I laid the foundation. Now it is now the congregation's time to build on that foundation. They are up to the task. Gloria Dei! has special members. They have vision, commitment, faith, but above all, they love Jesus. When you put all four of those characteristics together, God will lead them to a bright future. It will be fun to watch from the sidelines as new ideas emerge, new programs arise, a new generation takes the leadership reigns, and a new pastor can go along for the ride of his/her life.

Peace I Leave With You

Peace I leave with you
now faithful you may live.
Peace I give to you,
Peace the world cannot give.
Peace I leave with you.

Love I leave with you,
To nurture and to tend.
Love I give to you,
To share with all my friends.
Love I leave with you.

Faith I leave with you,
To build and build my church.
Faith I give to you,
To spread throughout the earth.
Faith I leave with you.

Joy I leave with you
A joy the world can't bring.
Joy I give to you
A joy to make your heart sing.
Joy I leave with you.

1

Did I remember to tell you about God's love?

Nothing you do can make God love you more.
Nothing you do can make God love you less.

God, who is present, active, and trustworthy,
transforms our hearts
so, we can transform the heart of the world.

1. There are few constants in this life. We truly cannot count on too many things. The eternal is even more rare. One thing is both constant and eternal: God's love. God cannot not love. 1 John tells us "God is love." It is God's nature to love. To withhold love would be to go against God's nature. You do not ever have to wonder about God's love.

    Nothing you do can make God love you more.
    Nothing you do can make God love you less.

— 1 —

Christianity is not so much a philosophy of love as it is a love affair. God loves you, and God's love flows through you. The questions you must answer are, "How will God's love be made visible in my life?" "What does God's love look like in me?" "How can I become the living expression of God's love?"

The New Testament uses three words that mean love: "eros," "philia," and "agape."

Eros or erotic love is love between lovers. Philia is usually translated brotherly love as in Philadelphia, the city of "brotherly love." It is love between friends. Philia is love that involves mutual giving. Agape is one-sided love. It is love that gives unconditionally. It rises from a heart overflowing with the holy.

Agape, is how God chooses to relate to you. Unlike eros or philia, agape does not seek anything in return. It spends itself on the object of its love. God's love for you is not motivated by your worthiness or lovableness. Neither is it driven by what God might receive in return. God does not expect or demand a return on God's investment of love. Unlike ancient Greek or Roman gods, you do not have to seek God's favor. Agape is love for the lovable and the unlovable alike. It is love for the deserving and undeserving. It is even love for the enemy.

2. When I was in the monastery in 1998 the abbot, Father Ambrose, remarked that "the greatest graces come when we least deserve them." It is then we realize how much we do live by grace. Grace is all around you. Let it embrace you as a mother cuddles her child.

3. We believe in an intimate God who is accessible, responsive, and transforming. Our Lord is also all compassionate, all giving, and

all loving. God, by abiding in us, not only challenges us to live a godly life, but also empowers us to live loving lives beyond our wildest dreams and our natural limitations. We can, if you will, touch the divine and be grasped by the holy. The church fathers (most notably, St Irenaeus and St, Athanasius) wrote, "God became what we are in order that we might become what God is." God invites us to become "partakers in the divine nature." (2 Peter 1:4) God is present, active, and trustworthy, and transforms our hearts so we can transform the heart of the world.

4. Before his crucifixion, Jesus commanded his disciples, "Love one another as I have loved you." In I John the author writes, "Beloved let us love one another, for love is of God and is born of God. Whoever loves is born of God and knows God. Whoever does not love does not know God, for God is Love."

    All human relationships: parents and children, husbands and wives, lovers and friends, or members of the same church, are signs of God's love. Jesus' love for you is the full expression of the Father's love. Your love for each other can be the full expression of Jesus' love for us. St Paul wrote to the Corinthians:

> If I speak in human tongues or angel tongues, but have not love, I am a noisy gong or a clanging cymbal. And if I have prophetic powers, and understand all mysteries and all knowledge, and if I have all faith, so as to remove mountains, but do not have love, I am nothing. If I give away all my possessions, and if I hand over my body so that I may boast, but do not have love, I gain nothing.
>
> Love is patient; love is kind; love is not envious or boastful or arrogant or rude. It does not insist on its own way; it is not irritable or resentful; it

does not rejoice in wrongdoing, but rejoices in the truth. It bears all things, believes all things,

hopes all things, endures all things. (1 Corinthians 13)

In this text, St. Paul explains in exquisite imagery what love looks like. On our own, the kind of love about which Paul speaks is not possible. Our love is finite because we are finite. The source love is not within us, but within God. <u>God empowers us to love as Jesus loved.</u> God will grow divine love within you and me. We, however, need to give God the space, time, and opportunity to do this transforming work in us through prayer, meditation, and worship.

5. Edward Farrell went to Ireland on vacation to celebrate his favorite uncle's 80th birthday. One morning, on the blessed day, they stood on the shore at a Lake in Killarney. His uncle stood silently and just got lost in the sunrise. They stood motionless and silent for some twenty minutes. Then his elderly uncle began to skip along the shoreline and sing. "Uncle, you look so happy. Could you tell me why?" "Yes, lad." With tears streaming down his face he said, "You see, the Father is very fond of me. O so very fond of me." God's love is transformative and healing.

May you experience God's love today. You see, God is very fond of you.

6. Years ago, I read a book entitled *Happiness is an Inside Job*. It was pretty interesting. Another book could be written—*Spiritual Growth is an Inside Job*. Americans, as a rule, do not value the inner life. We are an active lot. Our motto is, "Don't just sit there—do something." We busy ourselves with activities. "I just don't have time to pray," is a refrain spoken quite regularly. Being alone with God, however, reaps a rich harvest. You

experience the grace of God. You discover your true identity.
In God, you discern your purpose for life. You develop a rich
relationship with God. And you grow in love. Love prayer. It
is the key that unlocks the door to a rich and fulfilled life.

7. Your life reflects what is going on inside. God lives within. God
    wants to draw you to that place where spiritual growth takes
    place—in your secret heart. The Psalmist wrote, "Bring me
    out of prison." He was not speaking about a physical prison
    but the interior prison that keeps you from experiencing the
    freedom a rich spiritual life can bring. The Lord is your refuge.

8. You grow cold within when your heart is distracted, when it
    clings to something other than God. Worry, anger, or self-
    pity becomes a shadow that follows you wherever you go.
    A rich interior life depends on the self-discipline of prayer.
    Hearts grow weary without it. Spend a few quiet moments
    every day with that God who lives within. The result is a
    rich interior life that is God guided and God supported.

9. God is light. In a way, light is the visible nature of God.
    Darkness cannot co-exist with light. In a battle between
    light and darkness, light always wins. It does not take much
    light to illumine the darkness. When I go to sleep, there are
    no lights on in the house, to speak of. The lighted face of
    the alarm clock is all there is. Yet, if I awaken in the night
    the slight light from that clock is enough to allow me to
    walk without stumbling. So, it is with the light of God. It
    illuminates your path and enlightens the darkness that is within.
    Sometimes when I am out of sorts, I will stop, sit down,
    close my eyes, and surround myself with the light of God.

    "In Jesus was life, and the life was the light of all
    people. The light shines in the darkness, and the
    darkness did not overcome it." John 1:14

May the light of God's presence, brighten your life's path.

10. Too late have I loved you,
　　O Beauty so ancient,
　　O Beauty so new.
　　Too late have I loved you!
　　You were within me but I was outside myself,
　　and there I sought you!
　　In my weakness I ran after the beauty
　　of the things you have made.
　　You were with me,
　　and I was not with you.
　　The things you have made kept me from you,
　　the things which would have no being
　　unless they existed in you!
　　You have called,
　　you have cried,
　　and you have pierced my deafness.
　　You have radiated forth,
　　you have shined out brightly,
　　and you have dispelled my blindness.
　　You have sent forth your fragrance,
　　and I have breathed it in,
　　and I long for you.
　　I have tasted you,
　　and I hunger and thirst for you.
　　You have touched me,
　　and I ardently desire your peace.
　　　　　St. Augustine of Hippo (354-430)

Finding God is like a sailor sighting homeport
after years of being on a sea voyage.

It is like a lost child feeling her mother's hand.
It is like a runaway rediscovering the
joy and peace of being home.
It is the heart finding its loving home.

St. Augustine knew that joy.
His life had been one long party. He was on everyone's
party list. He was a brilliant student and studied rhetoric and
philosophy. But none of that brought him true joy or eternal
happiness. Then the hand of God seized him. Finding God
came late in life for Augustine. "Too late have I loved you,"
he wrote. He did not find God too late in the sense that it was
"too late" to experience God. This prayer is the heartfelt cry
of the heart, "What took so long!" When your heart finally
comes home to God, the joy is inexpressible and the regret at
having been so lost is great. The joy overshadows the remorse.

11. Lord, You have formed us for yourself, and our
hearts are restless until they find rest in you.
Saint Augustine of Hippo

This petite prayer opens St. Augustine's book, *The Confessions*.
Humans were created with an intense desire for God. In
a sense, we are hard wired for God. Throughout history,
humankind has been on a quest for God. Some worshipped
the sun, others the creation, and still others handcrafted idols.
There has always been the belief that there is something
greater than humanity. Augustine was on that quest as well.
But he had looked for God in all the wrong places. He was a
hedonist and was part of a group called the hooligans. They
boasted about their sexual exploits and urged unsophisticated
young men, like Augustine, to gain sensual knowledge

through experience. He lived with a woman for some thirteen years and fathered a child by her. In 386, he underwent a deep personal crisis and converted to Christianity. He was transformed. His life was never the same after that. He discovered that he was incomplete without God. With God, he was whole—complete. In God, he found meaning and purpose. He found love, intimacy, peace and joy. The pleasures of this life are fleeting and they afford the heart only fleeting fulfillment. Only in God is there eternal rest for our hearts.

In baptism, God claimed you. God will not let you go. At birth, God planted an everlasting thirst, quenched only by God's Spirit. God gave you a personal letter of grace and created you to be God's personal epistle of love. God has written a message of love in the glow of the evening and the shadows of the moon. In the summer rain, comes the quenching water of life. In God, you will find rest.

"Lord, You have formed us for yourself, and our hearts are restless until they find rest in you."

12. Hope does not disappoint us, because God's love has been. poured into our hearts through the Holy Spirit that has been given to us. (Romans 5:5) What a thought: "God's love has been poured into your heart." What a gift! The greatest gift you can give another is your unreserved love. This seed of love, planted in the soul, grows into the tree of belovedness. As you grow in love you grow in holiness. Seldom do we use the word 'holy' to describe someone. We certainly never use it about ourselves. We do not want to be accused of being "holier than thou." Holiness, however, is not a bad thing. Holiness is merely attentiveness to God's presence in your life. It is discovering ways you can love God through service to humankind. It is a sacred life created by God. It is evidenced by an ever deepening love of God, self, and neighbor. St. Paul

describes it as a transformation of the mind whereby the mind becomes capable of discerning God's heart. It is the creation of a new heart—a holy heart. "God's love has been poured into our hearts." He audaciously proclaims that the spiritual person is a "new creation" (Galatians 6:15). He holds out the promise of a new life in which your old ways die, and Christ is formed in you (Galatians 2:20 & 4:19). Ultimately, he declares that a life that "lives by the Spirit" is "guided by the Spirit" (Galatians 5:25).

13. A journalist wanted to write a story about a particular monk. He travelled to the monk and asked, "Are you a genius as some people say?" "Maybe, in a sense", replied the old sage. "And what makes a genius?' asked the reporter. "The ability to see." The journalist was confounded. It was not what he expected the old man to say. He expected to be mesmerized by some brilliant answer. He muttered, "To see what?" The wise man quietly answered, "The butterfly in the caterpillar, the eagle in the egg, the saint in the selfish person, life in death, unity in separation, God in the human, Christ in you, and suffering as the form in which God has appeared."

Venture forth and let your genius eyes guide your day.

14. Not long ago a pastor told the story of a man walking down a New York City street. The hero of the story, however, was a little girl. As the man walked along, a piece of paper fluttered down before him. He looked up to see from where it had come, and there he saw a little girl pressing her face against the window of a tenement building. She looked lonely. She could not come out into the street, so she dropped her note from the window. The gentleman opened the paper and there in scrawled handwriting were the words, "WHOEVER FINDS THIS – I LOVE YOU!"

God sent a love note in the form of a Son.
It is a note like the little girl's.
"Whoever finds Jesus—I love you."

15. God created you with a natural longing for the divine. Yet, it
does not always feel like it. Sometimes it just feels like loneliness
or incompleteness, or a sense that something is missing. But,
if you sit still long enough, if you can reach that deepest part
of who you are, even briefly, you will find this longing for
God and you will find this God who loves and longs for you.
May you be one with our God who
calls us into a loving intimacy.

16. As long as there are people who try to recognize divine
love in themselves, there will be hope in the world.

17. During World War II, Hitler commanded all religious
groups to unite so that he could control them. Among
the Brethren Assemblies, half complied and half
refused. Those who went along with the order had
a much easier time. Those who did not faced harsh
persecution. In almost every family of those who
resisted, someone died in a concentration camp.

When the war was over, feelings of bitterness ran deep between
the groups, and there was much tension. Finally, they decided that
the situation had to be healed. Leaders from each group met on
a quiet retreat. For several days, each person spent time in prayer,
examining his own heart in the light of Christ's commands.
Then they came together. Francis Schaeffer, who later told of
the incident, asked a friend who was there, "What did you do
then?" "We were just one," he replied. "As we confessed our
hostility and bitterness to God and yielded to God's control, the
Holy Spirit created a spirit of unity among us. Love softened
our hearts and adoration of God dissolved our hatred."

18. When I was in the monastery the abbot, Father
Ambrose, remarked that "the greatest graces
come when we least deserve them." It is then
we realize how much we do live by grace.

19. The doctrine of the Trinity is not just a mathematical
puzzle or an academic formula for theologians to
debate. Instead, it is a belief born out of the experience
of ordinary Christians as a real-life answer to the
question, "Where do we find God?" It answers the
heart's question, "How does God show us love?"

The trinity is a mystery that is best understood
in the way God is present to us.

We know God in three unique ways.

God is creator – or Father
God is redeemer – or Son
and God is sustainer – or Spirit.

God is one. Yet, God is three.

God is here. Yet, God is everywhere.
God is mighty. Yet, God is tender.
God is just. Yet, God has mercy.
God is spirit. Yet, God takes on flesh.
The three co-exist outside of time and space.
All three are in us in the here and now.

God is Spirit and the Spirit breathes life in me.
Yet, the Spirit abides in your heart as well.

The Trinity is God's Love Story that
swoops us up into God's heart.

20. Where there is no love, put love and there you will find love. St. John of the Cross (d. 1560)

21. St. Paul calls for nothing less than a spiritual revolution. To be a Christian implies that something is going on inside me. To be a Christian implies a certain behavior. It is a comportment that is born of an interior solitude. What I do reflects what is going on inside. If I feel angry or resentful, my actions mirror those feelings. If on the other hand, I am in touch with God's love, that love bubbles out like a spring welling up in my heart. Merton wrote, "When the world is made up by people who do not know an inner solitude it cannot be held together by love." The rhythm of a life of prayer helps create an atmosphere of love. Personal prayer and meditation give God the opportunity to work inside me.

I am convinced that by my sheer will I cannot create inner solitude. It is a gift of God. It is a fruit of prayer and meditation. It transforms my heart and mind. Tolstoy wrote, "Everyone thinks of changing the world but no one thinks of changing himself. Lord, rule my heart and mind so that it rules my actions.

2

DID I REMEMBER TO TELL YOU THAT YOU ARE GOD'S BELOVED?

You are God's tender loving presence in the world.

Be careful what you label good and bad, or right and wrong.
At some point in your life the bad and the wrong
will come back to haunt you.

1. The Bible faithfully reminds the reader that you are God's beloved child. That is your identity. That is who you are. That is your birthright. The world is not so kind. Rarely does the world say, "You are my beloved." Nevertheless, you are not who the world says you are. Neither are you what the world tends to turn you into. You are God's child—a beloved son or daughter of your Heavenly Father. That is the message Jesus came to teach.

   You can take Jesus at his word. Claim your belovedness.
   It is God's gift to you. Thenceforth, you can live
   out your birthright as God's cherished child.

— 13 —

Being God's beloved is God's gift to you. Behaving as God's beloved is your gift to God. Encouraging others to claim their belovedness is your vocation.

You are God's expression of love in the world.

2. God has loved you for all time. The Father birthed you out of his heart and while you are on this earth, you are never far from God's presence. God has loved you with an everlasting love. God cherished you before you were born, and blessed you with your gifts and talents. The gifts God gave you are the lumber with which you build your life. With them, you can build either a temple or a tavern.

Build a life worthy of your heritage.

3. You are God's unique expression of love in the world. God's love in the world is visible through you. The world knows about God's love by Christians who love. Periodically someone will say to me, "I wish I could be more loving like X." I usually reply, "You were not meant to love like anyone else but yourself. Do not measure your love with someone else. You are God's irreplaceable manifestation of love. No one else can love like you. You just need to learn to love like you can, not like someone else. Who you are is good enough."

4. *God Has Loved You Forever,* is the title of a book by Brother Alberic of Bolton Abbey. The title says it all.

5. Planted deep within you are the seeds of your identity and the life to which God calls you. Rooted within you is the Spirit of the God who formed and fashioned you. It is true for us all, yet there are millions who know nothing of God's presence. The seeds lay uncultivated waiting to blossom and bloom. They know something is missing but

not what or who is missing. They are unfulfilled. When this creative force is uncovered, you find deeper meaning in your life and greater purpose for your life. I pray that you know God who lives deep within you. May God grant you the blessedness to become the person God created you to be.

6. "A hungry person needs a meal, not a menu. A starving person needs rice, not a recipe. A sick person needs medicine, not a lecture on medicine. Too many sermons are menus, recipes, and lectures." Soren Kierkegaard (1813-1855)

7. My spiritual director told me, years ago, that people will listen to me only to the extent that I have experienced God. It shook me up a bit. Instinctively I knew it was true. The same is true about love. We can say, "I love you" but if the speaker doesn't live a loving life the words are hollow and meaningless. You are God's beloved. Live it and watch the world become more loving.

8. Sometimes I think my office is a refuge of the guilty. There is a lot of guilt out there. Some people feel guilty even after they have been forgiven. Henry Nouwen wrote, "One of the greatest challenges in the Spiritual life is to receive God's forgiveness. There is something in us humans that keeps us clinging to our sins and prevents us from letting God erase our past and offer us a completely new beginning." Guilt burdens a heart and afflicts a spirit. It disturbs our sleep and distresses us during the day. Forgiveness, on the other hand, lightens the load and frees the soul. Maybe my office is a place of forgiveness. At least I hope it is.

9. There is a lot to like in the Apocryphal Gospel of Thomas. There is a lot to read with a grain of salt too. I read this today: "A man is good when his will takes joy in what is good, evil

when his will takes joy in what is evil. He is virtuous when he finds happiness in a virtuous life, sinful when he takes pleasure in a sinful life. Hence the things we love tell us who we are."

Luther said that a soul lives more where it loves than where it resides. Jesus said, "They will know you by your fruits." We become like the things we adore. If we are full of joy and peace, we become even more peaceful. If, on the other hand, we enjoy creating chaos and conflict we become more disagreeable. Luther also said that we become like the *God* we adore. It is so true. If we worship a God who throws lightning bolts at sinners, we will do the same because it is a "godly' thing to do. Our lives are a mirror of who we are. Who we are is a reflection of what we do. It is a daunting thought.

10. Prayer is a way of walking in love. We all want to love. We also all want to be loved in our lives. . We want love in our lives. Prayer is a way of finding love and being found by love. How is this so? John tells us, "God is love." The most prayerful people I know are also the most loving. It is difficult to be in God's presence and not love others.

11. In 1996, I spent three months in a Catholic monastery in Ireland. They were Cistercians or Trappists. One of the resident monks was Father Albert. He entered the monastery at 17 in 1935. He may be one of the sweetest men I have ever met. He even smells sweet. What made him that way? I think prayer. Prayer warmed his heart and allowed it to grow. Irenaeus wrote, "Let the clay be moist." If God is to mold us, our hearts must be malleable. Prayer softens our hearts so God can mold us.

12. In 1996, seven Cistercian Monks in Algeria were executed. Right Wing Islamic radicals had seized them in March.

Their crime—being Christians. Evidently, the monks knew a month beforehand that they would be abducted. They spent time in prayer, to discern what to do–go or stay. They all decided to stay. If they left, it would have been a blow to the small Christian community in Algeria. The monks could not and would not desert them. They stayed and paid the ultimate price for their faithfulness. It has been said that the church was built on the blood of martyrs. The monks' courage, love, and faith in the resurrection are almost beyond my comprehension. Let us build on their fidelity.

13. Being in a monastery causes one to be reflective. Silence pervades a monastery. It cultivates silence. In the stillness, your heart confronts you. In 1996 while in residence, I wrote the following.

Through a Monastery Window I

I have been peeking at the world through this window for a week now. The window in my room looks out upon a field of green grass and contemplative cows on the hillside waiting Brother Louis to milk them. The cold wind and rain are chasing the blossoms from the fruit trees. It is quiet. I hear only the sound of the wind or a monk walk on the creaking floors in the hall. Occasionally, the phone rings and a voice booms over the loudspeaker, "Brother Antony, phone call." Then the footsteps are quicker and more determined. To be a monk is not to forget the world. It is to spend your life in prayer *for* the world. The world looks the same from a monastery. You still see its beauty and share in its joy. You still long for the companionship and seek love. You still see sin and evil. Monasteries are not immune from the ruins of the world. Nevertheless, to look at the world through a monastery window is to see the world through the eyes of God. It is to be able to see what God can make of me and what I can become. Seeing through the lens of a monastery window I can better see God's blessings in my life. I see the blessing of Faye and Kaaren and Erik, of my parents and congregation. Yes, the world appears a little different through the panes of a monastery window. I pray that I am able to bring some of this window back with me when I return home.

Three weeks later I wrote this:

Through a Monastery Window II

I look out my window. I count the blessings that I see in my family 3,000 miles away. I thank God for Faye. She has been at my side through triumph and trial, "the thrill of victory and the agony of defeat." I thank God for Kaaren and Erik. They are maturing and growing into intelligent, whole, sensitive, and caring people. I pray that they are happy. It's funny how much the happiness of our children means for parents. I thank God for parents who have given me everything and more— spiritual foundation, education, opportunities to play ball, learn music, and support for me. I see that more clearly through a monastery window. There is time here to ponder those things.

There is another window, however, in the monastery. It is not a window that peers out, but one that allows me to look in. It is the window to the heart. The window is smeared and smudged, because it shows the effects of time and storm. The first days of silence and prayer begin the process of cleaning a peephole that allows me to sneak a peek and see if I want to proceed any further. I wondered, "Is there anything in there that's worth pursuing? Is there any depth? Is there any love? Or do I just fake it? Is there a pastor's heart or a heart of stone? Is my heart black with sin, or is there some goodness? Is there any gentleness or is it hard with pride? Is the call to ministry still alive and beating in my heart, or have I been fooling myself all these years?" It is scary to peer through that window. It is covered with layers of self-defense and justification. It is smeared with the little hurts and big disappointments that protect me from feeling them too deeply. It is caked with grief and sadness from the people I've lost and dreams that have been shattered. It is sad to surround a heart with protection from the outside because a dirty window does not allow the heart's love to flow out as it could. It longs to love and share joy but is stifled, because it is imprisoned by all those little defenses that were built to protect it.

I opened a peephole today. Dare I look? I thought, "Maybe tomorrow." Days went by. Although I dared not peek in, the peephole was large enough for some unexplored joy, and love, and sadness to flow out. The window does indeed work both ways. One day, yesterday, I took a glance into that window. I saw pain and sin, sorrow and disappointment, failure and frustration, and joy and love, and peace and gentleness. It was all there, but more that—I found a hand. It surrounded the heart like a mother's hand cradles a newborn's head. It was the hand of God caring and cherishing, supporting, and forgiving—the Psalmist exulted, "Where can I go from your spirit? Or where can I flee from your presence? If I ascend to Heaven, you are there; If I make my bed in the depths of the earth, you are there; If I take the wings of the morning and settle at the farthest limits of the sea, even there your hand shall lead me and your right hand shall hold me fast." (Psalm 139)

Even in the scary journey, the hand of God is there.

Is there no place the Lord cannot be? Lord, your works are too wonderful, and you are always there to sustain me. You hold out your hand and beckon "come, I will give you rest." We are travelers journeying through years and exploring within. Behold, you are there.

There is still only a peephole. But it is large enough to allow some things to venture in and some inexpressible joy and love, and a tear or two, to wander out. And our God—is on both sides of the window. God just awaits a clean window.

Lord, I can only promise to polish the glass a bit at a time. Be patient with me and gather me into your love.

14. You are the apple of God's eye. (Psalm 17:8)
The world has appropriated this phrase. Sometimes we will say, "His daughter is the apple of his eye." It describes a special kind of love, and special kind of relationship. God has loved you with an infinite love. You are the apple of God's eye.

15. "Do not return evil with evil, or insults with insults. Instead, pray for blessing. You were called in order to inherit blessing," (I Peter 3:9)

When the Nazis overran Denmark in World War II, they told King Christian that all Jews would be required to wear a yellow star. The King replied that he too would wear one. The Nazis never enacted the law. Then the Nazis ordered the Danes to build a ghetto for the Jews. King Christian refused. He said if he were forced to build a ghetto for the Jews that both he and his entire family would leave the palace and move in with them. The ghetto was never built.

On October 1, 1943, (the Jewish new year) the Nazis planned to arrest all Danish Jews. The Danish government caught wind of the plot and alerted the citizens who searched for Jews and smuggled them into neutral Sweden. Through this non-violent grace-filled action, almost all of Denmark's 7000 Jews were saved. The notorious Adolf Eichmann said, "The action against the Danish Jews was a failure."

King Christian ran the risk that the Nazis would call his bluff. Nevertheless, he was willing to follow a course that his love of human dignity and justice dictated.

16. "Faith lengthens the soul, love widens it, and hope gives it height." Isaac of Stella (d.1178)

St Paul wrote, "Faith, hope, and love abide, these three, but the greatest of these is Love." (1 Corinthians 13) They are not three separate attributes but three that work inextricably together. Indeed, they are one. When we try to separate them we fail.

17. In God we live through faith, we move and advance through hope, we have our being, that is our fixed dwelling-place through love." William of St. Thierry (d.1148)

William was one of the great souls of the medieval church and a great friend of Bernard of Clairvaux, whom Luther called the greatest of all the saints. His sanctity helped elevate the church in the bleak times of the Middle Ages.

He wrote, "Love's birthplace is God. There it is born, there it is nourished, there it developed. There it is an indigenous citizen. Love is given by God alone and in God it endures." The deeper our love for God, the vaster our love for each other.

18. One day a visitor came to the home the great poet, William Blake, and knocked on the door. The visitor asked Mrs. Blake if Mr. Blake were at home. She replied, "Oh no, William is usually in paradise." Most of us find paradise elusive. We are stuck here on earth. Yet, enough paradise is within you that it can shine forth from you.

Blake wrote "And we are put on earth in a little
space, That we may learn to bear the beams of love."

What a nice phrase. The sun's rays illumine the earth. The
rays of your heart can illumine the lives of another. Love is
the result of letting the light of God's presence shine out of
you. What an honor it is to bear the beams of God's love.
May God's love spring forth from your beam of light.

19. Jesus not only reveals the true nature of God and the
    true nature of humankind; he bonds the human nature
    to the divine nature. The author of 2 Peter 1:4 writes,
    "Thus God has given us, through his precious and great
    promises, that you may become participants in the divine
    nature." You are as one to the Godhead as your hand is to
    your arm. You are branches on the vine that is Christ.
    You can live as if God inhabits your being, because God does.
    You can live in hope, because God is the source of all hope.
    You can live in love, because God is love.
    You can live in a peace that passes all understanding.
    You can have faith to move mountains.
    You will live with God throughout eternity,
    because God is eternal and overcame death.
    You can assume the veritable likeness of God.
    You can become the presence of God to the world.
    "Put on the new nature, created after the
    likeness of God." (Ephesians 4:24)

20. Martin Luther wrote, "The greatest sorrow is separation
    from God. The greatest joy is reunion with God."
    Intuitively, we know the truth of this statement. There
    are times when we feel close to God and times we feel
    distanced from God. God, however, is never far from us.
    God knew before you were a glint in your father's eye or
    moved in your mother's womb. Prior to birth your soul

gestated in the Father's heart. Consequently, God knows
you intimately. Indeed, God is more intimate to you than
you are to yourself. You do not have to generate this union
with God on your own. You do not have to climb to the
highest Heaven to attain it. God comes to you. God draws
near to you. God stoops down to you. With an open heart,
receive God who approaches you with outstretched arms.

O Lord, let me feel your abiding presence
and know you as I am known.

21. You are God's tender loving presence in the world.
   I wonder what percentage of all literature, art, and music
   is about love. I dare say more than we could calculate. We
   receive love and we bestow love. One of my greatest sorrows
   is to come across folks who have not been loved. They
   pay for it in sadness, grief, despair, and anger. Like infants
   who are not cradled in parental arms, they fail to thrive.

   Personally, I have received more love than I could have
   imagined. I cannot take credit for any of it. It is all a
   gift. It is all grace. Moreover, when I awaken in the
   night I can feel a sacred presence in and around me.
   That presence is God. That presence is also the residual
   love, people have shown me throughout my life.

   The church sometimes attracts people who are love hungry. It
   makes sense because the church is the vehicle God has chosen
   to be God's holy presence in the world. You are on a journey to
   holiness. You are on a journey to love. Prayer fuels the journey.
   Love prayer; love the silent times when you lovingly linger with
   the Lord. Love God's gift of love—yes—but love the Giver
   more. The result will be a heart more skilled in the art of love.

   You are God's loving tender presence in the world.

22. I remembered when I was in seminary trying to purchase the best stereo equipment I could. It seemed I was never satisfied. This one had too much hiss. That turntable had too much rumble, etc. I was not interested in the music as much as I was interested in listening for imperfections. I think all of us tend to see the imperfections in peoples' lives more than we are interested in listening to their sweet music and dulcet overtones. Look for the good. Look for the God in them.

23. Today I read Ephesians 5:14 from the Jerusalem Bible. *Everything exposed to the light itself becomes the light.* I hadn't read that translation before. I like it.

In prayer I bow to Holy sunlit face of God and I become a reflection of that the light for others. In the Sunday morning liturgy, we end prayers with the words, "through Christ our Lord." We do not so much pray *to* Jesus as we pray *through* Jesus, or rather he prays through us. We become the receivers of God' s presence and conduits of God's love.

3

DID I REMEMBER TO TELL YOU
ABOUT FAITH?

*Faith and humility are the truest signs
of spiritual maturity and love.*

Faith is the ability to grasp the gifts of God.

*Prayer changes the one who prays
and draws that person into the heart of the One
who hears our prayers.*

MY LORD, GOD, I have no idea where I am going. I do not see
the road ahead of me. I cannot know for certain where it will end.
The fact that I think I am following Your will, does not mean
that I am actually doing so. But I believe that the desire to please
You, does, in fact, please You. And I know that if I do this, You
will lead me by the right road, though I may know nothing about
it. Therefore I will trust You always, though I may seem to be

lost and in the shadow of death. I will not fear, for you are ever with me; and You will never leave me to face my perils alone.

Thomas Merton *Thoughts in Solitude*

1. THE THEOLOGICAL HERITAGE OF MARTIN LUTHER

    All great movements in the Lutheran Church claim Martin Luther as an authority. So great is Luther's influence, even upon contemporary Lutheran theology, that any Lutheran theologian must cite Luther to establish credibility. His shadow looms large. Yet, he is so complex that disparate Lutheran theologians can, with complete honesty, draw from Luther substantial underpinning for each respective theological position. Since Luther is not so easy to categorize, a variety of theological movements can refer to him as father.

Luther was a product of his times and the religious piety of his day. The teachings of home, school, and university were designed to instill genuine fear of God yet reverence for the church. Medieval religion held fear and hope in tension. Fear of hell drove Christians to the church, which held the hope of Heaven.

This is illustrated very well in On the Art of Dying, a popular book of Luther's day. In the book, graphic woodcuts depict a dying man and his "departing spirit" surrounded by demons that tempt him to commit the irrevocable sin of abandoning hope in God's mercy. To convince him that he was already beyond pardon, the neighbor whom he sinned against or the beggar he had failed to feed confronted him. A companion woodcut then gave encouragement by presenting the figures of forgiven sinners…, with the concluding brief caption, "Never despair. *Here I Stand* by Roland Bainton

Luther, like every medieval Christian, was terrified of hell. His search for a merciful God has been well chronicled. For him the greatest despair is separation from God, while the greatest joy is reunion with God. Luther, in his early years, found no joy—only despair. To assure his place in Heaven, Luther became a monk. "Monasticism was the way to Heaven par excellence." Luther wrote,

> I was a good monk, and I kept the rule of my order
> so strictly that I may say that if ever a monk got to
> Heaven by his monkery it was I. All my brothers in
> the monastery who knew me will bear me out. If I
> had kept on any longer, I should have killed myself
> with vigils, prayers, reading and other work.

Luther tried to satisfy what he felt were the demands of God to gain entrance to Heaven. However, success was impossible. Luther's problem is best illustrated by the dilemma he felt in the sacrament of penance. For a sin to be forgiven, it must be confessed. A sin not only must be remembered, it also must be recognized; otherwise it cannot be confessed. If there is no confession, there is no forgiveness. If there is no forgiveness, one cannot win Heaven. Luther's dilemma was, "How can I remember and recognize every sin?" His conclusion was that he could not. Therefore, there really is not complete forgiveness and Heaven is impossible to attain. Luther despaired and even hated God for setting up impossible demands. Luther would keep his Father Confessor for hours. On one occasion his confessor, Father Staupitz, exclaimed, "Martin, we have been here for hours and I have yet to hear anything remotely interesting." Another time, an exasperated Staupitz countered when Luther despaired of God's love, "Martin, God wants you to love him." "Love him?" Luther later wrote, "I hated him." After extensive Biblical study, prayer, and the experience of grace, Luther discovered that God did not set up these impossible demands, the church did. Luther needed to experience God's grace, which resolved the struggle with his own over scrupulous conscience. Only then could he understand sin in a new way.

Luther moved to define sin as condition rather than as act. Sin, for Luther, is not just a particular offense but involves the entire person. Human nature is corrupt. His despair was that there is nothing humankind can do to redeem human nature. His joy was the rediscovery of a Pauline doctrine that Christ redeems humankind by his action on the cross and in the resurrection. Luther recounts this in the following comments on Romans 1:17:

> I greatly longed to understand Paul's epistle to the Romans and nothing stood in the way but that one expression, 'the justice of God,' because I took it to mean that justice whereby God is just and deals justly in punishing the unjust. My situation was that, although an impeccable monk, I stood before God as a sinner troubled in conscience, and I had no confidence that my merit would assuage him. Therefore, I did not love a just and angry God, but rather hated and murmured against him. Yet I clung to the dear Paul and had a great yearning to know what he meant.

> Night and day I pondered until I saw the connection between the justice of God and the statement that 'the just shall live by his faith.' Then I grasped that the justice of God is that righteousness by which through grace and sheer mercy God justified us through faith. Thereupon I felt myself to be reborn and to have gone through open doors into paradise. The whole of Scripture took on a new meaning, and whereas before the 'justice of God' had filled me with hate, now it became to me inexpressibly sweet in greater love. This passage of Paul became to me a gate to Heaven…

The Lutheran movement began with Luther's experience of grace ("I felt myself to be reborn.") and it is grace that undergirds and informs all Lutheran theology since Luther.

2. Faith is simply experiential knowledge of God. You cannot will it or demand it of yourself. Neither can you create faith in another. Faith is a gift from God. We merely receive it. This does not mean, however, that we have no responsibility in nurturing our faith or instilling it in another. Luther said, "faith comes through hearing." He meant that people should be diligent in reading the Bible, prayer, and attend Sunday worship consistently. In other words, we need to give God the space, time, and opportunity to grow faith in us. We need to show up.

    Another word for faith is trust. The object of our faith is God. Faith is not belief in doctrine or some abstract acknowledgment of the existence of God. Rather, it is a relationship of trust, a relationship of intimacy, and a relationship of love.

    Pray for faith. Cherish it. Nurture it through daily Bible study and prayer.

3. In our earthly relationships, we think of give and take. You give something to me or do something nice for me. My response is to give something back to you. In the spiritual life, we think similarly. God has done good things to me what good thing can I do for God? Jesus died for me; what can I give him in return? Our relationship with God is not about give and take. It does not have to ask the natural question, "What can I give in return?" It is not a bad question; it is just an unnecessary question. God's gifts are free. They are grace filled. There are no strings attached to the gifts. God only wants to walk with you. God's fondest wish is to accompany you on your life's journey. We may give to the Lord because we love God. We just do not have to give out of obligation.

4. I love this quote from Merton in his *Thoughts for Solitude*. "The desert Fathers believed that the wilderness had been created supremely valuable in the eyes of God precisely

because it had no value to men. The desert was the region the Chosen People had wandered for forty years, cared for by God alone. They could have reached the Promised Land in a few months had they traveled directly to it. God's plan was that should learn to love him in the wilderness before they loved him in the promised land."

I think about the truth of this statement quite a bit. It is easy to love God in the Promised Land. It is easy to love life when everything is going well. It is easy to trust God when everything is good. It is harder in desert times. Trusting God is more challenging when life falls apart. Loving God when my world comes crashing down is difficult. Few people go through life in the Promised Land. All of us have desert times. That is when our faith is tested and that is when our faith grows. God wants us to learn to love him in the desert before we love him in the Promised Land.

I spoke with Brian Smith a couple of days after his wife died. Five days earlier Ana gave birth to a beautiful little girl. Ana had a stroke and died. Brian told me, "God doesn't always protect us from bad things, but promises to always to be present to give us strength." His faith is inspirational. Most of us will find that our path must lead through a wilderness. God's hand will lead us. Just ask Brian.

5. In essence, the purpose of the Christian life is twofold:

    1. To be in communion with God.
    2. To be in a caring relationship with all of creation.

The Christian life is one of connectedness. We are connected to creation because we are of the stuff of creation. We are matter and mass, in time and space. We are connected to God because the Creator fashioned us in God's own image and likeness.

There is another connectedness—a spiritual connectedness.
In the incarnation, God united with humankind in a
more intimate way. With the gift of the Holy Spirit,
God united with each of us even more intimately. The
Christian life is an unflagging attentiveness to God's Spirit
within others and within ourselves. It is a life directed by
the hand of God. It is seeing God in all that is. We see
the world as holy because God permeates all that is.

6. My second parish was Augustana Lutheran Church in northeast
    Baltimore. I was pretty green when they called me to be the
    solo pastor there. I had only been ordained a couple of years,
    and I was not prepared for the kind of ministry that was to be
    required of me. One of the first people I met was Margaret.
    Margaret was about 16 and full of trouble. Over the next years,
    the police station called me often because Margaret had gotten
    into trouble. Generally, I would bail her out and bring her to our
    home. One night she had a terrible argument with her boyfriend.
    She took her anger out on the windows of Belair Road. She
    threw rocks through a jeweler's window, a drugstore, and a
    car dealership. She was in real trouble. I got the call from the
    Northern District Police Station about midnight. When I arrived
    I found a drunk and injured Margaret. Her boyfriend had beaten
    her badly. Margaret never called me Pastor Tom. Her nickname
    for me was Paz. She looked at me and sobbed, "Paz, does God
    listen to drunks?" I told her, "God especially listens to drunks
    because they need God so badly." God listens to people drunk
    on liquor, drunk on success, drunk on pride. There is no state
    of drunk God will not listen to. We can trust that God will be
    present to us regardless of what we have done. Faith reminds us
    that God is present to us even when we are not present to God.

    Yes, God listens to drunks, Margaret. The prayer of a
    drunk Margaret moved me then. It still does now: intensely
    gracious, profoundly humbling, and tenderly received.

7. Margaret kept in touch with me even after I received the call
to Gloria Dei! in Arnold. She kept getting into trouble. She
would do well for a while then fall off the wagon, so to speak.
I kept wondering if she would ever find the beautiful person
I could see in her. She was caring, sensitive, wonderful to my
kids, but deeply wounded. She came from an abusive home.
She had been physically and sexually abused. She could never
get past the memories and they haunted her and followed her
like a stalker. Eventually, Margaret ended up on the infamous
Baltimore Block. The Baltimore Block is a stretch of bars, strip
clubs, and sex shops on Baltimore Street. I received numerous
calls from her when she was there. She had gotten into drugs
and was abusing alcohol even more. She'd always tell me, "I'm
trying, Paz. I just don't know how to get my act together."
She was not lying. One of the last times I saw her we prayed
together. She asked God to forgive her and to help her. A few
days later, I received word that she was murdered. It triggered
a faith crisis in me. Why hadn't God "fixed" her? Why hadn't
God helped her when she so desperately needed it and wanted
it? I still do not have an adequate answer. I do know that the
abuse she suffered helped set her on a road to disaster. Some
can get past it. Some cannot. I do know that God sent her to
me so that she could experience unconditional love a little.
God sent her to me so I could experience her unconditional
love. God sends us people all the time. We may not want to
get involved or spend the time and money that person may
need. Maybe, just maybe, you could be the one to demonstrate
what true love is. We may not understand all the whys and
wherefores, but we all can be conduits of God's grace. Faith
is not just about our belief in God. Faith is not just about
going to Heaven. Faith is being open to the opportunities
God places before us. We can either act on them or ignore
them. There have been others sent to me that I did not help.
I wonder if maybe I could have been the one they needed.

Rest in God's arms, Margaret. Now, you finally are whole. You finally know peace. Thank you for coming into my life.

8. I believe and trust that God is the Best Listener. God knows exactly where I am and who I am. I do not have to pretend to be someone I am not. I do not have to pretend to be holy. God's willingness to listen to my innermost secrets never ceases.

   We can pour out our hearts to God's attending ears when we are angry at misfortune, or hurt by something, or wracked with grief. At times like these, we occasionally do not even know what to say. According to the New Testament, when this happens, the Holy Spirit speaks to the Father for us, using a Heavenly language humans cannot know. "The Holy Spirit prays within us with sighs too deep for words." (Romans 8:26) Prayers like these can continue literally for years. We never pray deeply without being changed. **Prayer changes the one who prays and draws that person into the heart of the One who hears our prayers.** Our faith tells us that God never wearies of listening to the heart of God's children.

9. "It is one thing to be justified *on account of* faith and another to be justified *by* faith. In the former view, faith is the meritorious, in the latter, the instrumental cause." John Gerhard (Lutheran Scholar D. 1637) Faith is the ability to grasp the gifts of God.

   We are not justified *on account* of faith as a work, but by faith, which lays hold of the work of Christ.

10. Friend of Luther and co-reformer, Phillip Melanchthon wrote,

    You say you are unable to obey the voice of the Gospel, to listen to the Son of God, and to accept Him as your

Mediator? When a parishioner comes to you complaining of his inability to believe, you must tell him that you are not surprised at this statement; for no one can; he would be a marvel if he could. And you must instruct him to do nothing but listen to the Word of God, and God will give him faith.

Here is where Luther reveals his true greatness. He rarely appeals to his hearers to believe. Instead, he preaches concerning the work of Christ, salvation by grace, and the riches of God's mercy in Jesus Christ, in such a manner, that the hearers merely need accept what is being offered and they will find a resting-place on the divine lap of grace. Faith is the by-product of hearing the Gospel. The Gospel invites the listener into a life with Christ.

Luther preached the Gospel. He expounded on the message about Jesus Christ, who He is and what He has done. A good Lutheran pastor will follow the example of Luther and preach the Gospel. He will not command faith; rather he will use those means by which God has promised to create faith: preaching, Bible study, prayer, and the sacraments. Only the means of grace can create faith and only the means of grace can bestow the ability to receive faith.

11. Every human being longs to know whether there is more to life than the phenomena that we touch, taste, and feel. Hardwired into humans is the awareness that there is something greater than ourselves out there somewhere. Jesus is the embodiment of what that something else is.

God came down to our world in the person of Jesus. If you want to know who God is, *look* at Jesus. If you want to know who you can be, *look* at Jesus. In Colossians 1:15, St. Paul writes, *"Jesus is the visible image of the invisible God."* He is the discernable manifestation of the indiscernible God. He embodies God. He is God. He is the very substance of God. He is the total expression of God. Jesus reveals more than the will of God or the character of God; He reveals the fullness of God.

In John 14 Philip asked Jesus to "Show us the Father." Jesus replied, "Whoever has seen me has seen the Father."

One night a small little voice was heard from the bedroom across the hall. "Daddy, I'm scared!" The response came quickly: "Honey, don't be afraid, daddy's right across the hall." After a very brief pause the little voice is heard again, "I'm still scared!" Again a response: "You don't need to be afraid. God is watching over you."
This time the pause is longer … but the voice returns, *"Daddy, I need a God with skin on!"*

Jesus is God with skin on. So are you.

12. Jesus is an incomparable Lover, who
    caressed the untouchable leper,
    granted sanity to the monster living
    within a demon possessed man,
    gave sight to the blind,
    fed the hungry multitudes,
    embraced the tax collector,
    gave sturdy legs to the lame,
    and unburdened those besieged by guilt.
    He laid down his life, not just for his friends, but
    also for those who beat and murdered him—
    for those who hated and reviled him.
    Nails did not keep Jesus on the cross, his outrageous Love did.
    An outrageous Love that is for you and for me.
    Jesus is the gracious image of his gracious Father.
    He is indeed God with skin on.

One of my favorite hymns is *Amazing Grace*. That is not unusual. It is a favorite hymn of many. Amazing Grace astounds us in its generosity and purity, draws us near to Jesus, and completely disarms the enemy of our souls.

Jesus embodied amazing grace *as* he loved us and died for us even while we were yet sinners. He offers forgiveness, not as a reward for our own goodness, but as a precious gift. This sweet Jesus reveals the Father's Amazing Grace.

Because of him, we have the promise
of help in time of trouble:

Of escape, in the day of temptation;
Of joy, in the midst of sorrow;
Of comfort, in the darkness of distress;
Of victory over death;
Of life eternal, in the splendor of God, our eternal companion.
This Eternal Hope teaches us how to live and how to die.

Yes, Jesus *is* the image of the invisible
God and what a beautiful God he is.
The God of Outrageous Love, Amazing
Grace and Eternal Hope.

13. A small boy and his older brother, Henry, were standing before a large portrait of their father who had died when the younger boy was a mere babe. "Tell me," the younger brother said, "just what was Father like?" The older boy attempted to tell his little brother something about their father. He described his strength. He said he was a good man, kind and handsome. He was friendly, and people liked to be with him. He was always gentle with Mother. He made people happy. In spite of everything the older brother could say, the small boy could not form a satisfying picture of his

Father. He wanted so much to know what his father was like. At last, he interrupted his brother with the question, "Tell me one thing, Henry, was Father anything like you?" The older boy hesitated a moment, then said: "Well, friends of ours who knew Father best say that I'm the living image of him. And even Mother says the same."

With his heart filled with joy, the small boy walked away, saying: "Now I know exactly what my Dad was like. He was just like my brother Henry." Jesus came to our world as God in human flesh. Jesus is "the Son of God"–God of mass and matter and the thoughts of God made audible. Jesus himself said, "Anyone who has seen me has seen the Father" (John 14:9). If you have seen Jesus, you have seen God. Whenever you want to know what God is like, then look at Jesus as the Bible reveals Him.

Earlier in this chapter I wrote, "If you want to know who God is, look at Jesus."

There is a next step

If you want to know who *you* were meant to be, look at Jesus. St. Paul wrote, in Romans 8:29 "Let us be conformed to the image of Jesus." Indeed, let us be conformed to the image of Jesus so that the beauty of Jesus can be seen in each of us.

Now, do not hear these words of Paul as demand, but rather as a description of who we can become. Paul is saying, "You can become the image and likeness of Jesus. That is your true identity, as members of God's family."

Who knows, maybe someone will say,
"I know what God is like. God is like Jesus.
I also know what Jesus is like, he is like you."

14. Jacob Needleman, an American philosopher and theologian, wrote an intriguing allegory called the *Mountain Climb*. In it, he speaks of a very high mountain. At the top of the mountain is God. The base of this mountain is so broad that it extends out to several different climate zones. People in the arctic climate climb the mountain, wearing a parka with snowshoes and goggles, etc. The people in the tropical zone teach how it is necessary to wear short pants and a pith helmet with mosquito netting. The people in the Arctic, by the time they get halfway up the mountain find that it is warmer than they had thought, so they shed some of their outerwear. The people from the tropics find the need to go back to get a sweater. By the time they get to the top, they are all dressed in a similar way because there is only one top. Disagreements arise when people walk around the base of the mountain arguing with each other about the proper way to dress for the journey.

Sometimes we arrogantly declare that how we dress theologically, on our journey to God, is the only correct way. Yet, most agree that God is much bigger than our theology. Faith does not seek to comprehend fully who God is. It merely seeks to be present with the One in whom we have faith. It seeks to be embraced by the one who draws us to the mountaintop of the one we call God.

15. Monks are dangerous to the Church, capital "C." After the noon meal, Brother Alberic and I had a fascinating discussion. He told me that what the mystic experiences at the center of our being is nothingness. It is what the atheist believes as well. We just give that nothingness a name—God. That is why the Church, capital "C," is always leery of mystics, Lutheran or Catholic.

We had a discussion about Meister Eckhart. I did not realize that the Catholic Church still considers him a false teacher. Luther read and was influenced by him. Eckhart said that it does not make any difference that Jesus was born 2000 years ago if he is not born in your heart. It reminded me of his Christmas sermon. He said there are three births: God in the person of Jesus born in Bethlehem, Jesus born in me, and Jesus birthed out of me.

4

Did I remember to tell you to bring your kids to church?

One of the greatest gifts you can give your children
is the gift of a enduring faith.

Train up a child in the way he should go: and
when he is old, he will not depart from it. (Proverbs 22:6)

1. You are God's precious beloved children.
    You are the apple of God's eye.

Let me tell you a story. In 2013 one of Gloria Dei!'s members died. I will call her Alice. She had attended church her entire life and was a member of Gloria Dei! for decades. In July, Alice fell in her back yard and severely injured her left arm. She was rushed to Shock Trauma in Baltimore, where the doctors did emergency surgery. After a while she was sent to a nursing home where she was to do rehab. Unfortunately, she contracted pneumonia. The infection was so severe that the doctors were unable to combat it successfully. Doctors sent her home to die. All this time Alice reminded me that God was with her and that God's arms wouldn't let her go. A few days before she died, I asked her if she was scared. "Oh no," she replied. "I know I will be with my Father and your Father. What is there to frighten me?" Her faith was an inspiration to her family and to all who knew her. Alice had buried her husband and her only child. She knew heartache. She also knew God intimately.

She had brought up her son in the church, and in turn, he intermittently took his children to Sunday School but not worship. Consequently, they really did not understand how a congregation supports each other. Neither did they intimately know a God who is a continuing presence in their lives. Her grandchildren never took their kids to church at all. Those kids, now in their late teens, know almost nothing about the faith. At the funeral, I spoke about Alice's faith and asked everyone to pray the Lord's Prayer together. None of her great grandchildren knew it. When the service was over, one of the great grandchildren came to me and said, "I would like to have a faith like my great grandmother, but I don't know how to get it." In four short generations the family went from a person whose intimate knowledge of God buoyed her up on her most painful days, to great grandchildren who don't know that God loves them. The great grandchildren do not have the gift of faith. Neither do they understand how a congregation and pastor can support them in hard times.

Your children are God's precious and beloved sons and daughters. I pray they grow up knowing that. I pray that God becomes their best friend. I pray they get to know a Church that cherishes them. One of the greatest gifts you can give your children is the gift of a enduring faith. I encourage you to bring your children to Sunday School and Worship.

2. When I was the pastor of Augustana Lutheran Church
    in Baltimore, I served as a adjunct probation officer for
    some folks who got in trouble with the law. The judge
    would ask a defendant if he would mind reporting to a
    pastor. Some said yes. I will never forget the first man
    who was assigned to me. He just looked at me and blurted
    out, "Pastors are no earthly good because they are too
    Heavenly minded." Fortunately, things got better.

    Another young man the judge assigned to me, had a profound
    effect on my life. His name was David. He was 16. David had
    gotten into trouble with drugs. The court assigned him to me
    the first week in May 1974. The first time we met, David was
    argumentative and defensive. Yet, somehow, we connected. I
    was to meet with him once a week. When school let out for
    the summer David began showing up every day. He was bright,
    despite the poor grades he received in school. He would come
    into my office and look through my library, and scan through
    some of my books. He loved to read, even some of my boring
    books on theology. He would greet me every morning and if
    I did not show up, my secretary, Lucille, would just put him
    in my office. I thought to myself, "If this kid is going to be
    here every day, I am going to put him to work." I had a pretty
    extensive library of over 1000 books. I asked him if he would
    catalogue them. To my delight, he agreed. We made up our
    own catalogue system. We divided up the books according
    to kind. The 10s are reference books and commentaries. The
    20s are Old Testament books. The 30s are New Testament
    books. The 40s are theological works and so on. He worked
    every day. I think over the course of that summer David was
    in my office sixty days. He was there five or six hours at a time.
    We became very close and he began showing up for worship.
    He changed. So did I. I began to look at people differently. I
    did not only see who they were but who they could become.
    I began to look for the inner Christ. I loved David. He had a

profound influence on my life. I cannot pick up a book without thinking about him, because on the binding is a catalogued number. He changed by being with me. I changed because I was with him. David moved in the fall of that year and we lost touch. Too bad, I would like to see him. I miss him.

So, it can be with your children. They can begin to see not only who they are as humans but also who they can become as children of God. In the meantime, parents can discover their own identity as Christian parents of beautiful children.

3. Train up a child in the way he should go: and when he is old, he will not depart from it. Proverbs 22:6
    My Mom is having some dementia problems, so I never know what I will find when I get there. Sometimes she is clear and sometimes she is very confused. One Wednesday morning she couldn't remember if she had been married, but she still knew the above verse—*"Train up a child in the way he should go: and when he is old, he will not depart from it."* She repeats that verse to me every time I see her. I think about it when I see my kids and watch them with their kids.

    We all hope it is true. In some ways, it is, and in some ways, it may not be. Our kids will all find their own truths and their own way. They will understand God in a way that makes sense to them. They may even leave the church for a while. My uncle left the church for forty years. He came back. I know the words that my grandma must have been thinking. *"Train up a child in the way he should go: and when he is old, he will not depart from it."* She taught this to my mother, who taught it to me. Sometimes, when we parents worry about our children, we need to hang onto these words. I have been doing this job for a long time and have followed families for a couple of generations. What we teach our kids matters. They will remember it even if they leave the church for a while.

What we teach them about God matters a lot.

Their image of God can shape their worldview. It can shape how they understand themselves. Teach them about a vengeful God and watch them become angry people. Luther said we become like the God we adore. It is true. Let us train our children to understand a God who cherishes each of them as precious and pray they never depart from that knowledge.

5

DID I REMEMBER TO TELL YOU
ABOUT THE ATONEMENT?

*When the cross is the predominant focus of the atonement,
sin and depravity are the central theological themes.*

*When the resurrection is the predominant focus,
hope and new life are the dominant theological themes.*

—

*The purpose of Jesus' mission was to make
the reign of God visible
and to vanquish the forces of evil
that resist God's rule.
Jesus accomplished this through his death and resurrection.*

Forewarning: To be certain that I am clear in my argument, there is considerable repetition in this chapter. Unlike other chapters, please read this at one sitting so that the argument is fully comprehended.

Introduction: The discussion of the atonement centers around theological reflection about the reconciliation of humankind that God accomplished through the cross and resurrection of Jesus Christ. There is no set doctrine of the atonement because the church has never come to a final definitive statement. Rather, there are many theories of the atonement that have been postulated over the centuries. A person's explanation of the atonement shapes his or her worldview and image of God. It is impossible to overstate the importance of the interpretation of the atonement. It informs all of our theology. It shapes how we understand ourselves in relationship to God and others. *I reject any understanding of a penal substitutionary view.* God did not kill his own son because we were so sinful. The death of Jesus was not necessary for forgiveness. God forgives because it is God's nature to forgive. The death and resurrection of Jesus destroyed the power of death to separate humankind from God, and is the first fruit of our own resurrection. The death and resurrection of Jesus demonstrated that the powers of God and life are greater than the powers of evil and death. Evil and death do not have the final word. God does.

TWO DIFFERING VIEWS OF ATONEMENT

I gleaned some of what follows from the groundbreaking book *Christus Victor* (Christ the Victor) written by Swedish Lutheran Bishop, Gustaf Aulen (d.1977)

1. CHRIST THE VICTOR

1. The mission of Jesus made the rule of God real in the lives of humnakind. (Luke 17:20-21) (Matthew 4:17 & 23, 6:7, 10 & 33) (Romans 14:17)

2. The incarnation of Jesus made the reign of God visible. The powers of darkness and death could not overcome the light that is Christ. (John 1:4) "I am the resurrection and the life." (John 11:23)

3. Atonement is the reconciliation of humankind to
    God because of the life, death and resurrection of
    Jesus. (Romans 5:10) Atonement is the restoration of
    our relationship to God. (2 Corinthians 5:18-19)

4. Sin is bondage to the forces of evil. Sin is not
    necessarily act, but a wrong life orientation. (Romans
    7:19) The progenies of this bondage to sin are, fear,
    lack of trust, pride, selfishness, and cruelty.

5. The power of evil killed Jesus. The death of Jesus was the
    power of evil's radical rejection of the reign of God. (I
    Cor. 2:8) "Give us Barabbas," was the cry of the crowd.
    (John 18:39-40) It is the absolute rejection of a kingdom
    ruled by God's love. (I Peter 5:6 and II Peter 1:3-4)

6. The loving and merciful God, who sent his Son to make
    visible the rule of God, reveals the depth of divine love in the
    suffering and death of Jesus. Mercy triumphs over judgment.

    Humankind is about death; God is about life. God's
    answer to the radical rejection and death of Jesus is
    resurrection and life. God's answer to our death is
    likewise, resurrection. "Because God raised Christ from
    the dead we too may live a new life." (Romans 6:4)

7. Evil did its worst – killing Jesus – God, in
    resurrecting Jesus, demonstrated ultimate authority
    over death, the last enemy. (I Cor. 15:51-57)

8. This victorious resurrection and the defeat of evil are
    invitations to transfer our allegiance from the powers of
    evil and the world to the kingdom of God here on earth.
    It is an invitation to enter into a new life, transformed by
    the reign of God. (II Cor. 3:18) (Gal. 2:19, 3:27, 4:4-7)

9. The resurrection of Jesus reveals the true balance of power in the universe and God's will for Jesus and for us – life. (Eph. 1:3-10) (Col. 3:14-15, 3:5-10) (John 10:10)

Summary – Atonement is an invitation to participate in the Kingdom of God, to recognize Jesus as Messiah, to overcome the forces of evil and sin, and reconcile sinners to God. The resurrection of Jesus, not his death completes this act of reconciliation. Jesus calls us to act as people of the Kingdom of God. In essence, he calls to discipleship.

2. CHRIST THE VICTIM

Satisfaction/substitution – God's holiness cannot tolerate anything less than purity. (Ex. 33:17-20)

1. The sin of humankind demands the penalty of death. "Therefore, just as sin came into the world through one man, and death came through sin, and so death spread to all because all have sinned" (Romans 5:12)

2. Jesus bore the punishment we deserve. (Romans 3:21-26) (Eph. 1:7) (Heb. 9:15)

3. Sinful humankind can obtain salvation because Jesus died in our place. This satisfies divine justice.

4. Jesus is sacrificed to the Father for us. In short, God arranged for the death of Jesus; thereby God is reconciled to humankind.

Summary: the satisfaction theory paints a picture of a vindictive God who demands a sacrifice to "redeem" humankind from God's vengeance. Instead of humankind being reconciled to God, it is God who must be reconciled to us. In this view, Jesus is sacrificed to the Father. When

Luther spoke of sacrifice, however, it always indicated what it cost Jesus, not that Jesus was sacrificed to God for us.

Substitutionary atonement focuses on our guilt and the need for punishment. In the Christus Victor model, hope, forgiveness, and eternal life are the foci: for the resurrection of Jesus liberates us from the hostile powers of evil, depravity, and death. The satisfaction theory of atonement separates the work of the Father from the Son, as if they have competing concerns—the Father with judgment and punishment, the Son with sacrifice, and reparation. Ergo, the Son saves us from the Father's wrath. While the satisfaction or substitutionary theory may seem biblical, it is not. It promotes a juridical relationship with God instead of a familial relationship where God is a loving Father. It thereby distorts the life and work of Jesus, and the message he proclaims about the Kingdom of the God.

1. Jesus died on a cross. This is merely an historical statement. To say that "Christ died for our sins" (1 Cor 15:3) or that "he was handed over to death for our trespasses and was raised for our justification" (Rom 4:25) is to offer theological interpretations of the meaning of that death. It asserts that there is something unique about the death and resurrection of Jesus. Jesus' death and resurrection accomplished something no other death achieved–namely the salvation of the world. That is what we mean when we speak of Christ's death and resurrection as the "Atonement."

2. The hypothesis of the atonement undergirds, informs, and shapes your entire theological system, your concept of God in particular, and your worldview in general.

In the eleventh century, Anselm of Canterbury, wrote a little book entitled *Cur Deus Homo,* or *Why God Became Man. It may be the most damaging book ever written.* Yet, it may be the most influential treatise on the atonement ever penned. His thesis is as follows: Every bad act demands satisfaction paid to the recipient of the bad act. Human sin has dishonored God. Satisfaction or reparation is required. Furthermore, human sin cannot be forgiven until recompense is rendered to God.

Repayment or satisfaction must be according to the measure of the sin committed, which, since it was committed against God, is essentially infinite. Because the sin is so grave, only a sinless human can make the required compensation for the sin. The repayment, obviously, is beyond the power of any created being to give. Only God can give such infinite compensation. Humankind committed the sin. Consequently, only a human can make the payment. Hence the dilemma; there are no sinless humans. Why did God become Man? To make the payment. Accordingly, only a person who is both God and human can make adequate reparation and satisfaction. He must be God, so he can make an infinite payment, and human, so that the actual son of Adam makes the sacrifice.

Jesus is substituted on the cross for sinful humankind. The death that humans deserve is perpetrated on Jesus. He dies in our place. The death of Jesus, the God-man, outweighs all sins. The death of Jesus restores God's honor. The reward for the satisfaction cannot go to the God-man because he has no need for reward. The reward is given as salvation to those on whose behalf the satisfaction is made: humankind. In this plan of salvation, justice and mercy are thus fully reconciled and magnified. God shows that he accepts payment of Jesus by raising him from the dead.

For Anselm, it would be unjust and unfitting for God to outright forgive the transgressions without any repayment or satisfaction. In essence, God would not be just, and thus God would not be God. Justice demands that the guilty be punished.

St. Paul understands the atonement differently. There is no payment to God. The problem lies in the understanding of how Paul uses the word s*in*. Anselm understood sin in judicial terms; every bad act demands satisfaction paid to the recipient of the bad act. For Paul, sin is not merely an act of disobedience. Sin is a demonic power that enslaves and ensnares people. It is an evil cosmic force. Sin is in the world and rules people. (Romans 5:13 & 5:20) People can serve sin. (Romans 6:6.) People can be enslaved to sin and die to sin. (Romans 6:17 & 6:11) Moreover, people can be freed from sin and be slaves to righteousness. (Romans 6:18 & 22)

For St. Paul, the paramount predicament is not simply human disobedience ("All sin and fall short of the glory of God" Romans 3:23) but enslavement to the power of evil. People are under sin's control and evil's domination. (Romans 3:9) The solution is for Jesus to end the power of sin and evil's reign over death and the world, and bring reconciliation, deliverance, and victory. (Romans 5:10 & 11, 2 Corinthians 5:19)

In Anselm's cynical view, salvation comes through Jesus who paid the penalty for our sin. In St. Paul, it comes by participating in the death and resurrection of Christ. "If we have been united with him in a death like his we will be united with him in a resurrection like his." (Romans 6:5) "Just as sin exercised dominion in death, so grace might also exercise dominion through justification leading to eternal life through

Jesus Christ." (Romans 5:21) "Thanks be to God who gives us the victory through our Lord, Jesus Christ." (Romans 15:57)

All this has profound implications for our entire understanding of God and our relationship **with** God.

In Anselm's model of substitutionary atonement, the cross as reparation for sin is the focus. St. Paul emphasizes the resurrection and the power of God to overcome death and the cross.

Now, do not misunderstand. Like St. Paul, "We preach Christ crucified." (1 Corinthians 1:23) The cross is one of the cornerstones of Christian theology. On the cross, the sin of the world, as separator between humans and God, died and was buried with Christ. Jesus could have avoided the cross, had he wanted. After all, he is God. Nevertheless, he chose to allow the forces of evil to take him, scourge him, whip him, humiliate him, and nail him to a cross. He chose to die on a cross. As Paul said, it was a stumbling block and foolishness to the Jews and Greeks. On the cross, Jesus fought a cosmic battle with the forces of sin and evil. His blood was spilled and the sacrifice made. It was not, however, a sacrifice to God. It was sacrificial in that it cost Jesus dearly—it cost his life. When Jesus died, it appeared that evil had won. It, of course, had not. Three days later, the battle was over. Evil's power over life and death was vanquished. Then comes the cornerstone of Paul's theology; "as Christ was raised from the dead by the glory of the Father, so we too might walk in newness of life." (Romans 6:4)

When the cross is the predominant focus,
sin and depravity are the theological themes.

When the resurrection is the predominant focus,
hope and new life are the themes.

"So if anyone is in Christ, there is a new creation: everything old has passed away; see everything has become new!" (2 Corinthians 5 17)

"But now that you have been freed from sin and enslaved to God, the advantage you get is sanctification. The end is eternal life. For the wages of sin is death, but the free gift of God is eternal life in Christ Jesus our Lord." (Romans 6:22-23)

3. The purpose of Jesus' mission was to establish the sovereignty of God and to vanquish the forces of evil that resist God's rule. In his actions, Jesus brought healing, deliverance and restoration to the victims of oppression. People's relationships change when they are governed by the reign of God. Jesus challenged the structures that tyrannize and dehumanize people. When he encountered evil or violence, he refused to respond in kind, thus exposing and breaking the cycle of hatred and revenge. Violence originates with humans not with God. Jesus was ready and willing to die for the sake of his mission. Nevertheless, death was not the goal or culmination of the venture, even if it was an inevitable consequence of resisting the powers of imperial Rome and the Jewish hierarchy. These powers were so threatened by Jesus that they conspired to kill him. The sin of rejecting God's reign nailed Jesus to the cross. Jesus acquiesced to their violence rather than meeting it on its own terms, thus showing that the rule of God does not depend on violence. He died a violent death. God raised him from the dead, demonstrating that God's power is greater even than the dominance of death that comes from the exercise of violence. Jesus' resurrection serves as objective evidence that the fundamental balance of power in the universe has now shifted.

4. I dare say there hardly can be anyone who is not awed by the cross of Jesus. Crosses adorn necks of the faithful around the world. I have worn a Celtic cross around my neck for more years than I can remember. I wear it under my shirt and against my chest. Its presence constantly reminds me of the sacrifice Jesus made for me.

Crosses come in all shapes and sizes. Roman Catholics generally display a crucifix. The hanging body of Jesus reminds the faithful of the price Jesus was willing to pay so that we might have life eternal. Protestants normally display an empty cross. The vacant cross reminds Christians of Christ's victory over death. In Gloria Dei!'s sanctuary, we have a cross that depicts Jesus with his hands outstretched as though he were offering a blessing. This is the victorious Christ demonstrating his dominance over death, while reminding us of the sacrifice Jesus was willing to make. "{We} are justified through the free gift of {God's} grace by being redeemed in Christ Jesus who was appointed by God to sacrifice his life so as to receive reconciliation through faith."(Romans 3:25 New Jerusalem Bible)

5. The Father has created a dwelling place for each of us in Heaven. The kingdom for which the disciples clamored was established. Additionally, Jesus declares, *"If you want to know the heart of the Father, gaze into my heart. They are one and the same." (John 14)*

The world is about death. God is about life. The "*YES*" of our Beloved God counters the "*NO*" of the world. The eternal "YES" of resurrection obliterates the "NO" of the power of death. On the cross, the sin of the world, as separator between humans and God, died and was buried with Christ. To be a disciple is to say "YES" to the Kingdom—"YES" to life with Christ and "YES" to discipleship. The Son in whom the Father abides has revealed the truth of who God is. That same truth can reside in us. Cherish it as a mother treasures her child. Teach it as though it were the most important thing in your life. It is.

6. Jesus did not die to appease some wrathful God because of our sins. God does **not** will death. In Deuteronomy 30:19 the LORD decrees, "Today I have set before you life and death, blessings and curses. Choose life that you and your descendants may live." We worship a God who cherishes us, not condemns us. We worship a God who wills life, not death.

   The crucifixion of Jesus is humankind's emphatic "*NO!*" to the Kingdom of God Jesus came to establish. It is a resounding "*NO*" to the sovereignty of God. The crucifixion of Jesus was inevitable not because it was decreed by God, but because the world could not endure the holiness of Jesus. He was a threat to their worldview, and a danger to their comfortable way of life. The only possible conclusion to the story of Jesus was: *Jesus must die.* The natural response of a God who *'chooses'* life is the *resurrection of Jesus.* The world can slow down God's divine will, but God's plan will ultimately succeed. God's response to a world that crucifies is resurrection. God's reply to death is life. God's response to the cross is the empty tomb.

   The entire Gospel of St. John is a commentary on the words, "In him was life, and the life was the light of all people." (John 1:4) Death is not the ultimate victor—life is. Jesus declares, "I have come that you may have life and have it in abundance." (John 10:10)

7. Lutherans love paradox. Our theology tends to hold two seemingly disparate ideas in tension with each other. For instance, Luther said that we are both sinner and saint. His famous dictum in Latin is *Simil Justus et Peccator.* It simply means

simultaneously justified and sinner. The same is true for his understanding of law and Gospel. To understand the depth of Lutheran theology, as it pertains to salvation, it is essential to understand the distinction between law and gospel.

> Wherever the Gospel is presented as if it had requirements attached to it, there the Gospel is not rightly preached. Whenever the Law is preached as if it offered some kind of free gift, it is not rightlypreached. The law merely commands. It grants neither the ability nor the desire to meet its own requirements. Indeed, the more the law is pressed onto a man apart from the gospel, the more he hates both the law and God himself. In the law, God commands the impossible.
>
> Martin Luther

In his book, *Lectures on Romans*, Luther distinguishes between law and gospel in this way: "The law uncovers sin; it makes the sinner guilty and sick; indeed, it proves him to be under condemnation . . . The gospel offers grace and forgives sin; it cures the sickness and leads to salvation." Any text that unmasks sin and brings guilt is law. For Luther, the ultimate culmination of guilt is that the sinner feels "sick," despairs under its weight, and recognizes his inability to meet the requirements the law sets before him. At that point, the sinner needs the gospel, which is found in any text that frees him from such oppression by offering gracious forgiveness. Despair vanishes as salvation is applied.

Essentially, any text that carries a command is law. Any text that teaches grace is gospel.

Luther underscores the individual's inability to obey the commands of the law perfectly. Yet, for him, the main goal of the law is not obedience, but repentance and joy in the free grace of the gospel. Sometimes law and gospel get mixed up. Years ago a member wrote a letter to the church council saying that I do not preach the gospel. When I visited him in his home, I asked him what the gospel is. He replied, "Accept Jesus Christ as your Lord and Savior and be saved." I said that I understood what he meant but that his statement was law not Gospel. Any statement that commands is law. Luther wrote, "Wherever the Gospel is presented as if it had requirements attached to it, there the Gospel is not rightly preached. Whenever the Law is preached as if it offered some kind of free gift, it is not rightly preached." (Lectures on Romans)

The most salient point is this: *The Law* always commands and ultimately *condemns; the Gospel* always *saves*. Lutheran theology emphasizes this consistently. What does it mean? Simply put: it means that these two doctrines, found throughout Scripture, have entirely distinct meanings and different usages. One cannot intermingle law and gospel while remaining true to either doctrine. The cross and resurrection of Jesus are pure gospel. They are pure promise.

8. Satisfaction atonement theology rests on the idea of a God who endorses violence. Indeed, it sanctions a God who requires violence in order to satisfy God's own honor or justice. The accumulated actions of our evil deeds are balanced by God's retributive punishment of Jesus on the cross. Contemporary theologian Denny Weaver asserts, "Make no mistake about it, satisfaction atonement in any form depends on divinely sanctioned violence that follows from the assumption that doing divine justice means to punish."

9. In Christ, evil did its very worst and Christ died. God raised him from the dead, and in so doing triumphed over

the power of sin and death and the power of evil. "The death he died he died to sin, once for all," (Romans 6:10) with the result that "death no longer has dominion over him." (Romans 6:9) Moreover, those who by faith are united with Christ in his death share in his liberation, "so that as Christ was raised from the dead by the glory of the Father, we too might walk in newness of life. (Romans 6:4) This newness of life brings freedom from the fear of death, on which violence feeds, and participation in a new civilization in which enmity dies and "the things that make for peace" (Luke 19:42) are pursued.

10. Atonement can never separate the work of the cross from the incarnation. They are inextricably joined.

Christmas thoughts on the incarnation
and the atoning work of Jesus

God wanted to make it explicitly clear that
Jesus came to each of us as we are,
where we are. God comes to the cold dark
corners of our existence, the desperateness, the
loneliness, the rejection, and the pain.

He comes to unswept barns and the lonely nights of despair.
He comes because he understands them.
He comes to the tragedies in Columbine, Colorado: Virginia
Tech University: Oklahoma City: and Newtown, CT.
He knows them intimately and came to deliver us from those
raw stables to life. He comes to bring authentic life: life that
the Christmas angels proclaimed and humans long for.
And what is the life we long for?—-It is simply to be
loved, genuinely loved by God in spite of ourselves.

God reaches out to us, not merely at those
occasional moments of high spirituality, but
wherever we are and however we may be,

God, who sees us at our worst and offers us God's best–Jesus.

The essential message of Christmas is not addressed only to
those who bask in good times. The message of Christmas
is for those in need, for the lonely, the outcast, for those
who know sorrow, and those whose world has been turned
upside down. Christmas is a stable of water where we
dip our poor tired bodies in the cool springs of hope.

The Christmas story is a sprig of joy blossoming in the most
desperate and drought-filled deserts of times: when there is no
room in the inn, even for a young woman giving birth. Nevertheless,
the angels appeared to forlorn shepherds, and proclaimed:
"Fear not, we bring tidings of great joy. A Savior is born."

The Savior is for those in need, for those whose world
has been turned inside out or those who know sorrow.
The significance of that first Christmas is that hope
can break into desperate and tragic times. The child
that comes Christmas night is truth and grace.

He comes to a world overcome with darkness
to be the light that that will forever shine.

He comes to a world overrun by the senseless noise
of violence to sing the melodic refrain of peace.

He comes to your life and my life as a priceless gift. It is
the only gift that really matters, to stand the world's value

system on its head, to take away the hard edges, and make us tender. It is a message of salvation for the world.

11. A Palm Sunday reflection

It is Palm Sunday and Jesus rides, rides
on a donkey to dark Calvary.
His legs drag on the ground as he sits astride a borrowed colt.
He rides through palm branches and shouts of joy.
He rides past swooning crowds who
do not grasp his destination.
He looks at the Holy City and weeps
over our inhumanity and sin.
He rides through a Temple that excludes
foreigners, women, and lepers.
He rides to a last meal with friends,
offering a cup of forgiveness.
He rides to the garden where torches
and swords interrupt his prayer.
He rides to Judas' betraying kiss and arrest.
He rides to Peter's denying lips.
He rides to Pilate's unjust indifference.
He rides through the Chief Priests' jealousy and fear.
He rides through the High Priest's declaration:
"that it is better that one die than many."
He rides into every holocaust, genocide,
abuse, racist word, and sin.
He rides to a crown fashioned from
thorns wearing a mocking robe.
He rides towards the cross and the taunts, spit, and wounds.
He straightens himself and pleads: "Almighty
God, forgive them: they have no idea."
And then he will ride into death…
Into Hell
Into the fire where the hoof-beats shake creation.

He rides to the hungry, the thirsty, the naked, and the ashamed.
He rides to our tables, cubicles, keyboards, and empty souls.
He rides to sinners, deniers, and liars.

He rides up from grave.
He rides through death's door on Easter.
He rides with all Heaven's company dancing wildly.
He rides to a weeping Mary Magdalene and calls her name.
He rides into rooms of fearful followers calling:
"Peace be with you, do not be afraid."
He rides into our hearts where he will abide
and whispers to us, "ride with me."

6

Did I remember to tell you to be diligent in your daily devotions?

"The Bible is alive, it speaks to me;
it has feet, it runs after me;
it has hands, it lays hold of me."
Martin Luther

1. What are Devotions?
Two Ancient Models

Built into the deepest part of the human spirit is a desire for intimacy. We desire for affection from other humans. As good as human love is, it is not eternally satisfying. We desire the eternal—we desire God. The Psalmist says it this way:

As a deer longs for flowing streams,
So my soul longs for you, O God.

My Soul thirsts for God,
For the living God. (Psalm 42:1-2)

This desire, longing or thirsting for God, is both similar and dissimilar from desire for intimacy and community with other humans. God saw that "It is not good for the man to be alone," and made a companion for him. (Genesis 2:18) This text not only illustrates the creation of family, but also communicates something much deeper. Humans have a natural inclination to be in community. Woven into the created fabric of humankind is the need to be in a relationship with other people. Similarly, we humans aspire to a relationship with something greater and more infinite than we are. In short, we long for God.

While maintaining relationships with other humans is difficult, at least one can see, smell, touch, and speak to another person. God does not appear to be so easily accessible. Even if we are not proficient practitioners at the art of discussion, we at least understand how human communication takes place. How does one communicate with God? Indeed many seem to ask an even more basic question: Can we communicate with God at all? Certainly, God speaks to us through the scriptures, sacraments, sermons and the words of Jesus. God also speaks to us through prayer. Prayer is nothing more than dialog with God. Just as most individuals need help fine-tuning their communication skills, so do people need help with prayer. What follows are two models for prayer.

An Ancient Devotional Model

In the early monastic movement, the monk's prayer life was described by four simple words: Lectio, Meditatio, Oratio and Contemplatio.

Lectio or Lectio Divina (literally Divine or Spiritual Reading) refers to a recitation of some sacred text by memory. Since most ancient people were illiterate and owned few, if any, books, they committed large portions of the Bible and other spiritual writings to memory. During daily work, the monk would recite some meaningful text, usually from the Psalms or the Gospels, quietly over and over. Lectio Divina, however, is not simply mindless recitation. Lectio includes being open to God's revelation. The monk understood that God communicated intimate truth about God's self through those recited texts. Lectio, then, was listening to the revealing word of God. Monks described it as tasting the words of God and allowing them to fill our senses. After a while, the words moved from the mind to the heart, where they germinated and bloomed into the blossoms of love and faith.

A natural result of this recitation is reflection upon the text or meditation. Meditation or Meditatio includes more than just thinking about the text. It is a prayerful interiorizing of the text's meaning so that it may be assimilated into one's life. For instance, the monk might meditate on a Psalm; as a deer longs for flowing streams, so my soul longs for you, O God. (Psalm 42:1) The monk might reflect on times when he was depressed or ill and God lifted him up. He might recall dry spiritual times when he drank of the water of life. In this context, the purpose of meditation was to ask the questions, "What is God saying to me through this text?" and "How does this text apply to my life?"

The monk believed that as he recited the text the words would pass from his lips into the mind for prayerful reflection, and then into its final destination, the heart. He knew God has the power to change the heart. A changed heart produces a loving faith-filled response to God and others. This response to God takes the form of both actions and speech. Actions take the form of good deeds. Speech to God is Oratio. Oratio, or oral prayer, is the spontaneous response to the text that was recited and reflected upon. This oral prayer may take the form of confession, petition, intercession, or simply thanksgiving and praise. Oratio is the oral response to the encounter of the presence of God in the text.

Finally, there is Contemplatio, or contemplation. When the monk had run out of words and thoughts, but the desire for God remained, the monk would simply rest in God's presence. In this resting or loving lingering with God, the mind and the heart begin to experience the God whom they had been seeking. It is the thirsty soul drinking in the presence of God. What they experience is an intimate and loving knowledge of God. Allow me to illustrate by analogy.

When my children were toddlers, they would quite regularly ask my wife or me to lie with them while they went to sleep at night. First, they would tell us of their day. They would share exciting incidents, sad moments, and relatively insignificant events. After a while, they would run out of things to say and would cuddle up close. They stopped speaking. They would simply close their eyes and rest in our arms. If we would try to leave before they were asleep, they would refrain us. At these moments our words were not important–our presence was. Our presence communicated safety, warmth, and a feeling of belonging. Contemplatio is similar. Let me share another story.

When my son Erik was five years old, we discovered he had Juvenile Diabetes. Erik had not been feeling well and had been losing weight. Consequently, my wife, Faye, took him to the doctor. With one quick test, we knew the awful truth–Erik was diabetic. We rushed him to the hospital where Erik became acidotic and went into a coma. For days, Faye and I took turns being with him in the Pediatric Intensive Care Unit. We held his hand and stroked his forehead. We said little. There was little to say. We lingered lovingly with him. He drew strength from our presence and from our being with him. Not only were words unnecessary, they were an encumbrance. Our presence spoke strength and hope more loudly than words ever could.

Prayer is similar. After a while we run out of things to share, things to ask for, etc. We run out of words. We linger lovingly with the Lord and allow God to communicate with us in the silence of our minds and hearts. St. John of the Cross (d. 1591) calls it the *Prayer of Loving Attention*. It is but a loving gaze upon our Lord who lingers near to us.

The early monks' prayer life had a natural rhythm. It began with the heartfelt desire to drink of the Water of Life. It grew out of a desire not to know more about God, but to know God more intimately. The result was an experiential knowledge of God.

The Prayer Life of Martin Luther

"To be a Christian without prayer is no more possible than to be alive without breathing." Martin Luther

It was Martin Luther's experience of God's grace through prayer and the study of scripture that set in motion the movement that culminated in the Reformation. Martin Luther not only reformed the content of doctrine, but he restored to prayer a simplicity of form and intent–that of being with God.

The medieval devotional and penitential system was designed to reform the believer's life as a way of preparing him for union with God. The church felt, as Aristotle had taught, that if you "do the good you become the good." Luther reversed this. He declared quite clearly that the Holy Spirit must train the "inner man" before the "outer man" can serve. Union with God is not the result of work but a gift given before any work begins. For Luther, any initiated movement in the relationship between God and humankind comes from God- even prayer. *Our prayer is always response to God's call. When we feel the desire to pray, God has already begun the prayer within us.* Prayer is a God–initiated response to God's call. It is unceasing attentiveness to God working in us. Our works do not reform the "inner man." The working of God within us changes us. Hear Luther in his own words:

1. A person does not come {to God} unless the Father draws and teaches him inwardly, which he does by pouring out the Spirit. The light of the Spirit sets Christ forth so that one is immersed in love and yields passively to God's speaking, teaching, and will.

2. If God works in us, the will is changed by being gently breathed upon by the Spirit of God. This is the most active working of God in which he has the sort of will that God has given him and that God carries along by his own momentum.

3. The true way to salvation is to be subject to God, to yield to him in faith, to stand silently before him and yield ourselves to God's guidance so that he can work in us and not we ourselves.

4. I believe that by my own reason and strength I cannot believe in Jesus Christ, my Lord, or come to him. But the Holy Spirit has called me through the Gospel, enlightened me with his gift and sanctified and preserved me in true faith....

Luther's theology of prayer begins with a statement of faith: just as the actions of God bring me into salvation, so also does the action of God draw me into prayer, bring me into a relationship

with God, and transform me from the inside out. Luther reversed
the conventional thinking of his day. Medieval wisdom and practice
believed that outer actions transform the inner person. Paul's theology
in Romans and Galatians convinced Luther that while we have some
power over our external behavior, we have no power to change the
"inner man". In that sense, there is no self-salvation. God's work
in us transforms the inner person. This interior transformation
initiates a positive change in our outer actions. In St. Paul's words, we
are justified and made righteous by grace through faith and not by
good works. Luther's theology of prayer grows out of his theology
of justification. Prayer offers to God the time and space for God
to work in us. In that regard, prayer is more than our speaking to
God. It is also, in Luther's words, "standing silently before God
and yielding ourselves to God so that God can work in us."

Luther not only spoke of the importance of prayer, he was a
man of prayer. He is purported to have said, "I pray three hours
a day, except when I am busy. Then I pray six hours." When
asked by his barber and good friend, Peter Beskendorf, for some
practical guidance on how to prepare oneself for prayer, Luther
responded by writing a brief tract, *A Simple Way to Pray*, first
published in the spring of 1535. After 500 years, his instruction
continues to offer words of spiritual nurture for us today. In this
book, he converted his theology into practice, and, as will be
noted, restored prayer to an ancient monastic simplicity. Though
Luther used different language than lectio, meditation, oratio, and
contemplatio, he incorporated each in his own personal prayer life.

Luther begins his prayer time with recitation or a kind of lectio. He
would recite the Ten Commandments, the Creed, a Psalm, and some
"words of Christ or Paul." These are, he says, "God's words of comfort
and instruction." He tells his barber, Peter, that he should pray as soon
as he awakens in the morning and as the last activity before sleep.
Luther also says that whenever he becomes cold or joyless, "I take my
little psalter, hurry to my room...I say quietly to myself and word for

word the Ten Commandments, the creed, and, if I have time, some
words of Christ or Paul or some Psalms, just as a little child might do."

Luther reflects and meditates on each of the words. He tells Peter,
"Blessed is he who meditates upon his law day and night." (Psalm
1:1-2) Recitation and reflection "warm the heart." Luther tells Peter
that when the heart has been warmed, he should kneel or stand with
folded hands and with eyes toward Heaven begin to pray. The content
of oral prayer is confession, thanksgiving, petition, intercession
and praise. This is nothing other than oratio. Luther's prayer does
not end there, however, because he knows that contemplation,
or a prayer without words, is also part of the prayer time.

> if in the midst of such thoughts the Holy Spirit begins to
> preach your heart with rich, enlightening thoughts, honor
> him by letting go of this written scheme; be still and listen to
> him who can do better than you can. Remember what he says
> and note it well and you will behold wondrous things…"

Indeed, Luther loses himself in such prayer. He "listens in silence"
and tries not to obstruct the teaching of the Holy Spirit. He
wrote, "in the silence it is the Holy Spirit who preaches, and one
word of the Spirit's sermon is far better than a thousand of our
prayers. Many times I have learned more from one prayer than
I might have learned from much reading and speculations."

Finally, Luther reminds Master Peter that prayer is really an
attitude of the heart and that the heart must be eager and ready
to be in God's presence. He writes that as Peter concentrates and
focuses his attention on the razor and hair when he is shaving
or cutting, so must he more concentrate on the "singleness
of his heart" (in German auffrichtigkeit) on God "if it is to
be a good prayer." John Doberstein (20th century) translates
auffrichtigkeit as "prayer possessing the heart exclusively." I
love that translation. For Luther all we have is gift. Faith is gift.
Correspondingly, prayer is gift that possesses our hearts.

This document from Luther is a great treasure for the Lutheran
Church. It deserves to be widely read. All too often, we
stress Luther's doctrine without understanding the devotional
practice that spawned it. This is dishonest and dangerous. It
is dishonest because Luther's active spiritual life informed
and shaped his theology. It is dangerous because *theology
without spirituality degenerates into formalism, theological legalism and
rationalism.* For Luther, prayer is the foundational act of the
Christian's life. The prayerful root system causes the tree of
our lives to blossom. Remove the roots and the tree dies.
"Dear Master Peter:" Luther writes, "I give you the best
I have. I tell you how I myself pray. May our Lord God
grant you and everyone to do better! Amen."

2. A Usable Model Based Upon Ancient Practices

What follows in this section is a practical application, using
the ancient model of the monks' rhythm of prayer and
Luther's insights. The text we will use for the basis of the
devotions is John 10:11: "I am the Good Shepherd. The
Good Shepherd lays down his life for the sheep."

Lectio

Recite the text six, ten, or twelve or more times so that you are
familiar with every word. You might want to include yourself
and the name of Jesus into the text. It would then read, "Jesus
is the Good Shepherd. Jesus lays down his life for me." Repeat
portions of the text. "Jesus is the Good Shepherd." Repeat it
slowly. Emphasize different words. "Jesus is the Good Shepherd."
"Jesus is the Good Shepherd." Feel the different nuances of
each recitation. Try not to analyze. That will come later.

Repeat the second half of the text. "The Good Shepherd lays down
his life for the sheep." Say it quietly and slowly a number of times.

As above, emphasize different words. "The Good Shepherd lays down his life for the sheep." or "The Good shepherd lays down his life for the sheep." Personalize the text. "The Good shepherd lays down his life for me," or "Jesus lays down his life for me."

There are almost an infinite number of variations on this one text alone. It is possible to use this text for the basis of devotions for a week or more. Each day, lectio could focus on a different portion of the text. One word of caution: there is an inclination to begin reflection on the text too soon. Try just to repeat the text or its variation without any reflection. Let the words flow through you. Allow the words to speak for themselves. Lectio is simply a time to bathe in the Word.

Meditatio

Meditatio is the time to reflect upon the text. It can take many forms and have different intensities. The form and intensity depend upon the personality, spiritual maturity, and the circumstances surrounding the one who is praying. It is important that this time of reflection does not lapse into an intellectualization about the text. Meditatio is not a time for critical study. It is a time to prayerfully ask, "What is God saying to me in this text?" or "What message does this text have for my life?" It is a time for personal reflection. It is a time for brutal honesty. For instance, we may reflect upon times when we have felt alone and needed a Good Shepherd. We may remember God's hand lifting us up. Alternatively, we may recall times we could not feel the presence of the Good Shepherd.

We might want to think of other shepherds in our lives: parents, friends, mentors, etc. We may want to reflect upon times when we were shepherds to others. We could remember opportunities when we failed to be proper shepherds. Underneath this reflection, we are reminded of Jesus, the Good Shepherd, who undergirds us in all times and all places. Allow yourself to pursue particular thoughts or feelings. They may be God directed. Sometimes it is necessary to abandon our own agenda. The best devotional times are often the moments we become God directed. Indeed, sometimes we might abandon our prescribed text altogether or change texts in the middle of our devotions. As Luther says, "that's when the Holy Spirit speaks to us—so listen. One word from the Holy Spirit is better than a thousand words from our own lips."

Oratio

While lectio and mediation serve to bathe us in the word, oratio is a time to empty our mind and heart of those things we need to share with God. Oratio may come at any time in the devotions. This model for devotions should not be so rigid that we short-circuit oral prayer. Indeed, we may feel the urge to pray any time during the course of the day. When a prayer arises; pray it. God is calling you into prayer. After all, God initiates prayer. Whenever we feel the urge to pray, the prayer has already begun with the call of God.

Oral prayer can be divided into five kinds of prayer: Confession, Conversation, Intercession, Petition, Thanksgiving, and Praise. After immersion in the text, these prayers will come naturally.

Confession: Still using the Good Shepherd text as the basis for our devotions, one might confess those times when we did not want a shepherd. We might confess that we not only hid from the shepherd, but we hid from the flock or used the flock for our own purposes, etc. We might not only confess our negligence to be sheep in God's flock, but our failure to shepherd those flocks we tend (i.e. family, friends etc.)

Conversation: Quite often we just want to share with God our hopes, desires, disappointments, and even some of the trivial things that occur during the day. We can speak with God, as we would with any friend. Conversation may not seem to be important, but it is essential in deepening our friendship with God. It is simply a time to share with God things that are on our mind.

Intercession: It is natural for us to think about certain people when we are in prayer. We all know people who need the Good Shepherd. Intercession lays them before the Good Shepherd. We know that the Good Shepherd will lay down his life for them. What better place can we bring our loved ones, than the arms of the Good Shepherd who leaves the 99 and seeks out the one who is lost, alone, ill, or in despair? Indeed, we may even imagine the Good Shepherd carrying our loved ones in his arms.

Petition: If intercession is prayer for others, petition is prayer for ourselves. It is quite appropriate to pray for yourself. We all need it. We all want it. We all have some things that require the presence and actions of the Good Shepherd. We may be ill. We may be worried about work or family and friends. The Good Shepherd cares for each sheep—including you.

Thanksgiving and Praise: When we pray to the Good Shepherd, God hears our prayers. We may also thank God for those times the Good shepherd heard us in the past. It is natural to give thanks. This might be a good time to read a Psalm of thanksgiving like Psalm 103. "Bless the Lord, O my soul and all that is within me bless God's holy name!"

Contemplatio: resting in the embrace of God

Everything up to this point is preparation for contemplation. Unfortunately, this supreme form of prayer is often misunderstood, neglected, or even maligned. It, however, may be the deepest form of prayer. As mentioned previously, contemplation is simply a resting in God or a loving lingering. Another name might be, the Prayer of Adoration. In our context, it is simply a time for the sheep to snuggle up next to the shepherd. It is a time to lovingly gaze upon the Good Shepherd who neither slumbers nor sleeps. Let me illustrate with two examples. I owned a golden retriever named Amber. She was gentle, obedient, and loving. She was always at my feet, always by my side. I do not know what she got out of it. She merely wanted to be near me. Similarly, we need to be near God. In 1973, my wife gave birth to our first child, Kaaren. As an infant, Kaaren slept much of the time. Faye would quite often get a chair, place it near the crib, and just gaze upon Kaaren. It was a loving gaze; it was a gaze of adoration. Such is contemplation.

We live in a time when people are seeking. They seek peace of mind, financial security, meaning and purpose, joy, hope, etc. It is incumbent upon the church to direct people to the only one who can give these gifts–God the Good Shepherd.

May God grant you the ability, desire and courage to develop your prayer life in such a way that God becomes as one with you as your hand is to your arm.

3. Silence is the friend of prayer. In fact, it is prayer's best friend. In the silent heart, God speaks to us.
   In the silence, we find ourselves.
   In the silence, we find our vocation.
   In the silence, we are found.

4. Occasionally, if we are quiet long enough, we become the vehicle of that which wants to be said. After I had been at Gloria Dei! for a year or two, one of our members, Ruth, was dying. She was in the hospital in Annapolis. About two o'clock one morning I received a call from her nurse. "You'd better get here soon," she implored. I got up, drove fast, and got there in record time. These kinds of visits are difficult, and I wanted to be present to her as well as I could. As I was getting out of my car, I felt the need to be silent for a while. I prayed,

"Lord, I am not certain what I will find or what I need to say. Be my mouth so I may speak words of comfort and grace."

Indeed, Ruth was bad off, but she was still coherent. She looked at me and said, "Oh, Pastor, thanks for coming. I need your help." Without even thinking I blurted out, "I know it. You're afraid you are going to Hell." I could not believe what I had just said. Where did that come from? It certainly was not part of my training. Before I could add anything else, she responded, "Yes, that's it. How did you know?" I was stunned. I had prayed for God to speak through me, yet, when it happened I was unprepared. Fortunately, I did not let her know that, and we had a long discussion about God's embracing arms of mercy. As I returned home, I knew that God had surrounded that discussion. Ruth died in peace the next day. I know God's arms swooped her up and carried her to her Heavenly home.

5. Late in my ministry I began ending letters or emails with the words, "May you rest in God's embrace." I have grown to love that phrase. One Christmas a member of Gloria Dei! gave me a carving of a little boy resting on God's palm.

The prophet Isaiah wrote, "I have engraved you on the palm of my hand." (Isaiah 49:16) When I am anxious or the cares of the world weigh me down, I take my little carving and hold it. I know that I can rest in God's embrace. Sometimes it is all the prayer I need.

6. "By reading and pondering the scriptures, we learn to know Christ, who speaks to us through them. Christ is both our teacher and the lesson we learn."
St. Bernard of Clairvaux (d.1153)

Luther called Bernard the greatest of all the Church Fathers. It is difficult to overstate his impact on the medieval church. He was founder of dozens of monasteries and was advisor to popes. He was a man of great intellect and deep faith. Like all of the great spiritual leaders, he drew his inspiration from scripture. It is food people of faith eat and the drink that quenches the thirsty soul. Feed on scripture when your soul is hungry and your spirit craves water the water of life. It can sustain you in the most difficult days.

7. Jesus said, "Whenever you pray, go into your room and shut the door and pray to your Father who is in secret." (Matthew 6:6) There is a duality in humans. We are both exterior and interior. There is an exterior me the world can see and know. There is also a me the world cannot see or know. The interior me is invisible to the world, yet is the genuine me. Jesus speaks about two closets. One is made of wood. The other is the closet of the heart or mind. It is in the heart where God abides. Jesus said, "The kingdom of God is within you." (Luke 17:21) St Makarios of Egypt (4th century) writes, "The heart is a small vessel, but all things are contained within it; God is there, the Angels are there, and there also is life and the Kingdom, the Heavenly cities and the treasures of Grace."

Go to the inner closet of your heart and place your mind before the God who lives there. The reward is a deeper experience of God and a better understanding of yourself and others.

8. Above I mentioned that there is a duality in humans. We are both exterior and interior. There is also a duality in the interior me. There is a secret me that only God and I know, and there is an unknowable me that only God knows.
   It is there, in that undiscovered cavern of the unknowable, that God knows me most sublimely.
   It is there, in that exquisite habitation, that God is more intimate to me than I am to myself.
   It is there, in that stunning space, that God resides to undergird, encourage, and sustain me.
   It is there, in the space God carved out as God's home, we can rest in God's embrace.

9. Community worship does not only take place on Sunday morning. Daily devotions are the private and personal worship of the congregation throughout the rest of week. It happens whenever members pray. During the Second World War Dietrich Bonhoeffer wrote in his outstanding little book *Life Together* "Let him who cannot be alone beware of community... Let him who is not in community beware of being alone...." This is another little Lutheran paradox. Each by itself has profound perils and pitfalls. Those who want fellowship without solitude, wade into the shallows of noise and self-indulgence. Those who seek solitude without fellowship fall into the abyss of vanity, self-infatuation and despair.

Community and solitude are both essential for Christian growth. Some of us favor one over the other. Being alone is natural for me. I crave alone time. Nevertheless, God created me to be in community. Christianity is more than one's private spiritual journey. It is the spiritual journey of the community of believers.

Congregations are communities of individuals on a common voyage to spiritual maturity. That voyage demands community occasions and periods of personal solitude. We need to foster personal time with our God if we want to be with others meaningfully. We must seek fellowship and responsibility if we want to be alone in a deep and profound way. We nurture both if we want spiritual wisdom.

10. In 1957, the Army transferred my Dad to Germany. We did not travel concurrently, so my Mom, my sister and I lived with my grandparents in Michigan. I remember one Saturday watching Grandpa at the breakfast room table. He was having devotions. He read his Bible aloud, in Norwegian of course. Mom said, "Grandpa believed that if Norwegian was good enough for Jesus, it was good enough for him." He took the sick list from the church and prayed for each person by name. He prayed for each of his six children and their spouses, his sixteen grandchildren, his family in Norway, his neighbors by name, and for the church, in both Norway and the USA. I had never seen that side of Grandpa, and to this day, the picture of him in prayer is embroidered in my heart. May we all do as well.

11. I have music in my head all day. There is never a time when some melody doesn't ring in my ears. I like it. Good thing too, otherwise it would drive me nuts. Sometimes the songs are popular ones from the radio. Sometimes they are jingles from TV ads. Sometimes they are ones I wrote. Sometimes they are hymns or Psalms. At other times, I find myself singing or humming parts of the liturgy. I especially like part of the Compline service. I even wake to music resounding in my head. In a similar way, God is never far from my

thoughts. It is a devotion that has no beginning and no end. You may not have music in your head all the time, but you can have God in your head in some way. Maybe, it is seeing God in others. Maybe, it is having a picture of Jesus in your mind's eye. Maybe, it is a Psalm, hymn, or prayer that you have memorized. We can keep the presence of God ever before us in many different ways. Consequently, we can be in worship and in silent dialogue with God all day long.

12. Thomas Keating says that the spiritual journey is like the migration of English sparrows. "Each sparrow weighs about an ounce and a quarter. Yet, twice each year they take off en masse into the unknown, committing themselves to the air and flying over the ocean where there are no landmarks to give them any guidance. Without any hesitation, every fall thousands of them take off, and in the spring thousands return undergoing the same hazards."

Sometimes it may seem as if we have no idea of where we are going. We may encounter all kinds of obstacles on our journey. The birds commit themselves to the elements by way of blind trust in their instinct. Our journey is similar.

The spiritual journey is a journey of discovery. We encounter God who is more intimate than our breath. It is, however, not a journey we make alone. We must let go and let the Spirit take us where we are to go. There is no turning back once we have started.

13. St. Paul tells us that disciples of Jesus need inner training in "godliness." It is not, however, our work that changes us interiorly, it is God's work. We cannot "make ourselves godly." Only God can do that. After all, it makes sense. We are not godly or holy by nature. We can only become godly or holy if God, the Holy one, bestows the gift. St.

Paul steadfastly maintains that holiness and righteousness are gifts of God. The spiritual disciplines of prayer, confession, study, fasting, meditation, and service put us on the path to inner transformation. Furthermore, it is essential to remember that the path itself does not lead to this transformation. The spiritual disciplines merely put us in a place where God can work the change in us.

This inner transformation generates love, joy, peace, patience, kindness, hope, etc. It also creates disciples. Regardless of our employment, God calls us all to be disciples. Discipleship is an honor, a responsibility, and dangerous. It is an honor to be called by our Creator and Redeemer. It is a responsibility because we always represent more than ourselves. Disciples represent Jesus. It is dangerous work, because the work of God's people is so often counter cultural and the world may neither understand it nor respect it.

14. "The Bible is alive, it speaks to me; it has feet, it runs after me; it has hands, it lays hold of me." Martin Luther

It is possible to have a deep spiritual life without reading the Bible, but why would one do it? The Psalmist declares, "Thy word is a lamp unto my feet, and a light unto my path." (Psalm 119:105) Most devotions begin with scripture. It only makes sense. The Bible is the history of God's people who struggle to understand God. The Bible reveals the nature of God, the work of Jesus, and the blessings of the Holy Spirit.

The Bible is not a newspaper, history book, or science book. The Bible lies at the heart of western culture, and it still lays claim on us. We define our world and ourselves in relationship to it.

7

Did I remember to tell you to love prayer?

Prayer is a way of finding love and being found by love.

Prayer changes those who pray and
draws them into the heart of the one who hears our prayers.

We are not human beings on a spiritual journey,
but spiritual beings on a human journey.

1. The purpose of our entire spiritual life is total transformation. It seeks to replace old destructive habits of thought with new, life-giving habits. It transforms us into what we really are. **We are not human beings on a spiritual journey, but spiritual beings on a human journey.** Prayer is life creating and life changing. Our spirituality shapes, informs, and determines our humanity. St. Paul wrote that anyone who is in Christ is a new creation.

2. Prayer is an art. We become more proficient by practicing the art. Prayer demands silence. In the silence God speaks. True inner prayer is to stop talking and to listen to the voice of God within our heart. We are attentively alert. We are in God and God is in us. "Prayer is becoming to God what our hand is to our arm. You ask the sun, 'Why do you shine?' She answers, 'I can do nothing else.' It is our nature to shine because it is not we that shine but the light within us." (*The Theologia Germanica*) So, it is with us. When we are at one with God, we emit God's light.

3. There is a real spiritual poverty in the world. Poverty is not a bad word. It merely implies need. The church as a whole is losing members because it does not address the deepest longings, fears, hopes, and dreams of humankind. We are sidetracked by theologicalism, liturgicalism, ethicalism, and moralism. While they are important, they do not address the deepest longings of the human spirit. In a sense, they divert the church from the mission to create spiritually alive Christians ready to encounter life as it comes to them.

4. In order to begin a life of prayer we must first pray for the grace to want to pray. We learn to pray by praying. William Blake wrote, "We are to learn to bear God's beams of love." It happens slowly, however. God meets us where we are. God moves us along at our own pace. An occasional jogger does not suddenly enter an Olympic marathon.

5. To pray is to change. Prayer changes the one who prays. It does not change God. If you do not want to change, you will abandon prayer. Tolstoy wrote, "everyone is out to change the world but no one wants to change himself." God uses prayer to change us. It is God who does the changing, not we ourselves. Prayer puts us in a place where God can do the Divine work in us. Prayer gives God

the space, time, and opportunity to work in us. Prayer is
our gift to God. Transformation is God's gift to us.

It releases us from selfishness and brings freedom: free to
become who we were created to be; free to see through the eyes
of God, hear through God's ears, walk in God's footprints, hold
another in God's arms, and serve without counting the cost.

Through prayer, we fall in love with God and the world. The
world becomes God's precious gift to cherish. The world
lives in poverty of love because it is spiritually impoverished.
Your spiritual poverty is God's call to a deeper relationship.
Prayer trains us in the ways of listening and seeing.

We pray that we might be aligned with God's will—
to see God's will in a thing. We pray that we might
be led by God's guiding and supportive hand.
We pray that we might become God's compassionate
presence in the world.
We pray that God might speak love through us.

6. In 1970, I interned at Christ Lutheran Church in downtown
    Baltimore, Maryland. My intern supervisor, Pastor Ed Goetz,
    told me that one of the gifts of a life of prayer is "the ability to
    see God more easily." That thought is ever present. Prayer gives
    us the ability to see God in the morning sun, joy in suffering,
    and life in the midst of death. It is being able to see the Christ
    in another and the Christ in yourself. Our hearts see that God's
    grace is sufficient to go with us wherever the journey takes us.

7. The one who feels himself to be most destitute in virtue and in
    grace can be rich in both if he has the humility and charity
    to share the virtues of another by rejoicing in them as if they
    were his own. And the strongest and most virtuous of all

become stronger still by the humility, which makes them realize that their virtues are not due to their own efforts alone but to the prayers and encouragement of their others. Thomas Merton (d.1968)

Merton's writings have been important for my spiritual development for decades. His timeless truths ring out loudly and clearly long after his death. The echoes of his words still chime in the writings of contemporary Christian authors. His books still are best sellers. This little quote shines like a lighthouse on a dark and rocky coastline. In essence, he says that we can make another's joy our own by rejoicing in their virtues. How wonderful it is to share another's life without jealousy. Additionally, when we feel self-sufficient we need to remember that the virtues we possess are gifts. Others have prayed for us and their prayers have helped make us the persons we are.

Often when I visit one of our members they will say, "I felt the prayers of the congregation." Praying for others is essential for the life of the Christian. Remembering that others have prayed for us, keeps us humble and grateful.

> Gracious, generous God, I owe you
> my breath, my heartbeat,
> my mind's activity. You are the author of my being, the one who gives me life. I thank you for the multitude of gifts you have showered on my existence and
> for each person who has
> played a role in my growth. Help me now to have clear eyes to see and accept my part gracefully and humbly responding so that others might live, too. Thomas Merton

8. We long to see God. We long to know God intimately. The greatest gift that a lifetime of prayer gives the individual

is the ability to discern God's presence more easily and in more places. It does not mean that there is no struggle. It does mean that people of prayer are equipped with more than their own strength of will. God's grace is indeed sufficient. The gift of prayer is to know that grace, to be encompassed by its arms, and sustained by its blessing.

9. Spirituality is attentiveness to God's self-disclosure through prayer, worship, and study. It discovers ways we can love God through service to humankind. It is a holy life created by God.

    Spirituality is transformative. It is growth in holiness. It is evidenced by an ever-deepening love of God, self, and neighbor. St. Paul describes it as the transformation of the mind, whereby the mind becomes capable of discerning God's will (Romans 12:2). He reminds us that God creates new hearts in us. "God's love has been poured into our hearts." (Romans 5:5) He confidently proclaims that the spiritual person is "new creation." (Galatians 6:15) He holds out the promise of a new life, in which our old ways die and Christ is formed and lives in us. (Galatians 2:20 & 4:19) Moreover, he declares; a holy life "lives by the Spirit" and is "guided by the Spirit." (Galatians 5:25)

10. I have known a few holy people in my life. They are holy not because of some intrinsic quality they posses on their own. They are holy because they all have been people of prayer. God fully possessed them. Their influence on me has helped me become a better person and pastor.

    My Dad was the greatest influence in my life. His model for life and ministry were invaluable for my growth as person and pastor. While he was alive, I would call and say, "Dad, I have a problem." He would always listen. When I was a young pastor at Christ Church, I called and began to moan about this thing in the church or that person who was on my case. He listened for a while and then responded, "Tommy, I don't ever want to hear you complain about your congregation ever again. You are not there to be their judge. You are their servant called to love and care for their souls. I don't want you to complain about them to anyone, not even God!" With that, he hung up. At first it seemed harsh, but I have tried to live up to that standard. How I view my congregations turned around 180 degrees. It may seem harsh but it isn't.

My intern supervisor, Dr. Ed Goetz, was one such man. He had a great impact on me. His influence is chronicled in other chapters, so I don't feel the need to include him here. Let it suffice to say, helped me learn to love parish ministry and regard the calling as one of service to God by loving God's people.

Roy Oswald has been a great friend for almost forty years. We do not see as much of each other as we used to but he changed my life. When I was at Augustana, I had a depressive episode. He said, "Tom, I am going to change your life." I was overweight and overworked. I had a desk drawer full of Twinkies and a bed in my office where I slept when I had late nights and early mornings. He started me running and taught me to meditate. Both those things helped save my ministry.

Somewhere in the late 80's, Roy ran the Marine Corps Marathon. He invited a number of us to celebrate at his apartment in DC. I knew that Tilden Edwards was going to be there. I had known Tilden for a about ten years and just loved being in his presence. Tilden is a man of few words. Tilden had facilitated my spiritual growth and taught me to pray in a deep and meaningful way, and make it an integral part of my day. His presence spoke more than words could. I brought Faye to the party to congratulate Roy but also to meet Tilden. I told her of his special presence. When anyone came through the door, Faye would ask, "Is that he?" I kept saying, "When he comes you will know it. Stop asking." Finally, after we had been there about an hour, Tilden showed. "That is Tilden. I just know it." Of course she was right. Something about holy people is ineffable but noticeable. The numinous surrounds them.

Two monks have blessed me with their presence and knowledge. Father William from Holy Cross Abbey in Berryville was my spiritual director for many years. The other was Father Albert from Bolton Abbey who lived in the room next to mine when I made a two month retreat there in 1996. It is not possible to relate their impact on my life. Sometimes I would just want to be silent with them. At first you think to yourself, "These are simple and loving men, and I just relish being around them." After a while, though, you think, "These men must be pleasing to God," and your focus shifts from them to God and God's presence surrounds and embraces your time together. I can think of no greater accolade to pay to someone.

11. St. Augustine wrote:

> There is a different kind of prayer without ceasing; it is longing. Whatever you may be doing, if you long for the day of everlasting rest, do not cease praying. If you do not wish to cease praying, then do not cease your longing. Your persistent longing is your persistent voice. When love grows cold, the heart grows silent. Burning love is the outcry of the heart! If you are filled with longing all the time, you will keep crying out, and if your love perseveres, your cry will be heard without fail.

Augustine helps us better understand St. Paul's injunction, to "pray without ceasing." Prayer without ceasing is not prayer filled with words. It is prayer filled with longing, love, and praise. It is a heart that is attentive to God's presence in my life. One day, as my impending retirement became more real, I was anxious and unsettled. Cares of this world weighed me down. I told myself, "Tommy, just let go of it. This kind of worry does you no good and it changes nothing." I could not let it go. Instead, I heard a voice in the back of my head, "If you can't let it go, then let me help you carry it." It was my beloved Lord calling me to prayer. The rest of the day was, as St. Augustine described it, a "persistent longing." My heart reached out to God who was drawing me to God's peace filled side. My anxiety did not fall away like autumn leaves. It did diminish. I also knew that Jesus was beside me. My unease was a constant yearning for God. When I look back on that day from a distance, I remember my anxious heart less and God's presence more.

St. Augustine also wrote, "You have formed us for yourself and our hearts are restless 'til they find rest in you." Restless heart of mine, rest in the heart of Jesus. Rest in your Lord.

12. Ole Hallesby was an early twentieth century Norwegian pastor and writer. I grew up with his writings. In fact, when my paternal grandmother was dying she wanted my Dad to read from Hallesby's book, *Prayer*.

> To pray is nothing more involved than to open a door giving Jesus acces to our needs and permitting Him to exercise His own power in dealing with them. He who gave us the privilege of prayer knows us very well. He knows our frame; He remembers that we are dust. That is why He designed prayer in such a way that the most impotent can make use of it. For to pray is to open the door unto Jesus. Prayer by Ole Hallesby

A picture of Jesus knocking at a door hung in our
home when I was growing up. I always prayed that
Jesus would knock on our front door. Actually, he
did better. He knocked on the door of my heart.

13. Whenever you pray, go into your room and shut the
door and pray to your Father who is in secret; and
your Father who sees in secret will reward you.
(Matthew 5:6)

> In the morning, force your mind to descend from the head
> to the heart. Hold it there, calling ceaselessly in mind and
> soul: Lord Jesus Christ, have mercy upon me." Repeat it
> until you are tired. When tired, transfer your mind to the
> second part, "Jesus, Son of God, Have mercy upon me."
> St. Gregory of Sinai (d. 1360)

For the West, contemplation is almost a lost art.
Nevertheless, the great spiritual leaders of the church
have one thing in common—an uncommon prayer
life. St. Gregory was one in a long line of Hesychasts.
Hesychasm comes from the Greek word meaning stillness,
quiet, rest, or silence. It springs from Jesus' directive to
go into your closet to pray. Hesychasts taught that there
are two kinds of closets. The first is physical. It is that
quiet place where there are no external disturbances.
The other is that inner secret closet of the heart.
It is in that hidden place of the heart we
encounter God and God encounters us.
It is in that deep place that God does God's work.
It is in that fertile place that God cultivates
the rich ground within us.
When we are quiet and still long enough: when we can
lovingly linger in our inner closet, we can hear God

whisper, "You are my beloved." If we are patient, we
can feel at one with God and at peace with the world.

14. God seeks out the silent heart. Silence is the friend of
prayer. Silence is not so much lack of noise as it is a quiet
restful state. There is always some noise outside and inside.
Nonetheless, there can be silence in a deep place inside
us. A pastor in Virginia told me, "Be a contemplative
in the milieu." It is beginning to sink in. We can take
that quiet space with us everywhere and any place.

15. Noise and busyness are twin rivals for a deep interior life.
Noise sidetracks us from what is within, and busyness distracts
us from the work of prayer. The spiritual life craves silence
and solitude. They are twin allies that generate a deeper
knowledge of God, and an enhanced love of neighbor.

There is within us a great need for periods of silence and
solitude. Instinctively we all know that there are fruits
in silence. God whispers into the silent listening heart.
There is an inner space that cries out for God and yearns
for contact with the holy. To grow in intimacy with God
requires times of silence. We need to draw back from
business and noise into a place where God can catch us.

16. "Prayer is the fair flower of humility and
gentleness." Evagrius Ponticus (d.399)
In 2013 I made a three week retreat to a monastery in Ireland.
It was November, and it was cold. Except for a few radiators,
the chapel is unheated. Vigils is at 4 AM and it is cold in the
chapel. I dare say it did not get much above 50 degrees. One
morning I was particularly cold. Brother Alberic, who sat next
to me, noticed me shiver. After Vigils, he told me to follow him
to his cell (room). Now his room is Spartan and small. I guess
that is why they call it a cell. In his little wardrobe, he pulled

out a sweater. It was woolen and knit on the Arran Islands off the north west coast of Ireland. He said, "Tom, here take. I never use it. I don't need it. Please use it and keep it." It is a very attractive gray cardigan. He said, "Cardigans are for old people." Now Alberic is 85. I asked, "Have you looked in the mirror lately?" After he laughed, he said again, "Please it gives me great pleasure to give it to you." It did. When I wear the sweater, I feel the embrace of Brother Alberic. He is a fair flower of humility and gentleness. It is an honor to know him.

17. If I had a nickel for every time someone said, "All I want is a little peace and quiet," I could build my own golf course. We live in a world of noise and action. Our bodies and minds crave silence and peace. After all, that is why we sleep. Prayer is a time when we can rest our weary hearts and give our bodies a little respite from activity. The following is a description of a kind of prayer that puts us in God's presence and allows us to sit in silent adoration of our Lord.

Centering Prayer is a method of silent prayer in which we experience God's abiding presence within us. This method of prayer is both a method to experience God and a discipline to deepen our relationship *with* God.

Centering Prayer does not replace other kinds of prayer. It is a resting in God's presence and a loving lingering with the holy. Centering Prayer accentuates a personal relationship with God. Centering prayer moves us from conversation with Christ to communion with Him.

Centering prayer is as old as prayer itself. Its popular usage can be traced to Trappist Monks from The Abbey of St. Joseph in Spencer, Massachusetts. The method is simple, and the following guidelines describe its practice.

I spent two weeks with Father Thomas Keating at
a monastery in Snowmass, Colorado. What follows
are from the notes I took during that visit.

THE GUIDELINES as developed by Father Thomas Keating
with annotations from me.
1. Choose a sacred word as the symbol of your intention
to consent to God's presence and action within.

> You may choose any sacred word you like. I suggest
> you choose a special name you use when you
> pray to God: Lord, Father, Spirit, Jesus etc.

2. Sitting comfortably and with eyes closed, settle briefly,
and silently. Introduce the sacred word as the symbol of
your consent to God's presence and action within.

> It is best to sit in a straight-backed chair with
> your feet flat on the floor and your back
> perpendicular to the ground. Allow your hands rest
> comfortably in your lap and close your eyes.

3. When you become aware of thoughts, return
ever so gently to the sacred word.

> Our minds tend to wander. Thoughts fill our minds.
> Focusing on one thought is difficult. Do not despair.
> When your mind wanders, gently bring it back to your
> sacred word. You may also notice parts of your body
> that are stiff or even have an itch somewhere. Pay
> no attention but peacefully go back to your word.

4. At the end of the prayer period, remain in silence
with eyes closed for a couple of minutes.

I suggest you practice it for twenty minutes twice a day.

For westerners this may seem like a fruitless exercise that accomplishes little more than relaxing for a while. Not true. It is an act of faith, which gives God the space, time, and opportunity to do God's transforming work within us.

18. Abhishiktanda was a French theologian who lived in India. In his book *Prayer* he wrote,

> The human manifestation of Jesus is itself a sign and has to be left behind. To reduce Jesus to what his friends remembered about him would be to treat him as an historical object we can manipulate as we like and in so doing deny his mystery.

God is not something in the past to be studied but a presence to be cherished in the here and now. In the same way, the Bible is not merely the recorded history of God's people, but a book that is alive and current. It is more than a study of a God 2,000 years ago. It is an account of how God is present today. Many years ago, a congregation was looking to call a new pastor. A call committee was appointed, and it interviewed many candidates. One gentleman on the call committee asked the same question of every potential pastor. He asked each of them to recite the 23rd Psalm. One after another would recite it. None of the candidates received a "yes" vote from him. Finally, he voted for one of the prospective pastors. When asked why he voted for him and not the others, he replied, "They all knew the Psalm, but he knew the shepherd." Jesus is not someone merely to be studied. He is our Lord and friend to be treasured.

19. Mother Teresa of Calcutta wrote, "Prayer enlarges the heart until it is capable of containing God's gift of

himself. The more you pray the more you will love to pray. The more you love to pray the more you will pray."

In the final analysis we pray so that we might
become aligned with God's will.
We pray that we might see God's will in a thing.
We pray that God will take our large hearts
and give them to the world.

You are on a journey to Holiness. God is leading you. Walking with God in a life of prayer does enlarge the heart. Of course, I am speaking in metaphor. The heart does not actually grow. What does grow, through your walk with God, is the ability to receive the gifts God gives. An ever-deepening relationship with God permits you to receive the gift God makes of God's self. Consequently, your heart's capacity to love is enlarged.

Resolve to love your journey into holiness. Resolve to love prayer; to love the silent times you patiently linger with the Lord, to love the gifts—yes—but to love the Giver more. The result will be a heart more skilled in the art of love.

20. One of the books that has nurtured me for the past forty years is a book entitled *Prayer* by an old Norwegian pietist named Ole Hallesby. The book I own was first given to my father in 1941 from his parents. They gave it to him just before he went to the Philippines in WWII. Dad gave me this book when I entered seminary in 1968. I have treasured it for all these many years.

Hallesby says some things that cause us to pause and
reflect because at the outset they seem counterintuitive.
The following has proved to be difficult for many,
yet its truth rings out as we ponder its meaning.

Prayer is an attitude of our hearts, an attitude
of mind. Prayer is attitude to God. It is a
spiritual condition of the heart.

What is this spiritual condition? What is the
attitude of the heart that God recognizes as prayer?

In the first place it is helplessness. Prayer and helplessness
are inseparable. Only he who is truly helpless can truly pray.

My helpless friend, your helplessness is the
most powerful plea that rises up to the tender
father-heart of God. To pray is to open the
door unto Jesus and admit him in your distress.
Your helplessness is the very thing which opens
wide the door unto him and gives him access to
all your needs.

Now, obviously we are not totally helpless. We can, after all,
make a living, raise our children, and do the myriad of things
it takes to live in our complicated and complex society. We,
however, cannot make ourselves holy. We are helpless to
win the holiness game. The holy is God's domain. Hallesby
maintains that God causes us to grow in holiness. We cannot
attain it on our own. Holiness comes from God. It comes from
prayerfully placing ourselves in God's presence. It is pure gift.

21. God chooses to want us. In a way, God chooses to need
us. As we are incomplete away from God, God is not
satisfied to be separated or distanced from us. That is the
reason for the incarnation. That is the reason for the gift
of the Spirit at Pentecost. God wants to have an intimate
relationship with us. That intimacy brings joy and inner

peace. Indeed, God wants to be with us more than we want to be with God. God loves us more than the one who loves us most. God says, "You are worth searching for."

22. A rabbi asked his students, "When is it at dawn that one can tell the light from the darkness?"
One student replied, "When I can tell a goat from a donkey."
"No," answered the rabbi.
Another said, "When I can tell a palm tree from a fig."
"No," answered the rabbi again.
"Well, then what is the answer?" his students pressed him.
"Only when you look into the face of every man and every woman and see your brother and your sister," said the rabbi.
"Only then have you seen the light. All else is still darkness."

23. Amazing grace, how sweet the sound,
That saved a wretch like me.
I once was lost, but now am found;
Was blind but now I see.
John Newton

As I mentioned previously, I have a song in my head all day. Music is a constant companion. I am never without it. I wake up with a tune and I go to sleep to a melody. Sometimes the song is just a little jingle. One trivial one that keeps playing is, "I wish I were an Oscar Meyer wiener…." Don't know why that song keeps coming up but it does. It usually appears when I feel a little silly.

"Amazing Grace" is another song that resonates in my heart. At some point during each day, I find myself humming it. It usually happens when I am feeling a little blue or upset. The music in my head reflects the mood of my heart. In a way, all that goes on in our day exposes what is going on within us. Our interior life is generally richer than we think it is. Most of the time, we are unaware of it. We do, however, have more control over what is going on inside than we think we do. We can direct our hearts toward God who lives within. I find that when I am angry or upset, I will chant Psalm 139 or Psalm 23, or sing a hymn. It redirects and transforms the anxious spirit into an amazing grace. You do not need to do it with a song. Maybe a Bible verse can direct your heart toward God. Or maybe you can just picture Jesus with your mind's eye. I have discovered for myself that an upset or a troubled interior is God's call to prayer. Pay attention to your heart it lets your know what is going on inside and calls you to prayer as well.

24. There are at least five ways to look at petition and intercessory prayer.

1. **Regardless of my prayers, everything that happens is God's will.** That means when there is an automobile accident God determines who will live and who will die. Many of us have heard it said, "You just have to accept it, it is God's will. We may not understand it, but God has a higher purpose."

   When a dear pastor friend of mine lost his baby to death, one of his parishioners said to me, "Pastor, see this bouquet of flowers? Some of the flowers are in full bloom and some are only budding. So it is with Heaven. God chooses people who have had a long life and some who are young to beautify Heaven." Nice, huh? That is not the God I worship.

2. **If I have enough faith, God will answer my prayer the way I ask.** This is a relatively common understanding. After all Jesus said, "Truly I tell you, if you have faith as small as a mustard seed, you can say to this mountain, 'Move from here to there,' and it will

move. Nothing will be impossible for you." (Matthew 17:20) I cannot count the number of people who have been plagued with guilt because they felt a loved one's death was due to their perceived lack of faith. It means that the answers to our prayers depend on us. This kind of thinking declares that God has favorites and denies that all are equally loved and cherished.

3. **God sometimes answers and sometimes doesn't or sometimes God says "yes" and sometimes God says "no."** This credo is comparatively common as well. It makes sense after all. The problem is that it makes God's decisions seem rather capricious.

4. **God cannot change things.** This was the answer Rabbi Harold Kushner espouses in in best selling book, *When Bad Things Happen to Good People.* Evil exists in the world and God is powerless over it. I do not believe in a powerless God.

5. **We ask God, "What is it you want me to do in this situation? What is your will for me?"** This was the prayer Jesus prayed in the Garden of Gethsemane. It was not a prayer of resignation but Jesus' heartfelt plea asking, "Father, what is your will for me?" When I encounter a difficult situation—Maybe someone is ill or dying or maybe someone is in trouble. I always pray, "Lord, I need your guiding hand and wisdom. I am not certain what I should do. Help me understand what you would have me do. Help me understand what I should say." This kind of prayer trusts that God can use me and that God can speak through me. It reminds me *that prayer doesn't change God it changes the one who prays.*

We can become the very agents through which God works.

25. God is always present to us. There is never a time or a
place when God is not at hand. God is never more present
or less present. God is never more "here" or less "there."
In truth, God is ever present to us. God is ubiquitous.

Prayer simply recognizes God's presence. The ability to see
God is God's gift to us. God blesses us with the capacity
to catch a glimpse of God's glory and feel God's love.

26. Oftentimes we pray what I like to call "Prescription"
prayers. It is as if we expect God to be a Holy Pharmacist.
I prescribe —God fills the prescription. Sometimes, so it
seems, our prescriptions are not filled as we have requested.
Then, at other times, we do not receive "our" answers.

Prayer is more about the development of a relationship
than about "my" answers. A unique and sacred relationship
can calm my interior storms and lead me to quiet waters.

Prayer leads the one who prays to a new awareness, new
horizons, new visions of justice and peace. The great
saints of the faith are those whose prayer life led them
to a life of service to God. Is not our deepest need the
desire of the soul to find meaning through service?

God calls us to prayer before we even think about wanting to pray.
When I want to pray, God has already called me into prayer.
Our prayers are always responses to God calling us to prayer.

Through prayer, we discover God's presence.
In prayer, we comprehend God's desires to be with us.
Through prayer, we become responsive to God's authority.
Through prayer, we become open to God's guidance.
Through prayer, we become malleable in the hands of
God, as clay is malleable in the hands of the potter.

St. Irenaeus wrote, "Let the clay be moist." In God's holy hands, God can mold us into a unique expression of love in the world.

27. At the center of our being is a divine spark that is untouched by illusion, a point of pure truth, and a gleam that belongs entirely to God. It is inaccessible to the fantasies of our own mind or the vagaries of our own will. This little divine spark is the pure glory of God in us.

   Prayer allows us to catch a glimpse of that divine spark within us, and allows us realize it in our lives. Thus, we become a divine spark that coupled with other divine sparks can set the world ablaze with love.

28. Prayer is dangerous. Sometimes it demands that we look at the world in a different way.
   Thomas Kuhn, a philosopher of science wrote a book in 1962 called *The Structure of Scientific Revolutions*. In that book, he argued that growth in knowledge is not linear. Rather, there are paradigm shifts that in turn encourage an entirely different way of understanding reality. He says that a society will have one paradigm that will pretty much explain the world. Nevertheless, as time goes along it may seem that the world no longer fits that given explanation and seems to invalidate old paradigms – often at that point, a new paradigm is born. New paradigms, however, can cause controversy. In the 16th century, Galileo Galilei championed heliocentrism. The church could not abide this new paradigm and censured Galileo. For the church the earth not the sun, was at the center of the universe. It was not until decades later that the church acknowledged a heliocentric universe. Something like that happened when Jesus was born. His birth demanded a paradigm shift in how the world thought and acted. Think of the paradigm shift that happened for the three

Wisemen. They were not even Jews. They were pagans as
most of the world was. They had a paradigm, an explanation
of what was going on in the world.

Then came a star.

They were not quite sure what it all meant
but follow that star they did.
When they found Jesus their world changed.
Indeed, their worldview changed.
Everything was turned upside down.

They discovered a new paradigm.
This one has Jesus at the center. It must have caused
some serious introspection and self-examination.
Paradigm shifts are difficult.
They do not happen without some soul searching.

Sometimes, life demands that we re-examine
the way we look at the world.
There are demands for shifts that life springs on us.

You are dead set against abortion.
Then your 16-year-old daughter gets
pregnant and she wants an abortion.
You need to reassess.
Your position may stay the same.
You may change your mind.
But what kind of conversation do you have with your daughter?
Regardless, abortion becomes more real
and your worldview is challenged.
You go through life thinking that homosexuality is a sin.
Then your son comes home and relates that he is gay.
What do you do?

What do you say to your son?
It is time to reexamine your worldview.
Is it time for a paradigm shift?
Maybe.
Maybe not.
Regardless your paradigm needs readjusting.
You grow up thinking about God in a particular way.
You are very comfortable with your theology.
Then a crisis happens.
A child dies or you get cancer and your
view of God no longer works.
It is time to reassess your understanding of
who God is and God's place in your life.
You live without taking a stand on many issues because
you do not want to get into arguments. You really
do not want to get involved. Then 20 children and 6
educators are shot in Newtown Connecticut with an
assault rifle, and your world is turned upside down.
It is time for some re-evaluation and shift in your paradigm.
You cannot stand by the side of the road any longer.
If you do your life has no meaning—no purpose.

However, taking the step to get involved is difficult. It
causes a change in how you view your place in the world.
Author, Betsy Rogers, tells a story about driving somewhere
with her 5 year old son who was happily singing a song in
the back seat. They drove past a hitchhiker holding a sign
with his destination, but Mom did not stop. As they went by,
the little guy called out, "Sorry, Jesus." His mother wonders
how it is that he can see what she misses. She marvels at her
son who sees Jesus in the poor, homeless, and oppressed.
We live in a God-filled universe;
we just need to lift our heads and open our hearts to see it.
We must let go of how we want the world to be.

We need to shift our paradigm. When we do,
we can gradually come to see God's presence
everywhere—come to see a blessed universe.

29. *The nearer we are to the heart of God*
the more we long to make a difference to the heart of the world.
In the story of feeding the 5000, Jesus began with very
little: two loaves and five fish. There was not nearly enough
food for everyone. Yet, everyone ate. The more they ate
the more food there was. So much so that there was more
food when they finished than there was when they began.
Similarly, the more we, as a community, feast on the Bread of
Life the greater our capacity to receive more and the more there
is to feast upon. We cannot exhaust it. It keeps multiplying.

St. Augustine wrote that "material goods, unlike those
of the spirit, cannot wholly and simultaneously belong
to more than one person. The same house, the same
land, cannot belong *completely* to several people at
once, nor the same territory to several nations."
St. Augustine goes on. The same spiritual treasure can
belong in its entirety to everyone at the same time,
without any disturbance of peace between them.

Indeed, the more people there are to enjoy the Holy
Spirit in common, the more completely they are
immersed in the Holy Spirit. The same truth, the same
virtue, the same God, can belong to us all. Such are the
inexhaustible riches of the Spirit that they can be the
property of all and still satisfy the desires of each.

We only possess a truth completely when we teach it to
others and allow others to share our contemplation.
We only truly love a virtue when we allow others to love it also.

We only wholly love God when we desire
to make God loved by all.

Give money away, or spend it, and it is no longer yours. Give
God to others, and you possess God more fully for yourself.

The nearer we are to the heart of God
the more we long to make a difference to the heart of the world.

This truth, so simple and yet so sublime: material
goods and their acquisition tend to cause disunion.
Spiritual goods unite communities in
proportion, as they are loved.
The Gospel puts it very simply: "Seek ye first
the kingdom of God and his justice, and all
these things shall be added unto you."
If the world today is in trouble, it is because it has lost sight
of a fundamental truth that for every Christian is elementary.

The nearer we are as a community to the heart of God,
the more we as a community long to make a difference
to the heart of the world.

The remedy is this, and this only: to consider the one thing
necessary, and to ask God to make us a holy people who live
only on this thought; who will give the world the spirit that
it needs? God has always sent us saints in troubled times. We
need them especially today. Be that Holy person–that saint.

30. Everything exposed to the light becomes
the light. (Ephesians 5:13)
In prayer I bow to the Holy sunlit face of God, and I
become a reflection of that the light for others. In the Sunday

morning liturgy, we end prayers with the words, "through Christ our Lord." We do not so much pray <u>to</u> Jesus as we pray <u>through</u> Jesus, or rather he prays through us. We become the receivers of God's presence and conduits of God's love.

8

Did I remember to tell you about Heaven?

"Let not your hearts be troubled…
I go to prepare a place for you."
John 14:1

God did not make death;
God takes no pleasure in destroying the living.
The Book of Wisdom 1:13

1. People seldom ask about Heaven, except when a loved one dies or someone is gravely ill and is not expected to survive. Then Heaven becomes an important topic for discussion. Folks usually ask, "Do you believe in Heaven?" Well, yes I do. I do indeed. Afterlife has been part of human religion almost as long as there has been religion. We are all familiar with the Egyptian pyramids, and their notion of the afterlife, which caused them to be built. I am convinced that God built into

the human consciousness an awareness that there is something greater than this life. It is in our DNA to wonder about what happens after we die? Does death have the last word, or is there something beyond? What is Heaven like? Who gets to go? How can I be certain that my loved one is in Heaven? At our most vulnerable times, we long for answers to those questions.

2. Potential Lutheran pastors spend fours years at seminary studying theology, after they graduate from college. The third year is practical learning, spent in a pastoral setting. I interned at Christ Lutheran Church in Baltimore, Maryland. It was 1970, and one of my supervisors was The Rev. Dr. Ed Goetz. Ed, or Dr. Goetz, as I called him, was a man of deep faith. He knew his theology, but more importantly, he knew the Lord. I would tag along as he made shut-in visits and hospital calls. He had a Volkswagen Beetle named "schnooky." It was a miserable little car, but Ed loved it. He fastened a little saying to his dashboard: "If you're not part of the solution you're part of the pollution." I watched him interact with members and listened as he prayed with them. I saw him take the hand of the dying and give them peace and hope. He would always say to the folks we visited, "God's grace is sufficient for you." It is a quote from Paul's Second Letter to the Corinthians. I did not really ponder the verse very much. It was 1970, and I was caught up in the antiwar movement and the struggle for civil rights. Then Dr. Goetz's cancer returned. I had grown to love Dr. Goetz, and he and his wife Dorothy had grown to love Faye and me. They had no children of their own, so they kind of adopted us. Faye and I would go to dinner with them often and would visit them in their home. We were with them a lot.

Ed had beaten cancer about ten years earlier, and everyone thought he would be cancer free for the rest of his life. It was not to be. Cancer can be a relentless pursuer that stalks us until we are caught in its clutches. He got the news in January, and by April he was dead. Those few months I shared with

Dr. Goetz, were some of the most poignant of my life. I
was privileged and honored to see how a man of faith dies.
For the members of Christ Church, his faithfulness during
those months was his last and greatest pastoral act. One day,
I tentatively asked, "Dr. Goetz is there really a Heaven?" I
knew his answer of course, but I wanted to hear it from his
own lips. He began by talking about faith. "Faith," he said,
"allows us to see things as they really are without the veil of
this life covering them up. Faith allows us to see peace in a time
of violence, hope in a time of despair, and life in a time of
death." For Ed, Heaven was more tangible than the earth and
more real than this life. It is what we point to during this life.
It is the ultimate destination for a Christian, and the hope of
Heaven adds meaning and purpose to our lives. During his last
months, Ed repeated often, "God's grace is sufficient for me."

Ed spent his last days at The University of Maryland hospital.
During that time, I observed him pray with a nurse who was
having marital difficulties, and comfort his doctor, whom he
had known well and long. Two days before he died, Dorothy
leaned over to him and whispered, "Ed, I love you." He
replied, "I love you too, but I'm pooped." Those were his
last words. He then drifted into a coma. On the day he died,
I sat by his bed, held his hand, and prayed. I ended with the
Benediction. As I said the Benediction, he raised his hands just
as he had done when he blessed the congregation. Then he
died. I know that the angels in Heaven sang, and our Lord said,
"Well done, well done, thou good and faithful servant," as he
welcomed Ed into his Heavenly home. God's grace was indeed
sufficient for you, Ed and it is sufficient for us all as well.

3.   In 1996, I was in an Irish monastery for two months. There,
     I met Father Albert. Father Albert was one of those people
     you just loved to be around. Often at chapel, when I was
     supposed to be praying, I would gaze at him. I had a difficult

time taking my eyes off him. He was a holy man, and his holiness was palpable. My day got better just by being in the same room with him. He did not need to speak. In fact, I liked it better when we were just silent together. In some ways, words detracted from who and what he was. His presence spoke more about who he was than did his words. I once asked him if he was always so holy. The question genuinely embarrassed him. "Oh no," he sheepishly replied, "I am the least holy person I know." It was not false modesty. He really believed it. Holiness and goodness are qualities the holy do not think they possess. They are too humble. Father Albert died many years ago, and I was unable to attend his funeral. I bet the angels in Heaven could not wait to meet him. I am certain they knew of his great holiness. Our loss is Heaven's gain. Rest in peace, Father Albert. I know
your peace is alive in my heart.

4. The resurrection of Jesus is more than the raising to life of one who was dead. Resurrection is being born into a new existence. When Jesus raised Lazarus from the dead, he was "resuscitated." He went back to his old life. Lazarus would die again. Jesus was raised to a new life in a new realm. He is on the other side of death. So it will be with us. When we are raised from the dead, it will not be to this life on earth. We will be raised to a life with God. There will be no physical illness or infirmities. There will not be any painful memories, for the "old has passed away." There will be only joy, love, and peace. There will not be any need for faith and hope. Faith and hope have to do with trusting in the mystery of God. In Heaven, we will have *the certainty of knowing*. Paul says, "Now we see in a mirror dimly, but then we shall see face to face." (1 Corinthians 13) We will know God even as we are fully known. We will be birthed into the waiting arms of the Father in Heaven. Indeed, there is a place for us with Jesus.

5. The resurrection of Jesus was the restoration of the hopes
    and dreams of his followers. It was vindication of their faith
    in the eternal presence of Jesus. In the resurrection, Jesus
    reasserted the promise that "Lo I am with you always."
    The post-resurrection Christian knows that
    death is not an eternal void but a bridge to a
    more perfect relationship with God.

    The post-resurrection Christian knows concretely
    that the presence of God is eternal—unending.

    The post-resurrection Christian knows that the promises of
    God are unconditional. Death does not invalidate the pledge
    of presence, for even in death the promises are true and valid.

    Jesus is on the other side of death—
    yet he is alive and waiting for us.

6. Every once in a while, someone comes into my office rather
    sheepishly, and says, "Pastor Tom, you're going to think I am crazy
    but my Mom {who has died} visited me." Over the years, I have
    heard stories like that at least a hundred times. The first few times I
    thought, "Yup, you are crazy," although I did not say it. After a few
    dozen times I thought differently about it. I do not understand it,
    but I believe people when they tell me their story. Normally, their
    loved one's unexpected visit comforts the bereaved. It is as though
    the loved one comes and says, "I am ok. Don't be sad for me."

    Somewhere around 2000 a lady, I'll call her Alice, came in with a
    story that had a different twist. Her Dad had just died, but it was
    her Mom, who had died years before, who visited her. Alice and
    her mother had a big fight before her Mom died. Alice carried the
    guilt of that last conversation for years. She could not shake it. Alice
    came in and said, "Pastor Tom, you're going to think I'm crazy, but

Mom visited me. Mom came and stood at the foot of my bed. I
didn't know what to do, so I blurted out, 'Mom, I am so sorry for all
the terrible things I said to you.' Mom, just looked at me and replied,
'I don't know what you are talking about. Honey, don't you know
that in Heaven all you remember are the love and the joy.'" Her
guilt was snuffed out like an old candle. I do not understand it. I do
believe it. If it happens to you, cherish it. Don't try to figure it out.

In the fall of 2009, a young man, I'll call him Aaron, died in a
violent crash. He wasn't a member, and I didn't have the funeral.
I did know his parents. While the Dad was a person of faith, his
son really wasn't. Wouldn't you know it, but the deceased's Mom
called and asked if I would see Aaron's young son, who was
traumatized. The first words he uttered were, "Pastor Tom, you're
going to think I'm crazy but Dad has visited me a number of times.
Could it be that God sent him?" I asked him how he felt after the
visits. "I feel comforted. Is it real or is it just my imagination?"
If it happens to you, don't try to figure it out; just feel blessed.

7. When we are young, we do not think about Heaven very
    much. Death is so far away; we really do not dwell on it. The
    older I get, the more Heaven is on my mind. My mother is
    94, and Heaven is on her mind all the time. My Dad died
    in 2009. My mother is comforted by the knowledge that
    Dad is in Heaven. She says repeatedly, "Tommy, I really
    miss your father, but I know where he is, and that he is
    waiting for me." For Mom, Heaven has always been real.
    It was something she grew up with, and when her parents
    and siblings died, she was comforted by the knowledge
    that they were somehow cradled in God's loving arms.

Around 1990 a child from the congregation was hit by a bus
and died. He was in middle school, and his death stunned
the community. The mother was a wonderful woman, but
had a difficult time understanding Heaven. She had grown

up in the church, but, like many young people, did not really think about Heaven much. Now, the question that confronted her was, "Is there an afterlife of some kind?" She would ask me, "Are you sure my child is in Heaven?" No answer comforted her. She was haunted by the prospect that her son's body was just rotting in the grave. The question was never really fully answered for her, and she spent many distressing years worrying about it. She moved away, so I do not know if she ever resolved her dilemma. I sure hope she did so she can find some peace.

8. "So tell me, Pastor Tom, who goes to Heaven?" I may not get asked a lot about Heaven, but when I do, it is frequently this question. It is a big question. It is an important question, because it says a great deal about the questioner and a great deal about God.

That concern raises a difficult series of questions. These queries are born out of love and concern for friends, relatives, and the world at large. They center around the larger question, "Who will participate in the Kingdom of Heaven, and who will have eternal life?"

a. "Pastor, my son no longer attends church. He tells me he does not believe in God anymore. He says, 'God is a fairy tale like the Easter bunny.' I pray for him constantly. I have tried everything—yet he cannot believe. Will he go to Heaven?"

b. "What of those generations before Christ? The Jews, or the population outside Palestine who never knew God. Will they enter God's Kingdom at the resurrection?"

c. "What of those who have not heard the Gospel, and can't have faith? Will they be banned from Heaven?"

d. "What of those who lived in Africa in the seventeenth and eighteenth centuries and only knew a Christianity that came conquered, destroyed, and enslaved? They only knew an aberrant and violent faith, and rejected it? Will they be saved?"

e. "What of those young people who attended church and only learned of a Christian God of wrath, and hate, and rejected that God? Or those who were not allowed to experience the living, strengthening, nurturing, and transforming love of God? What will become of them?"

Upon what does the promise of eternal life depend? Who is responsible for the fate of those outside the faith? Is the promise of eternal life dependent upon the missionary work of the church? Is it dependent upon the right proclamation of the Gospel? Is eternal life dependent upon our faith? Or is eternal life solely dependent upon the saving work of Christ?

The New Testament witness gives no consistent answers to these difficult questions. I am not sure we are intended to know the answers. The answers belong to God alone. Consider the following scriptural passages:

For God so loved the world that he gave his only Son, so that everyone who believes in him may not perish but may have eternal life. Indeed, God did not send the Son into the world to condemn the world, but in order that the world might be saved through him. Those who believe in him are not condemned; but those who do not believe are condemned already, because they have not believed in the name of the only Son of God. (John 3:16-18)

Indeed, just as the Father raises the dead and gives them life, so also the Son gives life to whomsoever he wishes. Very truly, I tell you, anyone who hears my word and believes him who sent me has eternal life, and does not come under judgment, but has passed from death to life. (John 5:21&24)

Those who eat my flesh and drink my blood have eternal life, and I will raise them up on the last day; (John 6:54)

{Jesus} is the atoning sacrifice for our sins, and not for ours only but also for the sins of the whole world. (1 John 2:2)

For there is one God; there is also one mediator between God and humankind, Christ Jesus, himself human, who gave himself a ransom for all. (1 Timothy 2:5&6)

For while we were still weak, at the right time Christ died for the ungodly.

(Romans 5:6)

[Jesus] has made known to us the mystery of his will, according to his good pleasure that he set forth in Christ, as a plan for the fullness of time, to gather up all things in him, things in Heaven and things on earth. (Ephesians 1:9-10)

Then he looked up at his disciples and said: 'Blessed are you who are poor, for yours is the kingdom of God. (Luke 6:20)

'Blessed are the poor in spirit, for theirs is the kingdom of Heaven. (Matthew 5:3)

For we hold that a person is justified by faith apart from works prescribed by the law. (Romans 3:28)

Do you not know that all of us who have been baptized into Christ Jesus were baptized into his death? Therefore we have been buried with him by baptism into death, so that, just as Christ was raised from the dead by the glory of the Father, so we too might walk in newness of life. For if we have been united with him in a death like his, we will certainly be united with him in a resurrection like his.

(Romans 6:3-5)

Much more surely then, now that we have been justified by his blood, will we be saved through him from the wrath of God. For if while we were enemies, we were reconciled to God through the death of his Son, much more surely, having been reconciled, will we be saved by his life. (Romans 5:9-10)

Therefore just as one man's trespass led to condemnation for all, so one man's act of righteousness leads to justification and life for all. (Romans 5:18)

Salvation, where it is proclaimed, presupposes faith. One must not conclude, however, that for God salvation is not possible without it. God is quite capable of saving all of creation. How that happens, is God's business. We neither have the privilege nor the authority to set limits on God's saving actions. God does not work within the limits of our own preconceived notions.

Simply, some of these questions cannot be answered. We must confess, silently, that creation is under the redeeming, restorative, and saving hand of God. Faith needs a hushed reverence.

So what of our friends, relatives, and those
outside the faith? What shall we do?

Pray that the liberating presence of God
becomes part of their experience.

Place them in the nurturing embrace of our Lord. Place
them in God's care. Trust that God is able to achieve
God's salvatory objective, through the redemptive
power of the cross and resurrection of Christ.

Then what is the work of the church? You may ask, "Isn't
the work of the church to get people into Heaven?"
The church loses the capacity to proclaim the truth of
what is when it thinks its sole task is to "Make people
decide for Christ" so they can "get into Heaven." I
would suggest that the role of the church is fivefold.

  a.   To proclaim the transforming power
       of the cross and resurrection.

       "Anyone who is in Christ is a new
       being." (2 Corinthians 5:17)

  b.   To live as people transformed by
       the work of the Holy Spirit.

       "Let your light so shine before others that they
       may see your good works and give glory to
       your father in Heaven." (Matthew 5:16)

  c.   To work for the poor and destitute, and to promote
       peace and justice. St Francis of Assisi asserted,
       "Always preach the Gospel. Sometimes use words."

"Religion that is pure and undefiled before God, the Father, is this: to care for orphans and widows in their distress, and to keep oneself unstained by the world." (James 1:27)

d. Provide, the children of God, the opportunity, in word, Sacrament, and prayer, to experience God's gracious love. "Train up a child in the way he should go: and when he is old, he will not depart from it." (Proverbs 22:6)

e. The job of the church is to equip the saints— to help members make God a reality in their lives, always realizing that "God's grace is sufficient for us all." (2 Corinthians 12:9)

9. The Nazis arrested Lutheran pastor and scholar, Dietrich Bonhoeffer, in 1943. He had been part of a plot to assassinate Hitler. He died, under Hitler's orders, in Flossenburg Concentration Camp on April 9, 1945, just days before the Americans liberated the camp. Toward the end of his life, he wrote a series of papers and prayers from prison. This is his prayer written only months before his execution.

Death Come now, thou greatest of feasts on
the journey to freedom eternal;
Death, cast aside all the burdensome chains,
And demolish the walls of our temporal body,
The walls of our souls that are blinded,
So that at last we may see that, which here remains hidden
Freedom, how long we have sought thee in
discipline action, and suffering;
Dying, we now behold thee revealed in the Lord.

9

DID I REMEMBER TO TELL YOU THANK YOU? DID I REMEMBER TO TELL I LOVE YOU?

If I took away everything in my life
except for time I spent at Gloria Dei!
my life would be rich beyond description.

1. In June of 1981 I knocked on my first door. It was my next-door neighbor's door. I was very ill at ease. I am an introvert by nature and sometimes find new situations a little unnerving. I remember walking around for a few minutes before I got the courage to knock. For the next six months, I knocked on some 6000 doors. Every day was a new experience, and out of the 6000 doors, I did not have one bad moment. I was graciously greeted and warmly welcomed to the neighborhood. Those months were some of the best months of my life.

From that first door to my last sermon, I have been treated with love. Oh, there were a few bumps and bruises along the way, but they pale in comparison to the love that you showered on my family and me.

In December of that first year, my son Erik was diagnosed with diabetes. He was acidotic and fell into a diabetic coma. Faye and I took turns holding Erik's hand at St. Agnes hospital. When we would arrive home there would be food on our stoop and letters of encouragement in our mailbox. This was merely a precursor of things to come.

On behalf of Faye, Kaaren, and Erik, Thank you for 33 years of loving us. We take the memory of that love with us. When nights become cold, the vestiges of that love will warm our hearts.

2. As I mentioned earlier, Soren Kierkegaard wrote, "Life can only be lived forward but can only be understood backward." When I accepted the call to begin a new congregation I was anxious beyond anything I had ever experienced. The responsibility was almost too much to bear. My supervisor told me that fully half of new congregational starts failed. After a few months, my fears diminished. A group of dedicated people surrounded me, and I knew that God was working through us to establish a new congregation on the Broadneck peninsula. As I look back, I really should not have been so wary. God was present and active in our work. The more than 200 people who worshipped at our first service at the community college evidenced it.

3. I have always been competitive. It began with the relationship with my Dad. From the time I was a little boy we competed at something: golf, baseball, Scrabble, or just seeing who could stay up on water skis the longest. As I grew older,

the competition was with myself. If I shot 75 on the golf course today, I would have to shoot 74 tomorrow. I would grade everything I did. This class I taught was a "B-" or this sermon I preached was a "C+." Every day I had to be better than I was yesterday. Every sermon had to be superior to the last one. It was exhausting. It was stupid. I similarly figured that I had to accomplish more in my ministry. I had to progress through the ranks, as it were. To be successful meant achieving a self imposed set of accomplishments. You did not look at it that way. You only wanted to be loved and hear the gospel. You threw out my grade book.

Now as I look back on 42 years of ordained ministry, I realize that all I ever wanted was to be your pastor. There is no higher honor than to serve you. I could not wish for anything more.

4. The 33 years we were together were not always easy. We had some difficult times. Sometimes, we struggled mightily. Being servants of God is not easy. It requires honest reflection and personal resolve. We did not always agree. Even in our greatest disagreements, you loved me. Even in times when I was not on at the top of my game, you never abandoned me. We worked through those times, and were the stronger for it. Thank you.

5. Over the years members of Gloria Dei! have given of themselves and their money to many causes both at home and abroad. I could not be more proud to have served you. Neither the church council nor the many treasurers said, "We can't help this cause, or this family, or this sister congregation." Even in financially challenging times, you figured out ways to give and help others. You understand that ministry is not a choice, but an opportunity to live out Christ's challenge that when we serve the least of his brothers and sisters, we serve him.

6. Once in a while someone will say to me, "Why do we have to give our money to our sister churches so far away? Why can't we just help people at home?" My response is always threefold:

   a. We do serve people at home. The outreach committee does a good job identifying causes and programs to support. Additionally, I would say that I spend about 20% of my time is with folks who are not members of Gloria Dei!

   b. Jesus' last words to his disciples were, "Go in all the earth." (Matthew 25) We go in response to God's command.

   c. More importantly, however, there is no place where God is not home. How can we who profess Christ as Lord go to him in prayer and say, "Lord, I know there are needy throughout the world, but I am going to keep my money at home"?

   The church is not tied to one community or one nation. It is global. Everywhere is God's home and every home is God's abode. Everywhere is our home, and our home is everywhere. Thank you for knowing that. You have always been there to help and to serve.

7. Sometimes ordained clergy, think we are a gift to God's people, instead of remembering that ordained ministry is a gift to the pastor. You have been a gift to me. You have shown it in many ways. Some days I will go to my office and find a plate of cookies on my desk. It seems like a little thing. It isn't. Somebody had to take the time to bake and think, "I'm going to give Pastor Tom some cookies." Wow! I will miss your cookies. Sometimes, there will be a plate of deviled eggs. You know how much I like them. With all the devilled eggs you have made, you would think my cholesterol would be through the roof. It isn't. Good thing too, because I have eaten more than my share of

eggs. When I was sick and gone for three months to convalesce, you took charge and kept the home fires burning, so to speak. Over the years, I learned never to underestimate your love of the ministry at Gloria Dei! or your care for my family and me. You have demonstrated it repeatedly. Thank you. Well done.

8. True love allows those we love to be entirely themselves. True love does not bend another to fit our own idea of who they should be. Otherwise, we love only the reflection of ourselves we find in them.

    One of the things I have cherished about being your pastor is that you allowed me to be me. You did not try to recreate me into your own private image of what you thought a pastor should be. It was liberating, and allowed me to be creative in worship and work. You did not mind that I did not wear the collar or socks. (Actually, there was one who wanted me to put on socks. You know who you are :-) In fact, you helped me discover who I am as a pastor and person: what a wonderful gift you have been.

9. In 2009 when my father was dying, he asked me to sing to him. He wanted to hear old hymns of his youth, as he prepared to enter Heaven. His favorite song was this one.

    > My God and I go in the field together;
    > We walk and talk as good friends should and do;
    > We clasp our hands, our voices ring with laughter;
    > My God and I walk through the meadow's hue.
    > We clasp our hands, our voices ring with laughter;
    > My God and I walk through the meadow's hue.

    God was my dad's best friend
    That worked out well, because God wanted
    to be Dad's best friend, too.

In fact, God wants to be your best friend. The
importance of that friendship cannot be overstated.
St. Augustine said that "the highest good is friendship."
The best thing a human can do is to be a friend to others.
I hope I have been a good friend. I have great love for
you, and it has grown over time. Not many days go
by when I do not think of you or pray for you.
At Gloria Dei we sing each week,

> To be in your presence is all I desire
> To be in your presence and feel your fire
> Of love burning in my heart
> Love that ignites
> Bringing hope to a wounded world. (Kathy Sherman)

Our love of God is what brings us together.

St. Augustine goes on to say, "As good as love for another
is, it cannot bring eternal joy. Human love ends, because
humans die. Only God is eternal, and only love of God can
bring a love that has no end. Only God's love brings true
and eternal joy to the human spirit. Ultimately, only love of
God is fulfilling. We can, however, love God in each other."

Augustine goes on to say that love is like a wheel. A wheel
is round, and has spokes leading to the hub at the center.
The spokes get closer to each other the closer they get to the
hub of the wheel, to the center. God is the center. God is
the hub. We are like the spokes. The spokes of the wheel are
closest to each other at the center. The more we love God,
the closer we are to each other and more we love each other.
Something deeper than our shared humanity joins us together:
our love of God. It brought us together, and kept us as one.

The best thing we can do for God is to love each other.
The best thing we can do for each other is to love God.

Neither distance nor my retirement can limit that kind of love. Neither time nor place can restrict it. It resides in our hearts, where God lives, and our love cannot end, even with death.

Thank you for being friend to my family and me. Our lives are richer because of you.

10. Around 2006 I was ill and away from the congregation for almost three months. During that time, the church was broken into three or four times. The burglars pried open the door to the office and sacristy. Since the break-ins occurred Sunday nights, the prevailing thought was that they were after the offering. The council had many discussions about a response to the damage. They considered an alarm system and locking the front door. The door to the church had been open since the first unit went up in 1985. The council decided to secure the offering in a safe, but do nothing else. To this day, the door remains open. Over the years a great many people, members and non-members, have thanked me for keeping the door open. They like to go into the sanctuary and pray. Some just play the piano. One fellow I see periodically leaves a little offering near the altar. The church is not a museum that is only open during business hours, but a sanctuary for troubled souls, and a sacred space where someone can sit quietly and pray. Thanks for allowing members of the community to share our space.

11. A few months before I retired, I went to do my Saturday chores at church. I normally check the thermostats, sit in the sanctuary for prayer and meditation, and make certain everything is ship shape for Sunday morning. More times, than I want to count, I will go after I have run or worked out. I don't change from my running clothes. To be honest, I don't look socially acceptable. Most of the time no one is there. One Saturday recently, however, it seemed everyone in the congregation showed up. You didn't even blink. You just accepted how I was dressed. Thanks for not making me feel self-conscious, even when I do not look my best.

10

Did I remember to tell you to cherish God by loving and serving your neighbor?

The nearer I am to the heart of God,
the more I long to make a difference to the heart of the world.

Only love teaches love.

Everywhere is God's home and every home is God's abode.

1. A Christian man is the most free lord of all, and sunject to none. A Christian man is the most dutiful servant of all, and subject to every one. These two theses seem to contradict each other. If, however, they should be found to fit together they would serve our purpose beautifully. Both are Paul's own statements, who says in 1 Cor. 9[:19], "For though I am free from all men, I have made myself

a slave to all," and in Rom. 13[:8], "Owe no one anything, except to love one another." *On The Freedom of the Christian* (also titled *On Christian Liberty*) Martin Luther

As I have written previously, Luther loved paradox. This is another. The first statement in the paradox is what Martin Luther means by Christian Liberty: "A Christian is a perfectly free lord of all, subject to none." Once Jesus Christ frees a person, nothing on earth has true dominion over that person. "So if the Son sets you free, you will be free indeed." (John 8:36)

Nevertheless, for Luther, freedom is not merely being freed "from" external or internal coercion. It is being freed "for" some act of love. For Luther the human condition is selfishness. If I have a choice between doing something good for you, or for me, I tend to choose me. When Christ frees the inner person, there is the freedom to choose the other. A Christian is freed from selfish desires, so she is able to choose to serve her neighbor. Later in that same little book Luther wrote, "Good works do not make a good man, but a good man does good works."

The hallmark of the Christian is the freedom to choose service. Love, by its very nature, is always ready to serve, and be subject to the one who is loved. To be a Christian is to be "other" minded. A Christian never asks, "Should I serve?" Instead, she asks, "Whom shall I serve?" or "How shall I serve?" We cherish God by loving and serving our neighbor. Jesus put it this way, "whoever wishes to be great among you must be your servant, and whoever wishes to be first among you must be your slave; just as the Son of Man came not to be served but to serve." (Matthew 20:26)

2. When the Son of Man comes in his glory, and all the angels with him, then he will sit on the throne of his glory. All the nations will be gathered before him, and he will separate people one from another as a shepherd separates the sheep from the goats, and he will put the sheep at his right hand and the goats at the left. Then the king will say to those at his right hand, "Come, you that are blessed by my Father, inherit the kingdom prepared for you from the foundation of the world; for I was hungry and you gave me food, I was thirsty and you gave me something to drink, I was a stranger and you welcomed me, I was naked and you gave me clothing, I was sick and you took care of me, I was in prison and you visited me."
Then the righteous will answer him, "Lord, when was it that we saw you hungry and gave you food, or thirsty and gave you something to drink? And when was it that we saw you a stranger and welcomed you, or naked and gave you clothing? And when was it that we saw you sick or in prison and visited you?" And the king will answer them, "Truly I tell you, just as you did it to one of the least of these who are members of my family, you did it to me." (Matthew 25)

Matthew 25 not only depicts the relationship between my neighbor and me, but between my neighbor and God. What I do to the least I do to God.

One day, after the Sacrament of Holy Communion, Mother Teresa of Calcutta, spoke to her sisters about the day's work. She asked, "Did you see how tenderly and lovingly the Priest handled the Bread and the Wine? He did so because they were the Body and Blood of our Lord. When you go into the streets today, cherish the poor and the dying in the same way, because they are also the Body of Christ."

3. *The nearer I am to the heart of God, the more I long to make a difference to the heart of the world.*

You are not members of a church merely to cultivate your spiritual life for yourself alone. You are a living prayer for the world. A little community, like Gloria Dei!, seems like it can have very little influence in the world. Yet, communities like Gloria Dei! help hold the world together. I remember reading a story about Thomas Merton, who when he visited a bustling and busy and noisy Lexington, Kentucky, said, "I have to hurry and get back to the monastery. We are holding the world together." It may be a little overstatement, but it is the prayers of religious people throughout the world that keep it from falling apart anymore than it already has.

4. Luther said that a soul lives more where it loves than where it resides. This is a statement that seems to ring true but requires some thought. Of course, we live in the world. Yet, if our world shapes us, we lose something of the holy. Luther reminds us that when God shapes and fashions us we become holy instruments of God's grace. I mentioned in another chapter that we are not human beings on a spiritual journey, but spiritual beings on a human journey. The more we are in touch with our spiritual self, the better we are able to become holy water vessels for a world thirsty for love.

5. The Church is a school of love. The Christian Church is a living symbol, sign, and image of God's love. The world knows of God's love by the actions of the Church. St. Paul writes, "the Church is the Body of Christ,". (Romans 12:5, 1 Corinthians 12:27, Ephesians 4:12) This school, however, is more than books and lectures. **Only love teaches love.** One learns to love by example. We do not learn to love by reading about it. We do not learn to love by hearing great oratory. We learn by observing loving spirits and hearts.

I spent the first six months on the Broadneck Peninsula knocking on doors. We did not yet have Sunday morning worship. I would introduce myself and relate that I was beginning a new Lutheran Church on the peninsula. Quite often, someone would say, "My mother dragged me to church when I was a kid. I have been to church enough." After a while, I asked, "So, what happened when you were at church?" The response was pretty much universal. "Mom would tell me, 'sit still! Don't you know this is the house of God?'" Or "Billy, stop running. This is God's house not a barn." You get the idea. Part of the reason some do not have a relationship with the church is because they felt no love there. Church was a place "I was scolded." No wonder some do not want to join a church or even worship. Philip Yancey met a prostitute and drug addict, who related, "I really want to get my life together. I hate the way I am living." Yancey asked her if she had thought of going to a church. "Why would I do that?" she responded, "I feel bad enough already." The church can expound on God's love brilliantly and with great fervor. If the Body of Christ does not live what it professes, the words are hollow, lack substance, and are duplicitous. We learn by what we see. It holds true for what people feel within the walls of the church and by what the church does outside the building.

6. Jesus said, "They will know you by your fruits." Luther correspondingly said that we become like the God we adore. It is so true. If I worship a God who throws lightning bolts at sinners, I will do the same because it is a "godly" thing to do. If I worship a God who is judgmental and stern, I become the world's magistrate. If, on the other hand, I worship a God of love and forgiveness, I see love and grace as Holy traits to emulate.

    It is also true that I become like the comportment I adore. If I am full of joy and peace, I become even

more peaceful. If, on the other hand, I enjoy creating
chaos and conflict, I become more disagreeable.

Your life is a reflection of who you are inside, and your
interior mirrors what you do. A Christian's life, of loving
and unselfish service, reflects the God whom we adore.

7. The Holy Spirit has called each of you to ministry. Ministry
is distinctive in each place, because the needs are different in
every location. Similarly, you are all Spirit-led, to do ministry
where you live. Each of you is unique. Each of you has a
different gift and talent. Consequently, ministry for me does
not look like ministry for you. However, when everyone
pools their efforts the world's needs are met. Can you imagine
what the world would look like if every Christian lived
out his/her calling? It would be quite a different place.

8. Love comes out of God and gathers us to God in order to pour
itself back into God through all of us and bring us all back to
Him on the tide of His own infinite mercy. So we all become
doors and windows through which God shines back into His
own House. Thomas Merton *New Seeds of Contemplation*
Like an ocean wave God pulls us into the divine heart.
This enthralling love is deep within us and spreads far
beyond us. Sacred love poured into our hearts does
not return to God empty. Neither is it the private
possession of individuals. God's love is a universal
gift intended for the mutual good of the world.

There is an ascending quality to this love, for in God's
generosity, God imparts more love upon us. Love births love,
until we become incarnate signs of God's active participation
in the world. Those who behold this love stand in silent awe of
its beauty. It begets community and invites others to participate
in this sacred dance of service to the world. All Christian

service emanates from the heart of God. It flows from God through us and back to God, where it returns to us with greater glory. This holy transference enlarges our capacity to love and serve others. It is the basis for all Christian ministry.

9. Someone once told me that the one who has the greatest power is the one who can give it away. Boy, does that seem counterintuitive. Power is something to seek, hold onto, and sustain with all your cunning. In fifteenth century Italy, Niccolo Machiavelli, wrote his most famous work, *The Prince*. In it, Machiavelli maintained that it is a ruler's duty to stay in power. The book details how to do this. Over the years, most of us, while outwardly detesting the book, have silently paid it homage with our actions. We want to be in control. It is difficult to give anyone authority over us. It takes a lot of trust to give power away.

Jesus had many discussions with his disciples concerning power and authority. He declared at one point, "You know that the rulers of the gentiles lord it over them…. It will not be so among you but whoever wishes to be great among you must be your servant." (Matthew 25:26-27) It is a lesson that Jesus still needs to teach. He needs to instill it in our heads, and install it in our hearts like the multiplication tables or the alphabet.

In the last week of his life, Jesus demonstrated the potency of his power. Pontius Pilate, the Roman ruler, tells Jesus, "Don't you know that I have power over you to set you free or to crucify you?" In a restrained and silent response, Jesus exhibited his power over Pilate. He let Pilate have his way. His apparent abdication of power, however, was an illusion, for three days later he made his power and authority manifest in the empty tomb. Evil, for a time, might seem to have the upper hand. Yet, it has no staying power. Eventually, it will turn in on itself and perish. Ultimately, only the power of love endures.

10. When I was a seminarian, a saintly old professor told me, "If you have not prayed for the suffering people of the world you will never understand the suffering of Jesus." Initially, his words made little impact. Nevertheless, like so many maxims, the phrase stayed with me. My life, like so many in the United States, has known very little suffering. One-third of the world goes to bed hungry. Countless millions live in shacks or sleep on the world's streets. There are Christians who suffer persecution for the faith, and lay their lives on the line every day. We, who have both the means and voice, need to speak for them. To profess Christ as Lord is to stand for justice among all peoples. We can be the voices of those whose voice is never heard.

11. "Once you have experienced the mercy of God in your life you will henceforth aspire only to serve." (Dietrich Bonhoeffer)

    Christians are actively involved in the world. In becoming disciples, we surrender ourselves to Christ, and strive to be in union with his desires. Jesus calls us to follow him, not merely as a teacher or an example, but as The Messiah. Discipleship means obedience to Jesus, and faithfulness in service. Discipleship is not merely doing good works; it is following Jesus where he leads us. Christianity without discipleship is always Christianity without Christ. Without discipleship, Christianity remains merely an abstract idea. In such a religion, there is trust in God but no discipleship. To be a Christian is to follow Jesus.

12. Many churches have a foot washing on Holy Thursday. We did not have that tradition. I resisted. I admit it—I don't like feet. Well, that is not entirely true. I like my own feet. It is your feet I don't like. I think, "If I were to wash anyone's feet, it would be Jesus'." That is not the message Jesus gave to the disciples.

"Now that I, your Lord and Teacher, have washed your feet, you also should wash one another's feet. I have set you an example that you should do as I have done for you." (John 13)

It must have been perplexing, for the disciples, to see Jesus grab a towel and a water basin. I cannot envisage letting Jesus wash my feet. It goes against everything in my heart. We sympathize with Peter's quandary when he did not want Jesus to wash his feet, but knew he had to let Jesus do it.

St. Bernard of Clairvaux wrote, "The sign of the Christian is not the scepter but the basin and towel." Jesus, by his actions, demonstrated that we should not calculate the cost, but look for the best way to serve. Because Jesus did not count the cost, we have the priceless promise of life.

The world does not work this way, but it is the way of God's Kingdom. God invites us to live the kingdom way.

13. One of Dietrich Bonhoeffer's greatest gifts to the church is his book, *Cost the Discipleship*. He wrote the book, in the atmosphere of fear and intimidation, in Hitler's Nazi Germany. At that time, Christians had the choice, either to deny their faith and follow Hitler, or to stand up for the faith and face imprisonment and death. In Nazi Germany, Jesus was no longer the Messiah; Hitler was. The SS troops even placed Nazi banners over crosses in churches. To take them down meant risking imprisonment. Those were dangerous times for Christians.

Bonhoeffer begins his book in startling way with a discussion of cheap and costly grace.
   Cheap Grace is the deadly enemy of our Church.
   We are fighting today for costly grace. Cheap grace is preaching of forgiveness without repentance, baptism

without church discipline. Cheap grace is grace without discipleship, grace without the cross, and grace without Jesus Christ, living and incarnate. Costly grace is the gospel, which must be sought again and again.

Costly grace is costly, because it cost Jesus his life. It is costly for us, because it may cost us our reputation, our security, our standing in the community, or maybe even our life. Grace requires action on the part of Christians. We celebrate the graciousness of God by lives that validate that grace in service to others.

In his book, Bonhoeffer adds these ominous words: "When Jesus calls us he bids us come and die." We die to the way of the world, and live the way of the Kingdom of God. Sometimes, it means we literally die. The Nazis executed Bonhoeffer in a concentration camp, just days before the Americans liberated it.

14. Acts of love are timeless. What you do here and now can reverberate through time. You never know how God will use your good works even after your death. There is an old Celtic saying: "The well from which you draw water was dug by someone else." What we do, for good or ill, has lasting effects.

In fourteenth century England lived a woman named Julian. She resided in an anchorhold. An anchorhold is a room off the church that houses a permanent resident, called an anchor (male) or anchoress (female). Julian never left her room or the church. Hers was a life of prayer, meditation, and study. Moreover, England in her day, needed intercessory prayer greatly, for Julian lived in troubled times. The Hundred Years War raged. The Black Death killed entire villages, and a cattle disease caused a severe famine. Living, as an anchoress would seem to be a luxury the church could ill afford. Yet, her prayers helped sustain and inspire a nation. Her little book *Showings*, written in the anchorhold during this critical time, is a spiritual classic.

In that book, she professed the following: "God's love is so great that he regards us as partners in his good works." To be a disciple is to discern what work God has in store for you. The work is God's gift to you. Your gift to God is to do that work for which you were created. Your talents are the lumber you use to build your lives. Build a life that is worthy of your calling.

15. John of Forde wrote about Jesus, "You were a great light, hidden in the bosom of the Father; you came forth from your retreat into our marketplace." What a marvelous way to describe the incarnation. Notice, John did not say that Jesus came to the Temple; he came to the marketplace. That is where the holy person does her work. Our work is in the world. That is why the work of the laity is really the work of the church. The work of the clergy is essential in building up the body of Christ, but it is the laity, the body of Christ, who does the real work in the world. They are the ones who roll up their sleeves and get their hands dirty in the market places of the world. Notice, however, before Jesus was born he was light in the bosom of the Father. So it is with us. Before we can be a light shining in the darkness of the world, we must rest in the bosom of our Lord who will birth us out into the marketplace.

16. One of the fathers of faith that helped shape my understanding of the Gospel and ministry was an early 19th century Norwegian layman, named Hans Nielson Hauge. He is only a minor footnote in the history of Christianity, yet his influence upon me is great.

One day, while working on his father's farm, Hauge was overcome by grace. He described it this way: "It was a glory to which no tongue can explain; my soul felt something supernatural, divine, and blessed. I had a completely transformed mind, a sorrow over all sins, and a burning desire that others should share the same grace."

From that moment on, he worked as an itinerant lay preacher, and helped fuel a fire of religious renewal in Norway. Because he was not ordained or licensed to preach, the State Church jailed him. Yet, he persisted in preaching, even while imprisoned.

He called Norway to a living faith active in love. Those four words—faith active in love—define discipleship. Disciples are followers who live out their calling as a Christian. Their faith actively serves people where they are, and whoever they are. Someone needs your love today.

17. Has it ever occurred to you that one hundred pianos all tuned to the same fork are automatically tuned to each other? They are of one accord by being tuned, not to each other, but to another standard to which each one must individually bow. So one hundred worshippers together, each one looking away to Christ, are in heart nearer to each other than they could possibly be, were they to become "unity" conscious and turn their eyes away from God to strive for closer fellowship. W. Tozer

Ministry, in a congregation looking to Christ, is a beautiful thing to behold. Their service is in tune with our Lord, and with each other. For them, nothing is impossible.

18. Gloria Dei! has three sister congregations; one is in Slovakia, one is in El Salvador, and one is in Madagascar. Each of the congregations has a different personality and strength. All have distinctive challenges.

The congregation in Slovakia came through forty years of
communist control, where religion was against the wishes of
the State. To be a Christian was to give up health insurance,
state employment, and other benefits. People paid a high
price to follow Christ. The members of our sister church,
in Krajne, Slovakia, paid that price. As a result, the church
outlived the Soviets. The first time I preached at their church,
I commented that I should get down on my knees and
kiss their feet in appreciation of their sacrifice. The church
survived, because dedicated and faithful people put their lives
on the line to follow Jesus openly. The church now thrives.

The congregation in El Salvador battles a poverty that beats
them down. Prospects for a better future are very limited.
In addition, they also must do battle with the gangs that
control the neighborhood around our sister church and
the Lutheran School that operates there. The devotion and
dedication of the pastor and the staff of the school create
opportunities for children to escape the stranglehold of
poverty, and be safe from the violence of the gangs.

Gloria Dei! has two sister congregations in the extreme rural
south of Madagascar. Madagascar is one of the poorest
countries in the world. Eighty percent of the country lives on
less than $2.00 a day. You would never know it by the lives
of the people. Their joy of living is contagious. They are able
to live lives of value and purpose, regardless of their lack of
material goods. They do not really think of themselves as
poor. They have what they need, although most do not have
running water or electricity. Health care is minimal. A heart
attack is almost always fatal. They know how to help each
other, encourage each other, and work for the common good.

Over the years Gloria Dei! has helped our sister
congregations in a variety of ways. An organ was

repaired in Slovakia, churches were built, water was made available in Madagascar, scholarships were given, and new desks for the school in El Salvador were built. All this pales in comparison to the gift of love and inspiration they have given to Gloria Dei!.

19. Christianity means community through Jesus Christ and in Jesus Christ. No Christian community is more or less than this. Whether it be a brief, single encounter or the daily fellowship of years...

    Christian brotherhood is not an ideal, which we must realize; it is rather a spiritual reality created by God in Christ in which we may participate. The church is a Spiritual reality not a Human wish.

    Even devout men cannot cultivate a spiritual community. The community of the Spirit is the fellowship of those who are called by Christ; human community is the fellowship of devout souls. Excerpts from *Life Together* by Dietrich Bonhoeffer

    Bonhoeffer wrote *Life Together* in an underground seminary he began. The Nazis had censured him, yet he continued to teach and preach in defiance of their directives. The Nazis tried to define what the church should be. Bonhoeffer maintained, until his death in a concentration camp, that God called the shots. The church is not ours. Gloria Dei! is not yours—it is God's. We are the stewards of the church's mission, and mission is always other oriented. If it is not, it is not a church but a human fellowship of like-minded people.

20. "When you've done it to the least of these you've done it to me."
    (Matthew 25:40)

When Andrew Young was mayor of Atlanta, Georgia,
he decided to dress up in raggedy clothes, go out on
the streets, and be homeless for three days to see and
experience what the homeless experience. The people on
his staff said, "It'll never work. People will recognize you.
You are so well known they will know who you are. It
won't work." Three days later, he came back and his staff
asked him, "Well, how did it go? Did people recognize
you?" Andrew Young answered, "Nobody recognized me,
because nobody looks into the faces of the homeless."

21. I love the play by Lorraine Hansberry, "Raisin in the Sun." It is the
     story of an African American family, living in Chicago. When the
     father dies, he leaves a small legacy, about $10,000. Each family
     member has plans for the money. Beneatha, the daughter, wants to
     use the money to go to medical school. The mother has ideas about
     buying a little house. She always imagined flower boxes in front
     of the windows. Then there is the son, who said, "I've never had
     a chance. Could you give me the money? I have a friend and we'll
     go in business together, and we'll make something of ourselves.
     With this money, I will have a chance to be a businessman,
     and make something good for everybody in the family."

Against her better judgment, the mother gives her son
the money. Of course, his so-called friend is not a friend,
and skips town with the money, leaving him behind
with nothing. When he comes home and announces
his failure to his family, Beneatha yells at him, and
tells him what a loser and ne'er-do-well he is.

He's a failure in every respect, but the mother speaks, and
reminds her daughter, "I thought I told you to love him.'"

Beneatha responds, saying, "Love him?
There's nothing left to love."

Mama: "There is always something left to love. And if you ain't learned that, you ain't learned nothing. Have you cried for that boy today? I don't mean for yourself and for the family 'cause we lost the money. I mean for him: what he been through and what it done to him. And God help him. God help him what it's done to him. Child, when do you think is the time to love somebody the most? When they done good and made things easy for everybody? Well then, you ain't through learning - because that ain't the time at all. It's when he's at his lowest and can't believe in hisself 'cause the world done whipped him so! When you starts measuring somebody, measure him right, child, measure him right. Make sure you done taken into account what hills and valleys he come through before he got to wherever he is."

We have a God who loves us, not just when we are riding high, but when the world has whipped us, when we are feeling lower than can be imagined. He comes to us in our hours of need, and reminds us that he loves us.

Jesus calls us to that kind of love. For when "you've done it to the least, you've done it to me." Not merely least in terms of need, but also those who seem the least deserving. When all is said and done, it gets down to Jesus, and in Jesus, the kingdom comes. In Jesus, we find one who lives out the will of God perfectly. It is our responsibility to transform the world in the name of Jesus. Jesus fashioned a people, a kingdom people, who live out His love with justice, and who bring this love and justice to the rest of the world. You and I are an important part of that people and the work we do can have lasting effects on the world.

22. I bind unto myself today.
    The strong Name of the Trinity,

By invocation of the same,
The Three in One and One in Three.

I bind this day to me for ever.
By power of faith, Christ's incarnation;
His baptism in the Jordan river;
His death on Cross for my salvation;
His bursting from the spicèd tomb;
His riding up the Heavenly way;
His coming at the day of doom;
I bind unto myself today.
Christ be with me, Christ within me,
Christ behind me, Christ before me,
Christ beside me, Christ to win me,
Christ to comfort and restore me.
Christ beneath me, Christ above me,
Christ in quiet, Christ in danger,
Christ in hearts of all that love me,
Christ in mouth of friend and stranger.
(St. Patrick's Breastplate)

St. Patrick of Ireland left one of Christianity's most
enduring legacies. On March 17th everyone becomes
Irish. In Ireland, the faithful gather at Dublin's St. Patrick's
Cathedral for worship, or St. Patrick's Mountain in northwest
Ireland, where they pray their way to the summit.
St. Patrick's path to discipleship and sainthood began in
a most unlikely way. As a youth, marauding Irish pirates
invaded his home in England, captured, and enslaved him
for six years. He escaped from captivity, and returned home
half-starved. Around the year 435 Patrick, now a priest,
returned to Ireland. While he had little formal learning,
his simple message of God's abiding presence, and his
pastoral care of the sick, converted an entire nation.

God does not need brilliant or extraordinary people
to do the sacred work. God only needs willing people,
and God will do extraordinary work through them.
God can use you to do the work of a saint.

23. When one person acts honorably, it brings honor to us all.

Stories, surrounding the events of September 11, 2001,
are inspiring. On United Flight 93, passengers rushed
the hijackers, at their own peril, to stave off another
disaster. This plane was headed towards either the US
Capitol or the White House. The passengers could have
stayed in their seats, but they ran toward the danger,
toward the terror, toward death, toward honor.

When one person acts honorably, it brings honor to us all.

After the plane crashed into the Pentagon, Sergeant
Will Johnson saw a wall of plaster fall on one of his
co-workers. Everything was crashing down around
him, yet he ran toward that crumbling room, and
carried the frightened woman out to safety.

**When one person acts honorably,
it brings honor to us all.**

New York City police officers and firefighters acted
honorably that painful day. As people were fleeing the
crumbling World Trade Center, police officers, firefighters,
and others, at their own peril, ran towards the disintegrating
buildings screaming, "Run for your life." They knew
their lives would be in peril, but they knew their duty.

When one person acts honorably, it brings honor to us all.

In addition, we cry out, "Lord, don't let our sense of duty
be less for your Kingdom, than these beloved people
had for those who were perishing in the fallen towers.

We want to be among those that who do not run from the
danger, but run into the danger saying, "Run for your life."

Run toward a life that has meaning and purpose,
and away from meaninglessness.
Run toward a life that conquers evil with good.
Run toward a life that brings honor to the name of Jesus.
Run toward a life that brings honor to the name Christian.
Run toward a life that brings honor to the name American.
Run toward a life that brings others to faith.
Run toward a life that understands that
love is a higher calling than hate.
Run toward a life that lives by the creed, "forgive us our
trespasses as we forgive those who trespass against us."
Run toward a life that will not be persuaded to vengeance.
Run toward a life of service to others.
Run toward a life that does not run
away from our Christian duty.
Run toward the person God wants you to be.
Run toward the person you can become.

Expectations are lofty for those who make the high
profession of faith in Jesus. Naturally and rightly, more
is expected of the believer than of the unbeliever. There
is a high price to pay when you run towards Jesus. It
may cause you to run into a crumbling building.

You cannot let evil alone, for evil will not let
you alone. You must struggle against it.

The conventional inclination is to overcome evil with evil.
The Divine approach is to overcome evil with good.
**It is true, when one person acts honorably,
it brings honor to us all.**
Be that person.

11

DID I REMEMBER TO TELL YOU ABOUT GRACE AND FORGIVENESS?

The church is a school of grace.

We practice loving God by learning to love others.
We practice loving others by learning to love ourselves.

1. Forgiveness is necessary when there are sin and guilt. Every life has some burdensome secret. In the dark of the night, when you visit the secret caverns of your heart, guilt awakens, shows its fangs and assaults the spirit. The splendor of the Gospel is that God does not want us to remain filled with guilt. God does not desire us to make our past sins a jailer. Jesus seeks those tormented by guilt. Jesus regularly consorted with "sinners." He offered forgiveness. He even offered it to people who didn't ask for it. On the cross he cried out, "Father, forgive them for they do not know what they do."

— 151 —

Forgiveness is the pathway to personal liberation. When you learn to feel forgiven, and learn how to forgive others, you can let the burdens of guilt and anger go, and watch them dissipate like dew on a warm summer's morn.

2. Forgiveness is tough work. It is easy to get distracted. It is easy to take the part of the Christian faith we like and ignore the parts we do not like. Maybe this parable explains it.

A young man went to a church and said, "I would like to buy $5 worth of God, please, not enough to explode my soul or disturb my sleep, but just enough to equal a cup of warm milk or a snooze in the sunshine. I do not want enough of God to make me love the outcasts or pick beets with a migrant. I want ecstasy, not transformation; I want the warmth of the womb, not a new birth. I want a pound of the eternal in a paper sack. I would like to buy $5 worth of God, please."

You cannot buy the Spirit of Life for $5 or even 5 million dollars. The Spirit blows where it wills. You can choose to live your life in the image of God. The only cost is our readiness to be transformed into the image and likeness of God.

3. Author Philip Yancey maintains that grace is the last best word. Other words like love or faith are so secularized that they have lost their power and spiritual meaning. Yet, every English derivative of the word grace contains something of its original meaning and intent. In other words, the world has not "messed up" this word. Our understanding of grace comes from two words from two different worlds: one is Latin and the other is Greek.

The Latin word is *gratia*. There are a great many words that are its progeny. Grateful, gratified, congratulate, graceful, we can be in someone's "good graces', or we may say "she graced us with her presence. Even companies give us a "grace period." When something is free of charge, we say it is *gratis*. It connotes, politeness, elegance, thankfulness, goodwill, giftedness, and favor. Christians talk about grace as "the unmerited love or favor of God.".

In Greek, the word for grace is *charis*. We get our words charism, and charisma. Charism is a divinely conferred power or talent. Charisma is compelling attractiveness or charm that can inspire devotion in others.

We have been the recipients of God's grace. Our charism is to be gracious in our living.

4. The church is a school of grace.

    We don't like to admit it, but churches compete with each other. Congregations try to outdo each other in membership, or building, or programs. Maybe if we are going to compete at all, we should try to "out grace" each other. Wouldn't that be something?

    "And they said to him, "If you will be kind to this people and please them, and speak good words to them, then they will be your servants for ever.""
    (2 Chronicles 10:7)

5. Lewes Smedes writes that the first stage of forgiveness is to "rediscover the humanity of the one who hurt us." Nobody is the worst thing she ever did. The worst thing someone does, does not define who she is. When we can look at the whole person, we see a mixture of unkindness and graciousness, of lies and truth, of good and bad; we see the humanity of the person. We see someone who shares our own frailties and flaws. We discover someone who is as human as we are. Discovering

that is a blessing. Anger and resentment diminish our hearts.
Forgiveness allows our hearts to grow in size and grace.

6. Then Jesus said, 'There was a man who had two sons.
    The younger of them said to his father, "Father, give
    me the share of the property that will belong to me."
    So he divided his property between them. A few days
    later, the younger son gathered all he had and travelled
    to a distant country, and there he squandered his property
    in dissolute iving. When he had spent everything, a severe
    famine took place throughout that country, and he began
    to be in need. So he went and hired himself out to one of
    the citizens of that country, who sent him to his fields to
    feed the pigs. He would gladly have filled himself with
    the pods that the pigs were eating; and no one gave him
    anything. But when he came to himself he said, "How many
    of my father's hired hands have bread enough and to spare,
    but here I am dying of hunger! I will get up and go to my
    father, and I will say to him, 'Father, I have sinned
    against Heaven and before you; I am no longer worthy
    to be called your son; treat me like one of your hired
    hands.'" So he set off and went to his father. But while
    he was still far off, his father saw him and was filled
    with compassion; he ran and put his arms around him and
    kissed him. Then the son said to him, "Father, I have sinned
    against Heaven and before you; I am no longer worth
    y to be called your son." But the father said to his
    slaves, "Quickly, bring out a robe—the best one—and put
    it on him; put a ring on his finger and sandals on his
    feet. And get the fatted calf and kill it, and let us eat and
    celebrate; for this son of mine was dead and is alive
    again; he was lost and is found!" And they began to
    celebrate.

    'Now his elder son was in the field; and when he came

and approached the house, he heard music and dancing. He called one of the slaves and asked what was going on. He replied, "Your brother has come, and your father has killed the fatted calf, because he has got him back safe and sound." Then he became angry and refused to go in. His father came out and began to plead with him. But he answered his father, "Listen! For all these years I have been working like a slave for you, and I have never disobeyed your command; yet you have never given me even a young goat so that I might celebrate with my friends. But when this son of yours came back, who has devoured your property with prostitutes, you killed the fatted calf for him!" Then the father said to him, "Son, you are always with me, and all that is mine is yours. But we had to celebrate and rejoice, because this brother of yours was dead and has come to life; he was lost and has been found." ' (Luke 15)

Forgiveness is kindness in action. The fifteenth chapter of Luke provides the ultimate illustration of forgiveness in the Bible. It is impossible to read the story of the Prodigal Son without a heartfelt appreciation of the grandeur of God and the importance of mercy. I cannot imagine the father's sadness as he watched his young son walk away from his home. The father must have thought, "Will he return? Why would my son want to leave? What could I have done differently?" His broken heart followed him to bed and hounded him like a predator during the day. Then one day, his son returned. The father had a choice to make: receive him back into his home, or turn him away. The father did not think twice. When he sees his son, he took off on a dead run to greet him. The older son was not so forgiving, and he let his father know his disgust at throwing a party for his younger brother.

As we read the parable, we tend to identify with one of the two brothers: the irresponsible penitent young prodigal, or the conscientious and resentful older brother. Henri Nouwen takes a different approach. He wrote a book entitled, *The Return of the Prodigal.* It is an exceptional book. I have used it as a book study many times. In it, he maintains that while it is easy to identify with one of the brothers, it is the father we should emulate. The father is the hero. Of course, the father in the parable is God. We however, can, be "father" to others. We can become living symbols of God's grace.

7. Sometimes we get stuck on fair. Kids will scream at a parent, "It's not fair." Our reply sometimes is, "Well, life is not always fair." Even though we may say it, we don't like it. Grace and forgiveness are not fair either. In fact, sometimes they are downright unfair. There is nothing fair about a daughter forgiving an abusive parent. There is nothing fair about a Father forgiving a son who had taken his inheritance, and squandered it, as the prodigal son did.

  One Sunday after I had preached on the Prodigal Son, a woman ran to me after church and blurted out, "The son should have crawled on his hands and knees to his father. Then, maybe the Father could have forgiven him. It wasn't fair to expect the father to forgive him." She is right it was not fair. Fortunately, God is not about what is fair. God is about forgiveness. When the father saw the returning prodigal, there was true joy in the old man's heart. Forgiveness may not be fair but it sure can bring joy.

8. Brennan Manning is a Franciscan Priest and author of a dozen books. In one of them, *The Relentless tenderness of Jesus,* he wrote, "Over the past fifteen years, my ministry has been identified, more than anything else, with healing our image of God. Religion is not a matter of learning how to think about God but of actually encountering God." This encounter shapes our image of God as well how we think about God. In the

twentieth chapter of Matthew Jesus tells a parable that can shake our understanding of what is fair and just. It was harvest time, and the owner of a farm went into the marketplace repeatedly to recruit workers for his fields. Because there was so much to do, he went at the eleventh hour (5:00), and hired men for just an hour of work. At the end of the day, the farmer gave each laborer the same pay. Those that worked all day received the same wage as those who worked only one hour. Those that labored all day were incensed. "Those that came last have put in only an hour and you've treated them the same as we who have toiled in the heat of the day," they complained. The farmer replied, "My friends didn't we agree on your wage? Take your earnings and go. If I choose to pay the last as much as you, haven't I the right to do what I like with what I have?"

Jesus' image of God assaults our standards of justice and fair play. The parables of Jesus reveal a God who is consistently overgenerous with forgiveness and excessive with grace. His parables portray a magnanimous God cancelling a debt, a shepherd seeking stray sheep, and a father forgiving his prodigal son. God does not condemn but forgives. God accepts the sinner even before he repents. God beckons us all day and every day of our lives.

9. Corrie Ten Boom, said, "Forgiveness is to set a prisoner free, and to realize the prisoner was you." These are not the words of a woman who had an easy life. Corrie Ten Boom was a Dutch survivor of the Holocaust who helped many Jews escape the Nazis in WW II. In 1940, the Nazis invaded the Netherlands. By 1942, she and her family had become very active in the Dutch underground, hiding refugees.

In May 1942, a well-dressed woman came to the Ten Boom door with a suitcase in hand. Nervously, she told Corrie that she was a Jew. The Nazis had arrested her husband several months before, and her son had gone into hiding. Occupation authorities had recently visited her, and she was too fearful to return home. After hearing about how the Ten Booms had helped their Jewish neighbors, she asked if she might stay with them. Corrie ten Boom's father readily agreed. "In this household, God's people are always welcome."

Thus began "the hiding place." Ten Boom and her sister began taking in refugees. Some of the refuges were Jews. Others were members of the Dutch resistance movement sought by the Gestapo. There were several extra rooms in their house, but food was scarce due to wartime shortages.

The Nazis arrested the entire Ten Boom family on February 28, 1944. Corrie's father died ten days after his capture. Corrie and her sister, Betsie, were sent to a local concentration camp, and finally to the notorious Ravensbrück concentration camp in Germany, where Betsie died. Before she died, she told Corrie, "There is no pit so deep that God's love is not deeper still." The Nazis released Corrie on Christmas Day of December 1944. Her autobiography *The Hiding Place* became a best seller and ultimately was made into a movie.

"We will know the work of forgiveness is complete when we experience the freedom that comes as a result. We are the ones who suffer most when we choose not to forgive. When we do forgive, the Lord sets our hearts free from the anger, bitterness, resentment, and hurt that previously imprisoned us." Corrie Ten Boom

10. "To the Lord our God belong mercy and forgiveness." (Daniel 9:9)

Sometimes Christians talk about the God of the Old Testament as condemning and the God of the New

Testament as forgiving. Don't fall into that trap. The Old Testament God consistently demonstrates mercy and forgiveness. God does not change. In his parables, Jesus endeavors to heal the Jews' image of God as unforgiving and demanding. He wants to change the way they relate to each other by changing their image of God.

To some extent, we make our own images of God. Someone said, "God created us in God's image, we were so grateful we responded by making God in our image." In truth, our image of God makes us. Luther wrote, "We become like the God we worship." The God of love cultivates a loving people. Healing our image of God heals our image of others and ourselves. Through the prophet Hosea, God laments, "My people do not know me. It is love I desire not sacrifices; knowledge of God not holocausts."

When my children were small, we wanted to nurture a giving spirit within them. One day they both wanted the last piece of cake. They measured as well as they could to make sure that each half was the same size. Faye told them, "Jesus would give the larger piece to the other. Maybe you should take turns being Jesus." My ever-clever daughter, Kaaren, told Erik, "You be Jesus first." Healing our image of God helps us to grow more Godly.

11. "Let us make humankind in our image and after our likeness." Genesis 1:26

Many years ago, there was a sermon drama, in a Michigan church, put on by some actors from a local theater. Part of the play involved a wrestling match in the pulpit. The actors got a bit carried away, and they broke the marble railing of the pulpit. In some places it was shattered into pieces, in other places it was merely cracked.

The congregation hired a venerated old craftsman to repair the marble. He was a master of his trade. He made an adhesive from an ancient recipe he had learned as a young apprentice in Italy. It was not just glue. He had found a small piece of marble that had the same color and texture as the marble in the pulpit. With a file, he ground pieces of that marble into sand, and he added that marble-sand to the glue. With that glue, he filled in the gaps between the broken pieces.

He reassembled the jigsaw puzzle of broken shards. He filled the deep cracks with his compound of ground marble and glue. All of the gaps were filled in and made smooth.

He said, "Marble holds marble together." Like adheres to like. Thirty years later, the marble-sand glue he made is still filling in the gaps, still holding the marble of the pulpit together.

So it is with all of the gaps and divisions in the human community. All of the chasms that separate us, and all of the fractures that divide us and keep us apart, can be overcome when like adheres to like, when the image of God in one person adheres to the image of God in another. Feuding family members, quarrelling neighbors, or old friends that no longer speak to each other, can only be brought together by what they have in common. What is common to both is the image of God in each of them. If we can find that image in ourselves, and in the person who stands across the abyss from us, we have found the glue.

The obstacles that divide us, the deep fissures in the human community, the chasms that separate us, the broken places in the family of God's children, can all be bridged and mended when like adheres to like.

When we seek the image of God in every human
being, we can begin to forgive and to experience
forgiveness. We can bridge the divide. We can heal
the division, because we have found the glue.

12. My Dad told me, "Anyone who angers you conquers you."
Anger and I know each other very well. We used to be best
friends. Then I got wise to it. Anger was not a friend at all.
It is a bully who takes your soul into an alley, and beats it
until it hollers, "Uncle" in submission. Sometimes anger
masquerades as martyrdom. We conspicuously parade our
feelings, believing we are punishing the person who hurt or
wronged us. We get even by being so visibly miserable that
we are beyond consolation. It does not take too long before
we discover that course of action offers no real consolation.
Many years ago, one of our members had a heated argument
with another member. He stopped coming to church
and did not participate in any church activities. He was
determined to show folks how upset he was. The result was
that he cut himself off from the very folks who were his
supporters. In addition, he found no personal satisfaction.
The person he hurt the most was himself. It took a while,
but he finally came back. His life has been the better for it.
Anyone who angers you conquers you.

13. "Train children in the way they should go,
and when old, they will not stray."
(Proverbs 22:6)

I have a friend who understands grace. I remember telling him,
"You are lucky to have such a forgiving spirit." He replied,
"It really isn't luck. It was just the way I was taught." One
lady told me that she began teaching forgiveness while her
children were still on her lap. "Then forgiveness becomes a

habit," she said. We teach our children so many things: music, sports, math, etc. We also need to teach Christian life skills, like forgiveness. It is not enough to have a brother say, "I am sorry" to his sister. Our children need to see grace and forgiveness lived by example. Children need models of grace. They need to see forgiveness lived out in parents' lives. St. Francis said, "Always preach the Gospel. Sometimes use words."

The church needs to be a model of grace. Unfortunately, that is not always the case. Some awful things occur in the name of God. How can we teach children to live a grace filled life if they don't see it in their families or church? After the tragedy at Nickel Mines, (5 school children murdered) one Amish man wrote, "When I was growing up my parents taught me by example to think of others before myself. My father and mother always tried to make sure that the other person got the best end of the deal. With God's help, I hope we can pass this attitude on to the next generation."

14. You can't "out-sin" God's grace. You may have as many sins as sand on the beach, or stars in the sky, or pints of water in the ocean, but God's grace exceeds your sin.

15. We suffer injury from those we love, and we cannot avoid wounding those we want to love. It is a sad but true part of the human condition. We desire to love well, to care well, to understand, but before we grow old, someone will say to us, "You weren't there for me, when I needed you. You didn't care what I felt or needed, and you didn't try to understand me." As we feel the pain of those statements, maybe even deny them, we will also know they carry truth. It is at those times we realize the liberating power of forgiveness. At those times, it becomes apparent that the only one who loves us as we need to be loved, is God. This knowledge can free us to forgive those who have wounded us, and also let those we have harmed forgive us.

Forgiveness opens the door to reunion,
resolution, and inner peace.

16. Evagrius Ponticus was a fourth century hermit, writer,
    and spiritual leader who lived in the Egyptian desert. He
    wrote a wonderful little book of practical suggestions for
    the early desert fathers and mothers called *The Praktikos*.
    He wrote, "Do not give yourself over to angry thoughts so
    as to fight in your mind with the one who has vexed you."
    When I have disagreement with someone or someone has
    said something to hurt me, it is easy to think, "I should have
    said this." Or "The next time I see him, I will give him a
    piece of my mind." It is natural and easy to have arguments
    with people in our minds. We always win those arguments.
    Evagrius adds, "When we fight with someone in our mind,
    anger, like a wolf, snatches away the soul as if it were a
    fawn." Anger eventually turns in on itself and wounds the
    one who is angry. Forgiveness enlarges the spirit of the one
    who forgives. We all know it is true, but we have a hard
    time really believing it. Guess that is another paradox.

17. Then Peter came to Jesus and asked, "Lord, how
    many times shall I forgive my brother when he sins
    against me? Up to seven times?" Jesus answered, "I
    tell you, not seven times, but seventy-seven times.
    (Matthew 18:21-22 NIV)

    Therefore I tell you, whatever you ask for in prayer,
    believe that you have received it, and it will be yours.
    And when you stand praying, f you hold anything against
    anyone, forgive him, so that your Father in Heaven
    may forgive you your sins. (Mark 11:24-26 NIV)
    Forgive us our debts, as we also have forgiven our debtors.
    (Matthew 6:12 NIV).

A PARABLE

AS TOLD BY JEFF HOGAN

THE SUN WAS shining, and I was surprised at how warm I was getting. It was not particularly hot, but my load was heavy and awkward. About halfway up the hill, we paused for a moment on the gravel road and I turned to take in the view behind me. Looking out past miles of pasture and grassland, my eyes met the horizon and fixed on the mountains that stretched out as far as I could see in either direction. Turning back to our burdens, we started again up the hill.

When we had gone as far as the road could take us, we negotiated a small culvert and continued across country. The buckets made it difficult to traverse the steep incline of the hill, but by now the destination was only a few minutes away. As we neared the top of the bluff, I thought about the objects I was transporting.

I had only chosen a few rocks, but they were significant. Most of them were pretty close in size and weight but had unique physical characteristics. For example, one was really rough and abrasive–like sandpaper. Another was quite attractive on one side and black on the other. Every new rock caused me to consider the instructions that were given concerning their selection: "Each rock should represent a deep hurt someone has inflicted on you; a wound that you continue to carry." Every new rock made the lesson sink in more deeply. My final selection was exceptional. It was a wound that I had carried around for a very long time. No, it was actually several wounds that were all joined together with the common thread of one relationship. I knew it as soon as I saw it. Large, angular and sharp, this rock was as awkward and unattractive as the hurt that it represented.

"That thing doesn't even fit right in your bucket," Tamara said. "Are you sure you want to carry it all the way up the hill?" She was right. This one rock was as heavy as all the others combined. And since the diameter of my five-gallon bucket wouldn't accept all of the lopsided mass, adding it made the whole load awkward and top-heavy. But that was precisely the point. I didn't want to carry its weight, but I already was. It was perfect.

We arrived at the top of the bluff, set our buckets down, and peered over the edge of the cliff. The path we followed on our ascent had circled around so that we could see the mountains again. We could also see where we had begun. Ironically, although we now stood 40-50 feet above it, we really weren't too far away from our starting point. Had we not been carrying the stones, we could easily have made the same journey in less than half the time.

We just stood silently for a few minutes, looking at the mountains and enjoying the cool October breeze. Then, one by one, we took turns throwing our rocks off the cliff. With each toss, we expressed to God that we had forgiven the one who hurt us so deeply, and surrendered the burden of the wound to Him. When I got to my last rock–the big one–I stopped and prayed, "Lord, I've carried this burden around for so long that it feels like a part of me. But I don't want it, and I never did. I surrender everything about the situation to You, including the person. After hurling it over the side, I watched as my rock landed on an even larger one at the bottom of the cliff and was broken.

We all have our bucket of rocks to carry. I do and so do you. The good news that Jesus came to proclaim, is that God is principally in the healing business. And healing feels good. When we cannot forgive, we load ourselves down with burdens that can be much heavier than a bucket full of big rocks. If you are carrying a weight like this around, take it to the cross and let it go.

Life is better with an empty bucket.

18. Home is where we love and receive love.

One of the greatest challenges in the Spiritual life is to receive God's forgiveness. Something within keeps us clinging to our sins and prevents us from letting God erase our past, and offer us a completely new beginning.

Forgiveness brings joy in Heaven. God delights in restoring each of us to the full dignity of "sonship." Receiving forgiveness demands that we allow God to be God: to heal, restore, and renew. As long as we are unable to acknowledge total absolution, we remain but hired hands. God calls us to be sons and daughters with all the rights and privileges of that birthright.

God runs to you with an eternal embrace, and the kiss of intimacy. You are God's beloved child. Say it aloud until it sinks in, "I am God's beloved child. I am God's beloved child. I am God's beloved child." Amen. It shall be so.

19. A teacher once told each of her students to bring a clear plastic bag and a sack of potatoes to school. She instructed her students to write the name of every person they cannot forgive on a potato, and put it in their sacks. Some of their bags were quite heavy. She told them to carry this bag with them everywhere for one week, putting it beside their bed at night, on the car seat when driving, or next to their desk at school. The hassle of lugging the sack around made it clear what a weight they were carrying spiritually. After a while, the condition of the potatoes deteriorated to a nasty smelly slime. This was a great life lesson. They paid a high price for hanging on to their pain and unforgiving

attitude. Too often, we think of forgiveness as a gift to the other person. It clearly is for us as well.

20. One day a friend of mine was lamenting to a mutual acquaintance about his son. The friend said, "Frankly, if he were my son I'd throw him out." My friend, the father in the story, has the ability to see things others miss. He replied, "Yes, if he were your son I too would throw him out. But he's my son, not yours."

Sometimes an injured party will say to me, "Why should I be the one to take the first step?" I generally respond with a reply I heard from a wise old pastor friend, "Love is too precious to lose because of protocol."

21. There is an ancient Jewish tale about a rabbi who sent his students out into the world. He asked them to determine what human characteristic is the most praiseworthy. They all brought back different answers. One said, "ambition," another "hard work," yet another said, "tenacity and the will not to give up." What pleased the rabbi most was the young man who simply answered, "A good heart is the most praiseworthy characteristic a person can have."

So, what is a good heart? A good heart is generous, patient, kind, joyful, forgiving, and compassionate. When we look for a humane response from someone we plead, "Have a heart." A good heart is merciful even as our Father in Heaven is merciful. A good heart understands grace.

22. "Pray then in this way:
Our Father in Heaven,
 Hallowed be your name.
  Your kingdom come.
   Your will be done,
    on earth as it is in Heaven.

Give us this day our daily bread.
　And forgive us our debts,
　　As we also have forgiven our debtors.
　And do not bring us to the time of trial,
　　But rescue us from the evil one.
　　　For if you forgive others their trespasses,
　　　　your Heavenly Father will also forgive you;
　　　　　but if you do not forgive others,
　　　　　　neither will your Father forgive your trespasses."
(Matthew 6:9-14)

For many, Amish country is s tourist attraction. The Amish are a curiosity or an off-Broadway show drawing patrons by the thousands. In fact, they are deeply religious, with roots that go back to the Anabaptist tradition at the time of the Reformation. Central to the Amish way of life is forgiveness. One young man put it this way, "when you start looking in the New Testament, forgiveness is everywhere. That's what the Bible is all about: forgiveness. It says we are to take up our cross and follow Jesus. No matter what happens, we must follow him." Mainline denominations, like Lutherans, tend to fixate more about the content of our belief system than following Jesus. The Amish take literally Jesus' words, "For if you forgive others their trespasses, your Heavenly Father will also forgive you; but if you do not forgive others, neither will your Father forgive your trespasses." One young Amish girl said, "The first thing we learn as a child is the Lord's Prayer. And the Lord's Prayer teaches us to forgive as God forgives." The Amish recognize two things: 1. They believe that God's forgiveness is directly related to their ability to forgive. 2. They know that extending forgiveness to an offender is hard work.

Lutherans tend to soften this approach by adding that God's grace is so all encompassing that God forgives us more than we forgive. We can cite many verses that back up that view. Nonetheless, our prayer is always, "Lord, help us forgive as you forgive." It is a tall task. It takes spiritual maturity and practice.

23. Never was the concept of Amish forgiveness more tested than it was in a small community called Nickel Mines. At 10:30 A.M. on Monday, October 2, 2006, a distraught and sobbing teacher ran to a nearby farmhouse with the frightening report that a man with a gun was in the school. Charles Carl Roberts IV had taken ten girls hostage. He had never come to terms with the death of his firstborn daughter who lived only twenty minutes. She had died nine years earlier. Roberts told the girls, "I'm going to make you pay for my daughter. Realizing that Roberts intended to kill them, thirteen-year-old Marian told him, "Shoot me first." She hoped that this might save the little ones in her care. Roberts lined up the girls and shot. Five would die and five others were critically injured. Roberts then turned the gun on himself. As the parents began to gather together, one woman began singing, "Safe in the arms of Jesus / Safe on his gentle breast / There by his love o'er shaded / Sweetly my soul shall rest."

The Amish quickly realized that the Roberts family was also victim of the shooting. After a long search, they found the family at the home of Mrs. Roberts' father. "So we walked over to her father's house and Mrs. Roberts, her children, and her parents were there alone. So we just talked with them for about ten minutes to express our sorrow, and told them we didn't hold anything against them." That same evening an Amish man visited the killer's father. A friend of the Roberts' family reported, "He stood there for about an hour and held that man (Mr. Roberts) in his arms and said, 'We forgive him.'" During the next few days, many of the Amish visited the Roberts family, expressing concern for them.

A TV reporter caught one of the Amish.
Do you have any anger toward the gunman's family? She asked.
"No.
"Have you already forgiven them?"
"In my heart, yes."
"How is that possible?"
"Through God's help."

The most prominent response to the Amish expressions
of forgiveness was amazement. Reporters were astonished
that they could forgive, and forgive so quickly. Not everyone
believed that they really had forgiven them, or even that
they should have. Jeff Jacoby of the Boston Globe wrote,
"Hatred is not always wrong, and forgiveness is not always
deserved." Well, he was correct on one point: forgiveness
is not deserved. If forgiveness were deserved, it would
not be grace. What constitutes deserved forgiveness?
Groveling at the feet of someone? Grace is undeserved
love and forgiveness. It comes with no strings attached.
One mother, whose daughter died at Nickel Mines
School, acknowledged that forgiveness is an ongoing
struggle. "Forgiveness stretches out over time, but you
have to start with the will to forgive. The bitterness
may reenter your mind from time to time, and then
you have to think about forgiveness again."

If you do not have "the will to forgive," pray the
desire to want to begin the process to forgiveness.

When thirteen-year-old Marian asked Robert to shoot her
first, she apparently hoped to absorb his anger, and save
her classmates. She had learned the lesson of sacrifice and
selflessness well. These same traits allowed the Amish to forgive
and begin the long process of healing. Lest anyone thinks that it
came easily for the Amish, do not. It didn't. Nevertheless, their

forgiveness reveals the depth of their convictions, even in the face of devastating loss. Their belief system was fully tested.

Forgiveness sets us free from a past that continues to harm us. Forgiveness heals the forgiver more often than the forgiven. When the Amish forgave Roberts for killing and injuring their children, they did not excuse his actions; rather, they began the process of healing. Their graciousness included the Roberts family. That was a bonus. **They needed to forgive as a way of honoring the memories of the children.** They also made a conscious choice not to let the incident destroy their future. They redeemed the event. They took what was the most awful thing that could happen and reframed it. They replaced violence with grace. They did not "return evil for evil but overcame evil with good." (Romans 12:21)

24. After the Civil War, in which between 600,000 and 700,000 Americans died, Abraham Lincoln and Generals Grant and Sherman gave the South very gracious terms of surrender. Lincoln died only a few days after Lee surrendered, but had said of the south, "You lose an enemy when you make him a friend." Lincoln wanted that policy after the war. When General Lee handed Grant his sword at Appomattox Courthouse, Grant gave it back. He also allowed the southern soldiers to keep their weapons, and ordered that they be given rations for their trip home. General William Tecumseh Sherman, whose horrific "march to the sea" left a path of destruction, gave General Johnston even better surrender terms. General Sherman, in keeping with Lincoln's stated wishes for a compassionate and forgiving end to the war, agreed on terms of surrender that included the political issues. Both Grant and Sherman wanted to allow the southerners to return home, feeling that they had been treated with respect and dignity. Unfortunately, after Lincoln's assassination the Congress was less

generous, and set the stage for decades of bitterness. I wonder what would have happened had Lincoln lived.

Forgiving your enemies is no small task. But, it has the healing power to make a friend and mend past wounds.

"The glory of Christianity is to conquer by forgiveness." William Blake

25. The truth that many people never understand, until it is too late, is that the more you try to avoid forgiving, the more you suffer because small and insignificant things begin to torture you out of proportion to your fear of being hurt.

26. *THE SCHOOL OF GRACE AND FORGIVENESS*

Learn the lesson well:
FORGIVENESS is the essence of what it means to be a Christian.

What FORGIVENESS is
What FORGIVENESS is not

1. *FORGIVENESS* is a gift from God.
2. *FORGIVENESS* is the natural outgrowth of *GRACE.*
3. *FORGIVENESS* is grace in action. *GRACE* is love freely given. It is unmerited and looks for nothing in return.
4. The church is a school of *GRACE* and *FORGIVENESS.*
5. *GRACE* is a spendthrift.
6. "Before we can *FORGIVE,* compassion must be born in your heart."
   Tic Nhat Hahn
7. *FORGIVENESS* is a slow process.
8. *FORGIVENESS* makes God smile.
   Bitterness grieves God's heart.

9. *FORGIVENESS* removes the toxins from our hearts and we rediscover the humanity of the person who hurt us.
10. *FORGIVENESS* is a gift to oneself.
11. *FORGIVENESS* does not mean we forget.
12. *FORGIVENESS* can be a gift to another
13. *FORGIVENESS* moves beyond the gift to oneself to a concern and a compassion for others.
14. *FORGIVENESS* is an act of the will.
15. *FORGIVENESS* is a choice we make.
16. *FORGIVENESS* does not mean we tolerate what was done to us.
17. The only thing more difficult than *FORGIVING is not FORGIVING*.
18. No one has the right to demand that you **FORGIVE** another.
19. Learn to *FORGIVE* yourself.
20. *FORGIVENESS* is the decision to move beyond the desire to get even with someone who hurt you. Too often, we want to wait until the other person pleads on his knees before we *FORGIVE*. We need not wait for permission to forgive.
21. *FORGIVENESS* transcends revenge.
22. *FORGIVENESS* is a non-violent way to deal with wrongs.
23. No one "deserves' to be *FORGIVEN;* otherwise it is not *GRACE*.
24. In actuality, *FORGIVENESS* is unfair: it is *GRACE* and *MERCY*.
25. *FORGIVENESS* is the essence of what it means to be a Christian.
26. It is not necessary to tell someone he/she is **FORGIVEN**. Indeed sometimes it is ill advisable. They may not feel they need to be **FORGIVEN** for anything.
27. *FORGIVENESS* is a skill that improves with practice.
28. If you find it difficult to *FORGIVE*, pray for the desire to **FORGIVE**.

29. In the Lord's Prayer, we ask God to **FORGIVE** us only as well as we **FORGIVE** each other.
30. There can be **FORGIVENESS** without reconciliation.
31. There is a difference between **FORGIVENESS** and justice. Justice often is revenge dressed up in a nice word. **FORGIVENESS** is not judicial but psychological and spiritual.
32. Anger and the spirit of retaliation re-open your wound by reminding you of the offense. **FORGIVENESS** brings healing to an open wound.
33. When we **FORGIVE** we surrender the right to get even.
34. **FORGIVENESS** restores the other person's humanity.
35. We pray to **FORGIVE** as God has **FORGIVEN** us. "We all have had to make numerous withdrawals from the bank of **GRACE**." Rev. James Farmer
36. We **FORGIVE** because we need healing.
37. "We love God only as much as we love the person we love least." Dorothy Day
38. If you find it difficult to **FORGIVE,** pray for the ability to want to **FORGIVE**
39. Proverbs writes "A stone is heavy, and sand weighty: but anger is heavier than them both."
40. It takes courage to **FORGIVE.**
41. **FORGIVENESS** does not imply approval or acceptance of another's behavior.
42. **FORGIVENESS** is not easy. There are few indeed with the natural predisposition toward **FORGIVING.**
43. One of the reasons many do not **FORGIVE,** is that they have not had any role models of **FORGIVENESS** in their lives.
44. To withhold **FORGIVENESS** is to be a perennial victim of those who have hurt us
45. **FORGIVENESS** does not imply spiritual superiority.
46. We are all students in the school of **FORGIVENESS**. Jesus is one of our teachers.

47. We need to teach *FORGIVENESS* to our
children, grandchildren, and each other.

48. God moves us to *FORGIVE*. It begins
when we feel God nudge us.

49. **THERE ARE DIFFERENCES BETWEEN
FORGIVENESS AND REUNION**:
1. It takes one person to *FORGIVE*.
It takes two to be reunited.
2. *FORGIVENESS* happens inside the wounded person.
Reunion happens between people.
3. We can *FORGIVE* even if we do not trust
the person not to wrong us again.
Reunion can happen only if we trust the
person not to wrong us again.
4. *FORGIVENESS* has no strings attached.
Reunion has several strings attached.
5. We can *FORGIVE* a person who never says he/she is sorry
We cannot truly be united until he/she is honestly sorry.

50. In Mozart's *Requiem Mass* are these thought
provoking words: "Remember, merciful Jesus,
that I am the cause of your journey."

12

DID I REMEMBER TO TELL YOU ABOUT SALVATION?

We are not human beings on a spiritual journey.
We are spiritual beings on a human journey.

God became what we are so that
We might become what God is.
St Irenaeus Bishop of Lyon (d.200)
St Athanasius Bishop Alexandria (d.373)

What are the goals and purpose of salvation?
The salvation of humankind and the restoration of creation

INTRODUCTION:
WHEN JESUS WAS old enough, Mary and Joseph took him to the temple in Jerusalem. They presented him to the Lord, as was custom. In the temple, they encountered a righteous and devout man, whom God promised would see the Messiah before he died. "And inspired by the

Holy Spirit the parents brought the child. When Simeon saw the child
Jesus, he took him in his arms and blessed God and said,

> Mine eyes have seen the salvation
> You have prepared in the presence of all people.
> A light to enlighten the gentiles
> And the glory of your people Israel. (Luke 2:30-32)

The coming of Jesus signals the coming of salvation for the
entire world: Jew and Gentile. Indeed, the incarnation centers on
the mystery of salvation. What is salvation? The answer centers
around two basic and deep yearnings of the heart. Something
in the very fabric of our human nature tells us that we are
creatures whose being is in question in two different ways.

1. We humans have a basic desire to live. Once we have
   begun to live, we want to continue living. Humans do
   not want life to stop. We are, however, conscious that
   we are mortal. This creates distress and unrest.

2. At the same time we aspire to life, we realize that there
   is little reason to live if we are not complete, or if
   our lives lack meaning and purpose. There is more to
   life than the simple act of breathing. Our hearts have
   more to do than pump blood. Life needs direction.
   The basic desire then is twofold: 1. To eternity and
   2. To completeness or wholeness with meaning and
   purpose. After a time of searching studying and
   reflecting, we come to understand that there is no natural
   answer to this longing for eternity and wholeness.

The Good News is contained in Simeon's proclamation;
"Salvation has come before all people as a light for the
revelation of all people." (Luke 2:30-32) Salvation has
come in the God-man Jesus the Christ. God has come

upon us sharing with us the divine nature, completing our nature, and bringing deep meaning and purpose.

Authentic religion paints a picture of spiritual health and wholeness, and draws us to Christ, the bringer of salvation.

1. Every Sunday at worship, we confess in the creed, formulated by the Councils of Nicaea in 325 and Constantinople in 381, "For us and our salvation he came down from Heaven." Christians universally agree that God became human so that we "might be saved." Where Christians disagree is what salvation entails.

   In the second century St. Irenaeus wrote, "to follow the savior is to be a partaker of salvation and to follow light is to receive light." He went on to say, "God became what we are in order that we might become what he is." St. Athanasius, picking up the same theme 200 years later, taught that if Christ were not truly God then we could not be saved; if he were not truly human, He could not save us by dying and rising again.

   We must understand however, that the early church fathers did not think in terms of an individualistic salvation. They thought more universally. What are the goals and purpose of salvation: the salvation of humankind and the restoration of creation. In other words, God restores to humankind the ability to live out their created nature, "in the image and after the likeness of God." (Genesis 1) In I John 3:2 the author writes, "We shall be like him." II Peter 1:4 declares, "We become partakers of the divine nature." Paul prays, "May Christ be formed in you." (Galatians 4:19) And in Ephesians 4:22-24 he writes, "You were taught to put away your former way of life, your old self, corrupt and deluded by its lusts, and to be renewed in the spirit of your minds,

and to clothe yourselves with the new self, created according
to the likeness of God in true righteousness and holiness."

God restores us to our created nature. We become alive
in the image and likeness of Jesus. We become, in St.
Paul's words, "A new creation." (Gal. 6:15, 2 Cor 5:17)

Where discourse about salvation goes awry
in much contemporary literature is its individualistic approach.
God is about the business of saving the world.
The question, "Are you saved?" denies
that salvation is about the world.
It is egocentric when salvation conversation
is purely concerned with individual believers.
God thinks broader than that.

2. New Testament authors wrote in Greek, because most of
the world spoke Greek. It was the common language of
most nations in the Roman Empire. When Alexander built
his empire, in the fourth century B.C., he brought Greek
language and culture to the occupied countries. Rome
followed a different path. They allowed a conquered people
to retain most of their culture, including the languages
spoken. Correspondingly, most of the world spoke Greek,
not Latin. Translating is at best an art. The New Testament
writers wrote in Greek so that it would have an extensive
audience. The common languages in Palestine were Aramaic
and Hebrew. The authors of the New Testament did their
best to communicate the message of Jesus, in a language that
was not their mother tongue. Consequently, translation is, at
best, difficult because their Greek was a translation from the
Aramaic or Hebrew that Jesus and his disciples spoke. It would
be like me writing in Norwegian. Possible, but not beautiful.

The Greek word for the noun, salvation, is *soteria*. The Greek word for the verb save is *sozo*. In the Gospels, *Sozo* is variously translated: to save, to heal, or make whole. Likewise, *soteria* is translated: salvation, healed, or whole. Regardless how one translates the words, they bring with them the texture and tone of all the possible translations. To save is to restore health and wholeness to body, mind, and spirit. When one looks at the ministry of Jesus, that is precisely what he did. In some ways, the word salvation in all its richness has become flawed. When someone asks, "Are you saved?" They tend to mean, "Have you accepted Jesus as your Lord and Savior so you go to Heaven?" On the one hand, it is too individualistic, and on the other, it makes salvation something that is in a person's power. It effectively negates the work of Jesus because it relies on acceptance of Jesus. That understanding is unbiblical. Neither is it what the church has historically taught. God makes whole. God's love heals. God saves the world.

3. 1. In the hunger of the spirit
    And the thirst of my poor soul
    I call to the one named Jesus
    To touch and make me whole
    To touch and make me whole

> Safe in the arms of Jesus
> Secure in the hands of God.
> Nesting on the palm of mercy
> Embraced by the Lord of Love.

2. It is you Lord that I cherish
It is you whom I adore
Grasp me in arms so tender
Both now and evermore
Both now and evermore

Safe in the arms of Jesus
Secure in the hands of God.
Nesting on the palm of mercy
Embraced by the Lord of Love

3. Lord, lead me out of darkness
Good shepherd of the light
Wake up, O sleeping spirit
The dawn is in your sight
The dawn is in your sight

    Safe in the arms of Jesus
    Secure in the hands of God
    Nesting on the palm of mercy
    Embraced by the Lord of Love

4. Send to me your holy angels
To protect me in my night
Live within my spirit
Fill my heart with light
Fill my heart with light
    Safe in the arms of Jesus
    Secure in the hands of God
    Nesting on the palm of mercy
    Embraced by the Lord of Love

4. Salvation is deliverance from the forces of evil and the power of sin. It begins the process of transforming us into godly people. (Ephesians 5:8-9) Salvation is taking on a life marked and shaped by Jesus, who makes the reign of God visible in our lives. (Eph. 4:15) (1 John 3:8-10)

5. While salvation belongs to the world, it does have meaning for individual Christians. Jesus declared, "I have come that you might have life and have it abundantly."

(John 10:10b) Jesus indicates that humankind is lifeless without him. Jesus brings life. In fact, he proclaims that our lot is not just life, but life in abundance. This abundant life is salvation, and it has three main thrusts.

1. It improves the quality of life beyond measure. "My cup runneth over," announces the Psalmist. The creator of the universe, the source of all that is, the object of my love is within me. I was born with a certain capacity to love. God, who lives within, increases my ability to love, to be caring, and to show compassion. My cup runneth over with goodness and mercy. Jesus saves and delivers me from a meaningless life. He offers new life, and I become a new being. He transforms my life and gives me meaning and purpose. Salvation is a gift I receive in the here and now.

2. Salvation is a future event as well. Jesus said, "I am the resurrection and the life, whoever believes in me, though he dies, yet shall he live and whoever lives and believes in me shall never die." (John 11:25&26) If salvation can increase the quality of life, it also brings eternal life. "If the Spirit of Christ Jesus dwells in you, the Spirit will also raise you to eternal life." (Romans 8:11) Life and death are mutually exclusive. Where life exists, death is vanquished. Life exiles death, as light banishes darkness. Jesus, the life of the world lives in us, and his eternal living spirit loosens death's grip on us.

3. Therefore, we can become what we were intended to be at creation. We can become whole and holy. We can indeed become the children of God.

6. In 1972, Christ Lutheran Church in Baltimore called me as their assistant pastor. Part of my job was to visit the 350 members who were shut-ins. One of them was a dear lady in her 80's. I will never forget her face, but I cannot, for the life of me,

remember her name. It is a shame because she was important to me. I'll call her Helen. Helen was a lifelong member of Christ Church. She had sung in the choir, been a member of the Ladies Aid, and did various chores around the church. She was a model member. Every church should have someone like her. Whenever I visited her, I always came away enriched.

Helen became very ill and knew she was dying. When I visited her in the hospital, she told me that she was afraid of dying. I asked her, "What frightens you about dying?"
"I am frightened because I am going to Hell."
I couldn't believe my ears. "What makes you think you are going to Hell?"
"Well, when I was a young girl I had a baby out of wedlock (probably just prior to WW I). My Sunday School teacher told me that I would go to Hell."

I was speechless. In my own inexperienced way, I endeavored to explain forgiveness and grace. It did not help. Helen died a short time later thinking she was going to Hell. It still breaks my heart. After I used this story in a sermon, I received an email from one of our members who said, "I would have told her how happy and overjoyed I was for her–that she had such a wonderful surprise waiting for her–more wonderful then she obviously ever imagined." I wish I had had the experience to say something like that.

St. Paul said, "We are ambassadors for Christ."
That is a pretty awesome responsibility.

The church has the power to crush or heal. Choose to heal.

13

Did I remember to tell that the ministry of the church cannot fail, if you follow God's heart? Did I remember to tell endless possibilities fill your future?

"Once you have experienced the mercy of God in your life
You will henceforth aspire only to serve."
Dietrich Bonhoeffer d. 1945

Being loved is like being found after having been lost.
Love is transformative.
It turns the one loved into one who loves.

We practice loving God by learning to love others.
We practice loving others by learning to love ourselves.

1. The ministry of Gloria Dei! is not yours; it is God's.
    You are the stewards of that ministry. It is a humbling
    responsibility and not to be taken lightly.

2. In another chapter, I told the story a child who woke up one
    night after a frightening nightmare. She was convinced that
    there were all kinds of monsters and goblins lurking under her
    bed and in the corners of her room. She ran to her parents'
    bedroom, and after her mother had calmed her down, she took
    the child back to her own room and said, "You don't need
    to be afraid you aren't alone here. God is right here with you
    in your room." The little girl said, "I know that God is here,
    but I need someone in my room that has some skin on!"
    You are the skin of God.

    The world needs you.

    Jesus in the flesh is gone. He ascended to his Father, but he left
    the Holy Spirit and the Church to be the instruments of grace.
    We are the church.
    We are God with skin on, who bring healing and peace to
    a world sick with poverty, disproportionate distribution
    of wealth, anxiety, division, hatred, and strife.

3. The next pastor will be better than I was at some things, and
    not as good at others. Over the years, we discovered, together,
    what I did well and what I did not do well. Others did the
    things I did not do well. Similarly, the new pastor and you will
    have to determine how to do ministry together. It took time
    for us to figure it out, and it will take time again. However,
    if done prayerfully and patiently, it will yield much fruit.

4. Gloria Dei! is a music conservatory of love where
    we are schooled in the love's melodic and harmonic
    strains. An academy where we learn to love God more
    deeply, cherish each other more profoundly, and serve
    God's children around the world more fervently.

5. I will sing of your *loving-kindness*, O Lord, for ever;
        with my mouth I will proclaim your
    faithfulness to all generations.
        I declare that your steadfast love is established for ever;
        your faithfulness is as firm as the Heavens.
    (Psalm 89: 1-2)
    Loving-kindness—it has a nice ring to it, don't you
    think? It is a Biblical term. It was coined by Miles
    Coverdale when he translated the Old Testament in
    1535. It comes from the Hebrew word "*chesed.*" In
    Jewish theology, many scholars think chesed is the
    primary virtue, and is one of the names for God. The
    word also is translated as mercy, grace, goodness, or
    compassion. Sometimes it is translated as steadfast love.
    In texture and tone, it carries all those meanings with it.
    In Psalm 23, Coverdale concludes the Psalm this way,
    "surely loving-kindness and mercy shall
    follow me all the days of my life."

    Indeed, I pray that loving-kindness follows you
    all the days of your life. May loving-kindness
    lead you as you journey to life's end.

6. "Once you have experienced the mercy of God in
    your life you will henceforth aspire only to serve."
    Dietrich Bonhoeffer (d. 1945 in Flossenburg
    Concentration Camp)

Christians are actively involved in the world. As disciples, we surrender ourselves to Christ and strive to be in union with his desires. Jesus calls us to follow him, not merely as teacher or example but as The Messiah, the Son of God. Discipleship means obedience to Jesus and faithfulness in service. Discipleship is not merely doing good works; it is following Jesus where he leads us. Christianity without discipleship is always Christianity without Christ. Without discipleship, Christianity remains just an abstract idea. In such a religion, there is trust in God but no following Jesus. To be a Christian is to be a disciple. To be a Christian is to follow where Jesus leads. Too often, we lack trust and worry that God will lead us to a place we do not want to go. My experience is that God gives us the desire to go where he leads us.

"The Christian life is not a set of rules and regulations; it is a statement of the life we will live when the Holy Spirit is getting His way with us."
Oswald Chambers

7. As a Christian I can live on one of three levels.
I can return evil for good, which is the satanic level.
I can return good for good, which is the human level.
Or I can return good for evil, which is the godly level.

8. Congregational members all moving in the same direction are a wonder to behold.

In 2000, we began a relationship with our first sister congregation. It is located in Krajne, Slovakia. It is the hometown of the family of one of our members, John Remias. Both his parents were born there, and he still has cousins who live in the area. He was hoping to establish a sister congregation relationship with them. It took a bit for it to sink in what that would mean. After some discussion, we all agreed that it would be wonderful idea to have a relationship with his congregation. For me it has special meaning because it was behind the "iron curtain."

When I was in junior high school, we lived in Berlin, Germany. My Dad was the chaplain. He was transferred there because we were Lutheran. The army knew it was essential for the USA to have good relations with the Lutheran Bishop of Berlin. We were there before the wall went up and stayed long enough to watch it go up. Periodically, Dad would say, "Tommy, get your music you're going to go sing." Dad would smuggle butter, cream, milk, eggs, and other items East Germans found scarce. I grew to love and respect the East Germans who struggled to keep the church alive. For me, personally, a chance to have a relationship with Krajne was a blessing.

John mentioned that the congregation would like to repair their organ. The organ is a symbol for Slovakian churches of vitality and health. Moreover, they use it for concerts and gatherings of the entire community. It would cost $10,000 to repair a pipe organ, which had been neglected for over fifty years. It was against the law to make repairs to church organs. In 2000, my wife, our two children, and I attended the first concert and dedication of the organ. The mayor of the town shared, "You will never know what this means to our entire village. It is a great gift." At that time, the mayor was not a believer. When I returned two years later, the mayor sat in the "Amen corner" of the sanctuary and sang the hymns with gusto and fervor.

In 2004, a tsunami in the Indian Ocean devastated countries along its coastline. About 230,000 people lost their lives. One Sunday after the disaster, I asked, "How much money should we raise to help those effected by the tsunami?" Member, Jim Quigley shouted, "$25,000." There was an audible gasp from the congregation. One of the gasps was mine. I was hoping for $10,000. Another said, "Let's do it." In one month's time, we raised the money.

In late summer, 2012, we decided to replace all 110 desks in our Lutheran school in El Salvador and employ local craftsmen to do the work. It would cost about $11,000. We raised the money in less than a month. I was there for the dedication in March of 2013. Additionally, members pay the tuition for about a dozen kids so they can attend the school.

In 2013, ten of us visited our two sister churches in rural south Madagascar. It is very rural. Electricity comes from a diesel generator and is on for about four hours a day. Most do not have running water. We wanted to raise $10,000 to build a water catchment so villagers did not have to walk the three and a half miles to get water. Additionally, we wanted to put a roof on one of the churches, and erect a Sunday School building at the other one. A storm had destroyed the previous building. These projects gave work to 26 resident workers, thereby putting money back into the village. Money goes a long way in Madagascar. We sent them over $12,000.

A congregation moving in the same
direction is a wonder to behold.

9. When I was a young pastor in the inner city of Baltimore a 16-year-old girl named Sharon pounded on the exterior window of my office. Sharon was a troubled kid, and I had heard about her many exploits. I told her to come around to the door, and come into my office. "Oh no," she said, "I won't go in the building. Church just makes me feel guilty." Sharon was abused as a young child. Her mother knew, but did nothing. Neighbors knew, and did nothing. As she matured, she acted out in unhealthy

ways. Folks began to tell her that she was a big sinner, and that she had better straighten up if she wanted to go to Heaven. Even the sanctuary itself was not an abode of comfort but a place of condemnation.

Over the next few years I helped her out of jams, bailed her out of jail, and periodically brought her back to our own home. The congregation was determined that she experience some love and grace in her life. Sometimes, congregational members would house her. A couple of families would check on her every week. Occasionally I would find her beaten and bring her to the emergency room. There was not much grace in her life.

One night I received a call from a Baltimore City Police officer. "Pastor, you better come to Mercy Hospital. There is a young woman here who has your name and telephone number in her pocket." By the time I got to the hospital she had died. She had been shot in a drug deal gone badly. I wept as though I had lost one of my own children.

Sharon did not experience much love. I pray that she found grace from the congregation, my family, and me. She sure needed it.

10. God never calls you to a ministry that you can do without God.

11. Father Monchanin was a French Priest who founded a Christian ashram in Southern India. He wrote, "Let us keep alive the flame of love and service: they are one and the same flame. Let us communicate to those around us the desire to give and attend to their needs."

The great 16th century Spanish mystic, St. John of the Cross, wrote a poem and commentary entitled *The Living*

Flame of Love. I love the imagery. A flame is light, gives warmth, and when it is hot enough can spread. This year there were wild fires in the western US that firefighters could barely contain, let alone put out. It took weeks and in some cases months to restrain the blazes. Christians, alive with God's living flame of love and service can spread the fire of God's love that can never be extinguished.

12. An old proverb says, "The rose spreads its scent around." I guess it refers to people as well. Christians, indeed, leave the scent of good works and love behind where they travel.

13. A monastery is the keeper of the solitude. In that silent sanctuary, we sit in God's healing presence.

The church can be the same.

It can provide a consoling and comforting home, where people can explore the most secret and sensitive places of their hearts. It can provide a secluded and sheltering abode, where God can bring the divine curative touch to the most delicate and wounded spirits.

It is essential ministry.

14. Be my hands to grasp another's hand,
Be my ears to hear another's fears,
Be my feet to walk from shore to shore,
Be my hand to unlock every door.

Be my hands to grasp another's hand.
See my will relationships to build.
Be my voice, speak loving words and true.
I'll be there to keep on guiding you.

Be my child to all be reconciled.
Be my song and sing the whole day long.
Be my eyes and see how life can be.
Be my life to live out faithfully.

15. A famous folk tale that tells how our Lord returned to
glory following His Passion and Resurrection, still bearing
the marks of His suffering. One of the angels looked
at the Lord and said, "You must have suffered terribly
down there. Does the world know what you did for it? Do
they all understand how great your love is for them?"

"No," Jesus responded, "Not yet. Only a handful
of people, my followers in Palestine, know about
my divine love and works of salvation."

The angel seemed perplexed, "Well, what have
you done to ensure that all people throughout
the world will hear about you?"

Jesus confidently responded, "I commanded my disciples to
make it their business to share the Good News. They will tell
others, who will still tell others, until the farthest person of
the widest circle throughout the world will hear my story."

The angel looked especially doubtful now, for he knew well
what poor creatures humans were. "Yes," he said, "but what
if they forget? What if they grow weary? What if they ignore
their responsibility? What if, way down in the 21st century,
your followers fail to share the story of your love for the
world? What then? Haven't you made any back-up plans?"

To which Jesus responded, "No. I haven't
made any other plans. I trust them!"

Our Lord is counting on us to tell the story: to share His love. To offer a witness of the transforming power that comes through believing and following Jesus Christ.

Our Lord is counting on us to be His hands and feet, to be His instruments in passing on the Good News to the world! What if we grow weary? What if we say, "Enough, already?" What if we ignore our responsibility? Our Lord has not only given us a command, but a privilege. He has honored us with the responsibility of acting as his emissaries throughout the world to tell his story and to share his love. We each play an integral role in his plan of salvation for all people.

We cannot limit this universal love of God exclusively on a local level. "Charity begins at home" some claim. "We have to take care of our own. There are plenty of needs here. We can't solve the problems of the world." Guess what, you do a wonderful job here at home. The Outreach Committee is made up of dedicated and faithful members who take the responsibility to serve others.

And yet, Jesus says, "I haven't made other plans. I'm counting on you." We should never limit our Christian witness to an either-or decision. When people remain indifferent to the needs of the world, and allow their parochial worldview to question the necessity of supporting the global work and mission of the Church, they reject Christ's universal vision.

Divine love knows no boundaries and it never sets any limits.

Jesus calls us to "tell others, who will still tell others, until the farthest person of the widest circle throughout the world will hear His story." Since the divine love of God knows no boundaries, His people and the Church must make every effort to participate in witnessing God's love at local, national, and global levels, all simultaneously. It must never be an either-or proposition. This universal and holistic vision, acts as the antithesis of the egocentric temptation we all face in our lives, as well as the cure to the parochial, often ethnocentric or "spiritual ghetto" heresy our parishes often lead.

Fr. Thomas Hopko writes, "If a parish has no awareness and consciousness of being "sent" by God to speak His words, to do His work, and to accomplish His will in this world, then it is not a Christian Parish!"

We are not living up to our Christian identity if we do not fulfill this calling to "go forth" and become Christ's witnesses in the world around us.

16. JESUS CAME TO TEACH us the language of love—the language of grace.

JESUS CAME TO TEACH us to break our cycles of revenge. JESUS CAME TO TEACH us to forgive ourselves and other people, no matter how painful that may be.

JESUS CAME TO TEACH us to forgive ourselves and other people, no matter how challenging that may be.

JESUS CAME TO TEACH us not only to forgive our friends and people that we like, but also to forgive our enemies and people with whom we have deep conflicts.

JESUS CAME TO TEACH us that grace and forgiveness are the master keys that unlock the doors to all human relationships.

17. In 1949, Mao Tse-Tung banished all
Christian missionaries from China.
One of those missionaries was my college
history professor, Dr. Larson.
He told of the hardships, and yet he felt that he
had deserted the Chinese when the communists
forced him to leave. There were some 500,000
Christians at that time. Communists burned
churches or used them for other purposes and killed
countless people who professed Jesus as Lord.

There were no missionaries left. However, they left the
seeds of faith planted in the good soil of the people.

Like a seed growing secretly, it blossomed and bloomed.

Today, estimates range from 50,000,000
to 90,000,000 Chinese Christians.
A few seeds planted grew into a great harvest.
Well done, Dr. Larson.

18. The most important people in your life are the
ones who bring out the best in you.
They encourage you,
They motivate you,
They inspire you,
They promote you.
They stimulate you to give your best.
These are the true supporters and life coaches.
They enjoy your success.

Others will test you,
Some will use you,
Some will teach you.

But most importantly ...
Some will bring out the best in you.

Moreover, you can be that person to others.

Goethe wrote, "Treat a man as he appears to be, and you make him worse. But treat him as if he already were what he potentially could be, and you make him what he could become."

19. "A man knows he has found his vocation when he stops thinking about how to live and begins to live." Thomas Merton

20. Author Rachel Naomi Remen tells the story of being invited to hear a well-known rabbi speak about forgiveness at a Yom Kippur service.

Yom Kippur is the Day of Atonement, when Jews everywhere reflect on the year just past, repent their shortcomings and unkindnesses, and hope for the forgiveness of God. The rabbi, however, did not speak directly about God's forgiveness.

Instead, he walked out into the congregation, took his infant daughter from his wife, and, carrying her in his arms, and stepped up to the podium. The little girl was perhaps a year old and she was adorable. From her father's arms, she smiled at the congregation. Every heart melted. Turning toward her daddy, she patted him on the cheek with her tiny hands. He smiled fondly at her, and with his customary dignity began a rather traditional Yom Kippur sermon, talking about the meaning of the holiday.

The baby girl, feeling his attention shift away from her, reached forward and grabbed his nose. Gently he freed himself and continued the sermon. After a few minutes, she took his

tie and put it in her mouth. Everyone chuckled. The rabbi
rescued his tie and smiled at his child. Looking at us over the
top of her head, he said, "Think about it. Is there anything
she can do that you could not forgive her for?" Just then, she
reached up and grabbed his eyeglasses. Everyone laughed
aloud. Retrieving his eyeglasses and settling them on his
nose, the rabbi laughed as well. Still smiling, he waited for
silence. When it came, he asked, "And when does that stop?
When does it get too hard to forgive? At three? At seven?
At fourteen? At thirty-five? How old does someone have
to be before you forget that everyone is a child of God?"

21. When my daughter was just about three years old, we
went out of state to visit some friends. After a long day of
visiting, catching up and eating, we packed up and returned
home. It was a tiring day. When we reached our driveway
and stopped the car, I carried our sleeping three year old
to her bedroom. She opened here eyes, looked around
and let out a loud scream, *WHERE'S MY PEESY??*"
Now her "peesy" was a blanket she had since birth.
Don't think **that** didn't send a cold chill through my body, and
guess who made the long journey back to pick up that raggedy
and threadbare piece of cloth! Amazingly, this well-worn and
much loved blanket brings assurance, security and peace to its
owner. When she's upset or afraid, it's there for her. In good
times and in bad, but especially in bad, it is a *great comfort* to
her. Nothing can take its place. Just washing the thing can be
traumatic. On one occasion this peesy's owner dragged around
three imposter blankets, two towels, a washcloth, an afghan,
and three dishtowels – pacing back and forth in front of the
clothes dryer waiting for the *real* peesy to finish drying!
Now that's devotion!
Wouldn't it be great if there were something equivalent that
could bring this kind of comfort and assurance to us as adults?

Actually, for Christian people there *is* something that brings assurance, peace and comfort to our lives. It is the church. It can be there for people when all else fails. It can bring comfort and succor in times of trouble, and healing to an anxious heart. It brings the comforter of all–Jesus Christ, the great consoler of restless spirits.

22. We can understand more clearly God's vision for the church when we look at the two "Great Commissions.

In Genesis is God's call to Abraham.

"Go from your country and your kindred and your father's house to the land that I will show you. I will make of you a great nation, and I will bless you, and make your name great, so that you will be a blessing to all the families of the earth." (Gen 12:1-3)

The Commissioning of the Disciples

And Jesus came and said to them, 'All authority in Heaven and on earth has been given to me. Go, therefore, and make disciples of all nations, baptizing them in the name of the Father and of the Son and of the Holy Spirit, and teaching them to observe all that I have commanded you. And remember, I am with you always, to the end of the age.' (Matthew 28:18-20)

Christians are called to be globally minded. The last thing Jesus told his disciples is to go into all the world baptizing, teaching and making disciples. The Christian church has no choice but to be internationally minded. Ever since I was a little boy, I have been sending money to missionaries and ministries in Madagascar. Part of the

Sunday morning offering went to Church. The rest went to Madagascar. Going into all the world is not a decision we get to make. It is a command we either follow or do not follow. It is a mandate from Jesus, "go into all the world."

The reach of the arms of mission extends throughout the world. This is why St. John Chrysostom as bishop told his pastors, "There are two types of Christian leaders: those who say, "My parish is my world" and others who say, "The world is my parish."

23. When I think about your future, I am so excited for you that I can barely contain my joy. The only thing that will change at Gloria Dei! is the pastor. I know that God will send you a pastor who will lead you and love you. The biggest difference will be that the new pastor won't be so devilishly handsome. The congregational leaders will be the same, and there will be opportunities for new leaders to emerge. Each will bring new ideas for ministry. Think where you might be in ten years. Some things will remain the same. You will still care for each other and buoy each other up. You will still love our Lord and serve him through your ministry. What will change are the opportunities for new mission. I will watch from afar and pray for you each day. How exciting the future is for Gloria Dei! How limitless are the opportunities. Seize them and make them real.

14

DID I REMEMBER TO TELL YOU ABOUT THE WONDER OF YOUR BEING?

God holds the key to our identity
Your identity is hidden in God.
God has loved you forever

No one is beyond the reach of God's embrace.

You are a wonder of creation and God's creative masterpiece.

1. Psalm 139

> Lord, you search me and you know me,
> you know my resting and my rising,
> you discern my purpose from afar.
> You mark when I walk or lie down,
> all my ways lie open to you.

Before ever a word is on my tongue
you know it, O Lord, through and through.
Behind and before you encircle me,
your hand ever laid upon me.
Too wonderful for me this knowledge,
too high, beyond my reach.

Where can I go from your spirit,
or where can I flee from your face?
If I climb the Heavens, you are there.
If I lie in the grave, you are there.

If I take the wings of the dawn
and dwell at the sea's furthest end,
even there your hand would lead me,
your right hand would hold me fast.

If I say: "Let the darkness hide me
and the light around me be night,"
even darkness is not dark for you
and the night is as clear as the day.

For it was you who created my being,
knit me together in my mother's womb.
I thank you for the wonder of my being,
for the wonders of all your creation.

Already you knew my soul
My body held no secret from you
When I was being fashioned in secret
And molded in the depths of the earth.

Search me, God, and know my ways
Test me and know my thoughts.
See that I follow not the wrong paths

And lead me in the way of everlasting life.
(Translation from the Abbey Psalter)

I love this Psalm. I chant it at least once a day. I find
myself humming it, even when I am not conscious of
the words. The writer of this Psalm must have had an
extraordinary spiritual life. It takes a certain spiritual maturity
to feel God's presence in every moment and place.

No one and no place are beyond the reach of God's embrace.
Wherever I go, God is already there to greet me.
When I fall, God's hands are there to catch me.
If I cannot walk, God's arms will carry me.
In my darkest thoughts, God is there to bring light; "even
darkness is not dark for you and the night is as clear as the day."

We think the Psalm could not soar any higher,
could not be more majestic, could not possibly
describe a more intimate relationship. Then, like a
comet, it soars on and glows even brighter.

For it was you who created my being,
knit me together in my mother's womb.
I thank you for the wonder of my being,

God who is higher than the Heavens and dwells at the
end of the seas "knit you together in your mother's
womb." God is not some prime mover or a first cause.

God's creative finger fashioned and formed you.
Because of that you are a wonder.
You are a wonder of creation.
There has never been and there will never be another you.
You are God's masterpiece.
You are the cherry on top of the creative cake.

2. True Self/False Self
    Late in my ministry Susan Coale, who had been Gloria Deil's parish
    counselor and is a church member, and I were asked to lead a
    one-day pre-Lenten retreat for lay people. The title we chose was:
    Becoming Who You Were Created to Be. When we submitted the title to
    the pastor who invited us he said, "I'm not sure it is a good topic. I
    don't want some kind of pop-psychology." It is a shame that much
    of contemporary Lutheran theology ignores celebrating the divine
    gift of who we are. Becoming who we are, however, is no easy task.

    In 1996, I spent a couple of months in an Irish Roman
    Catholic Cistercian monastery. Cistercians are a contemplative
    order. They love silence and spend 6-8 hours in prayer every
    day. When I arrived, I noticed a Border Collie, named Jack,
    in a pen. I asked the abbot, Father Ambrose, if I could
    run in the fields with him. "Oh no!" he exclaimed, "We
    can't let him out of his pen very often. We bought Jack
    to help round up the cattle on their way to the barn every
    night. Border Collies are given instructions by a series of
    whistles. He had too many bosses and he got confused.
    Now all he does is chase the cows. We ruined him."

    Jack's talent was now lost and could not be regained.
    He had too many people giving him conflicting
    orders and he lost himself. He lost his true self. He
    no longer was the dog he was created to be.

    There are a lot of people like Jack. It isn't as if
    they have an identity crisis, they just have not
    been able to cherish the wonder of being.

    Here is what happens to so many of us. We get all
    kinds of people who are not shy about telling us who
    to be and how to act: parents, teachers, relatives, and

friends. Mom tells us to clean our rooms. She doesn't say it, but we may hear, "I should clean my room so Mom is happy with me. I want her to love me."

We go to school and see who the poplular kids are and what they are wearing and need to buy the same things so we can be popular too.

Billy goes over to Johhny's house because they have a pool, or some such thing, and we get the message that we are liked because of what we own.

We are also good at telling ourselves who we should be, who we should be like, and how we should act. Then comes the hard part. We expend a lot of energy trying to be that person. Down deep we know it is a lie, but we don't know what else to do.

I counseled a young man who grew up at Gloria Dei!. I've know him all of his life. He is a well-educated professional. Yet he is having difficulty, because he earns less than his wife, and does not feel his job carries as much prestige. His brother-in-law is an attorney in a large DC law firm, which makes him feel even more like a failure. He knows how silly this is, but can't seem to get past it. He isn't alone. We tend to get caught up in valuing our self worth by the prestige of our employment or the size of our bank account.

After the death of her father, a young woman tearfully confided, "My Dad never knew who I am." I asked, "Do you know who you are?" "No! I guess I don't." Her inability to get in touch with her true self caused her grief.

St. Paul writes about the Old, man, or self and the New, man, or self.

Romans 6:6
What then are we to say? Should we continue in sin in order
that grace may abound? By no means! How can we who died to
sin go on living in it? Do you not know that all of us who have
been baptized into Christ Jesus were baptized into his death?
Therefore, we have been buried with him by baptism into
death, so that, just as Christ was raised from the dead by the
glory of the Father, so we too might walk in newness of life.

Ephesians 4:14-16
We must no longer be children, tossed to and fro and blown
about by every wind of doctrine, by people's trickery, by their
craftiness in deceitful scheming. But speaking the truth in love,
we must grow up in every way into him who is the head, into
Christ, from whom the whole body, joined and knitted together by
every ligament with which it is equipped, as each part is working
properly, promotes the body's growth in building itself up in love.

Ephesians 4:17-24
Now this I affirm and insist on in the Lord: you must no longer
live as the Gentiles live, in the futility of their minds. They are
darkened in their understanding, alienated from the life of God
because of their ignorance and hardness of heart. They have lost
all sensitivity and have abandoned themselves to licentiousness,
greedy to practice every kind of impurity. That is not the way
you learned Christ! For surely you have heard about him and
were taught in him, as truth is in Jesus. You were taught to put
away your former way of life, your old self, corrupt and deluded
by its lusts, and to be renewed in the spirit of your minds,
and to clothe yourselves with the new self, created according
to the likeness of God in true righteousness and holiness.

Colossians 3:9-11
Do not lie to one another, seeing that you have stripped off
the old self with its practices and have clothed yourselves

with the new self, which is being renewed in knowledge according to the image of its creator. In that renewal there are no longer Greek and Jew, circumcised and uncircumcised, barbarian, Scythian, slave and free; but Christ is all and in all!

Martin Luther wrote, "I thought that the old man drowned in the waters of baptism, but I discovered the miserable wretch can swim." The great spiritual writer of the 20th century, Thomas Merton, wrote extensively about the difference between true self and false self.

For me to be a saint means to be myself. Therefore the problem of sanctity and salvation is in fact the problem of finding out who I am and of discovering my true self. To say 'I was born in sin' is to say 'I came into the world with a false self. I was born in a mask.' We may wear now one mask and now another, and never, if we so desire, appear with our own true face. But we cannot make these choices with impunity. Causes have effects, and if we lie to ourselves and to others, then we cannot expect to find truth and reality whenever we happen to want them.

The false self is who we think we are. It is our mental self-image and the social agreement most people spend their entire lives living up to—or down to. Once you learn to live as your true self, you can never be satisfied living out that charade again. It is too superficial and silly.

The journey to the true self begins by letting go of the need to be someone else. We may endeavor to be like someone we admire or envy, but the tendency to compare who I am with who someone else is, is a dangerous trap. We either come out on the short end and beat ourselves up for not being as good as the other person, or we determine that we are better and secretly superior. Either way we are not being true to our selves.

God has fashioned you with God's own hands.

You are an irreplaceable creation.

You are given gifts that allow you to live
out love in your unique way.

Here is the dilemma: you cannot become
yourself unless you know yourself.

This is where Psalm 139 is helpful: It was God
who created your being. It was God who knit
you together in your mother's womb.

God holds the key to your identity
Your identity is hidden in God.

**Before you can become who you really are, you must
become conscious of the fact that the person you
think you are, is at best an impostor and a stranger.**

The closer you are to God, the nearer you are to your true self.
As you discover who God is, you uncover who you are.
God desires you to be the person God created.
Finding your true self allows you to appreciate
your unique way of being holy.

There is not a flower that opens, not a seed that falls into
the ground, and not an ear of wheat that nods on the end
of its stalk in the wind that does not preach and proclaim
the greatness and the mercy of God to the whole world.

Your interior exploration is to realize that you proclaim God's
love by discovering how love is to be lived out in you.

We must make the choices that enable us to fulfill
the deepest capacities of our real selves.

3. I wrote the following letter to my daughter
    when she was in college.

Hi Honey,
You have been on my mind the last couple of days. I
have learned over the years not to ignore feelings like
that, so I thought I'd jot you a note. There are some
things I want to be sure I tell you about God.

You are known and loved by God. In fact, you came out
of God and God has loved you forever. You, God has
loved—just as you are with all your strengths and talents
and all your faults and perceived flaws. You don't have to
be anything more than who you are. Who you are, by the
way, is special enough. I pray that you can experience the
joy of who you are as much as those around you do.
Finding out who you are involves a certain amount of struggle
and pain, and for intuitive feelers like you it is a life-long
occupation. The sensitive ones seem to struggle the most.
Sensitive people struggle to please everyone. You can't. You
also can't find out who you are outside of God. God holds the
key that unlocks your true identity. I read somewhere that in
each of us is a captive child waiting to be free. God can see that
child of joy and wonder and awe. God loves you just the way
you are. Indeed, God fashioned and formed your inward parts.

It is just in "being" that you fulfill your life mission. We tend to
think it is "doing." Amber and Pike fulfilled their life mission
just being dogs. They didn't have to accomplish anything to
justify their existence. Just being is so important. The rest will
follow in its own time. Life unfolds before us each day and each

day we learn a little more about our place in the world. Now is your time to dream and hope and wonder. It is your time to dare and risk, to succeed and fail, and to make good choices and bad decisions. Through it all God is there with strength. I pray that you enjoy this part of your journey. Enjoy your friends and garden. Enjoy your work and sunshine. Play in the rain and slosh in the mud—your freed child is dying to do so.

I love and cherish you as my daughter.
Dad

4. I wrote a similar letter to my son.

Dear Erik,
I have awakened with you on my mind. I feel blessed that you are my son. You are also God's son.

God breathed life into your being. You have always been with God. God knew you from all time, and birthed you at the precise moment in history you were to live. You are more than you know. You're God's beloved. It was God who formed you as you are–loving, kind, filled with the joy of life, hopeful, concerned about the world, musical, and athletic (especially golf).

You are an original. You are unique in all creation. There never has been, and there never will be, another Erik. Who you are is God's gift to you. Now, you study and think, reflect and dream. You wonder about your place in the world and you dream about what life can be. You worry if you can cut the mustard—you can! The world is open to you and God will guide you and lead you. You can't, however, find your place in the world outside of prayer and meditation. Your Mom and I taught you to "do your pancreas [meditate]." One day you told me that, "Jesus moved from my pancreas to my heart. I like him there." Continue to "Do your heart." God will surround it with love and strength so no evil can harm you. Your heart is tender and filled with love. God's presence can help you deal with the hurts that come with just living. I thank God for the gift of you, son. So be yourself—after all, it is who you are.

I love you son.
Dad

5. Becoming your authentic self
God has known you from all time. God birthed you into the world. In fact, you came out of God, and God has loved you forever. God loves you just as you are, with all your strengths and talents, and all your faults and perceived flaws. You do not have to be anything more than who you are. Who you are is special enough.
Finding out who you are, however, involves a certain amount of struggle and pain. You cannot find out who you are outside of God. God holds the key that unlocks your true identity. The Psalmist declares:
For it was you who created my being,
Knit me together in my mother's womb.
I thank you for the wonder of my being,
For the wonders of all your creation. (Psalm 139)
You are more than you know. You are God's beloved. God formed you, and the Spirit matures you. The fruit of growing in the Spirit is love, joy, peace, patience, kindness, goodness, faithfulness, gentleness, and self- control. (Galatians 5:22-23) We have the choice of two identities: the external mask, which seems to be real, and the hidden, inner person, which may seem to you to be nothing. It, however, can become the truth of who you are.

6. If you know me at all, you know how I loved my Dad. Dad was my hero and inspiration. He was kind and patient,

compassionate and caring. He could also be a tough taskmaster. Nevertheless, he was always there when I needed him. People just loved him. When he was dying, I held his hand and wept. I wept because I knew he was going. I wept because as bright as my Dad was, he never really grasped the wonder of his being. He never felt as though he measured up. He was not alone, however, I come across many who never have been able to cherish who they are, who never appreciate the wonder of their being. I have met thousands of people over my forty-plus years in the ministry. Some are very successful at life. Some are not. Yet, all of them carry God's special spark. All are masterpieces in their own way. Some of those masterpieces have not been discovered. Some masterpieces have been painted over by the hardships of life. When my Dad was dying, I lay next to him and whispered, "be at rest, Dad. Be at rest. You lived a holy life. You loved God and cherished God's people. Well done, Dad. Well done, thou good and faithful servant." Dad was a good pastor and loving husband, a caring Father, and loyal friend. But Dad never really thought he fulfilled his potential. He never thought he did enough. It broke my heart when he was dying, and it breaks my heart now that he never really appreciated the beauty of his spirit. That is the way it is sometimes. The last person to appreciate someone's goodness is often the person himself.

7.   Your image of God forms your worldview, and your worldview decides your actions. If you have an image of a God who throws lightening bolts, it makes sense to become fierce with your enemies. On the other hand, if your image is one of gentleness, your relationship with the world is a bit more sensitive and kindhearted.

For most of us, if we were asked to describe God, our description would be that of a God of love because we have learned that is the right answer. Unfortunately, many understand a different

God. Gerard Hughes wrote a parable about an image of
God many have learned. He is a Jesuit priest in Birmingham,
England, and in this parable he describes God as a family relative
whom he has given the name, "Good Old Uncle George."

God was a family relative much admired by Mum and Dad,
who described him as very loving, a great friend of the
family, very powerful and interested in all of us. Eventually
we are taken to visit "Good Old Uncle George". He lives
in a formidable mansion, is bearded, gruff, and threatening.
We cannot share our parents' professed admiration for this
jewel in the family. At the end of the visit, Uncle George
addressed us. "Now listen, dear," he begins, looking very
severe, "I want to see you here once a week, and if you
fail to come, let me just show you what will happen to
you." He then leads us down to the mansion's basement.
It is dark, becomes hotter and hotter as we descend, and
we begin to hear unearthly screams. In the basement there
are steel doors. Uncle George opens one. "Now look in
there, dear," he says. We see a nightmare vision, an array
of blazing furnaces with little demons in attendance, who
hurl into the blaze men, women and children who failed
to visit Uncle George or to act in a way he approved.
"And if you don't visit me, dear, that is where you will
most certainly go," says Uncle George. He then takes us
upstairs again to meet Mum and Dad. As we go home,
tightly clutching Dad with one hand and Mum with the
other, Mum leans over to us and says, "And now don't you
love Uncle George with all your heart and soul, mind and
strength?" And we, loathing the monster, say, "Yes I do,"
because to say anything else would be to join the queue
at the furnace. At a tender age religious schizophrenia
has set in and we keep telling Uncle George how much
we love him and how good he is and that we want to
do only what pleases him. We observe what we are told

are his wishes and dare not admit, even to ourselves,
that we loathe him. (*Good Goats: Healing Our Image of God*
Dennis Linn, Shelia Fabricant Linn, Matthew Linn, p. 3)
Our image of God determines how we
live, how we love, and how we act.

8. God became what we are that we might become what he is.
St Irenaeus (130-202) and St Athanasius
Bishop of Alexandria (4th century)

These words were first written by the luminary St. Irenaeus and
picked up by St. Athanasius and others. (I wrote about them in
another chapter, but they are important enough to write about
them again.) For most of us in the West, these are very strange
words. They almost seem heretical. Yet, Athanasius is one of
the most influential people in the history of the church. We
Lutherans hold three creeds as expressions our theology: The
Apostle's Creed, the Nicene Creed, and the Athanasian Creed.
Such is his importance. So, what in the world is he talking about?
We understand the first part of this statement. God became
human in the person of Jesus born of Mary. The second part
of the equation, however, is almost as important as the first.
Obviously, we do not become God in nature. Nevertheless,
St. Paul writes, "It is no longer I who live, but Christ who lives
in me." (Galatians 2:20) In 2 Peter 1:4 the author writes, "we
become partakers in the divine nature." It simply means we
yearn to be possessed by God. It means we aspire to be godly
in our actions. It means the love of God is apparent in our
daily lives. The church in the West, describes this progress as
sanctification or simply growth in holiness. Growing spiritually
means deepening our relationship with God and allowing God
to take over our lives. Luther said we become "little Christs"
in the world. No matter how it is described, we can become
more than ourselves. We can reflect the love and mercy of our
God and leave our world a little better because we were there.

9.   I had to name the congregation. Naming the church was even more difficult than when Faye and I gave names to our kids. Gloria Dei! with the exclamation point seemed good. Irenaeus wrote, "The Glory of God (Gloria Dei!) is human fully alive. So, what is a fully alive human? I think it is simply the ability to discern my special role in the world, my special way to express love for God, others, and self. In the midst of doing that, I am fully alive. It means discovering who I am, or allowing God to show me who I am. I only have the ability to know myself in God. The ability to love becomes gift, not obligation or chore. When it is a chore, I am not fully alive. When love is as natural as breathing, then I am fully alive. Obviously, we don't make it in this life. But we can approach it once in a while. You are Gloria Dei!—the glory of God.

10. Where can I go from your spirit,
     or where can I flee from your face?
     If I climb the Heavens, you are there.
     If I lie in the grave, you are there.

     For it was you who created my being,
     knit me together in my mother's womb.
     I thank you for the wonder of my being,
     for the wonders of all your creation. (Psalm 139)

     The writer of this Psalm knew God.
     The writer of this Psalm knew that God knew him.
     The writer of this Psalm knew that the God who "knit him together in his mother's womb" was always present. There was no place he could go and not be found. There was no place he could go and elude the arms of his God. There was no place God was not.

     God is always present to us. There is no time or place in which God is not at hand. There are not times when God is more present or less present. There is no sense when God is more "here" or less "there." In truth, God is ever present to us.

The life of prayer is simply to recognize and rest in God's presence. The ability to see God is God's gift to us. God blesses us with the capacity to catch a glimpse of divine glory and feel sacred love.

When God's glory and love surround us, we are able to live in love's holiness and the goodness of God can shine through us.

11. You are God's piece de resistance. When God fashioned and formed you, there was an expression of joy and satisfaction on God's face. Find the wonder that God created. When you do, you will not be able to contain your joy. In Ephesians 2:10, St. Paul writes, "We are God's work of art, created in Christ Jesus to live the good life as from the beginning he had meant us to live." (The Jerusalem Bible) It is difficult to think of ourselves as a "work of art." Nevertheless, that is what you are. Cherish who you are. You are a masterpiece.

12. I am my beloved's and my beloved is mine. (Song of Solomon 6:3a)

The longing to be loved is an eternal longing. It arises from a deep center that only love can touch. Love sustains us even in the hardest times of our lives. John O'Donohue wrote, "Under the gaze and in the embrace of love, crippled hearts are transformed into long distance runners." When you are loved, you leap and run like a young colt who just found the joy of boundless movement.

Being loved is like being found after having been lost. Love awakens us from sleep and transports us into a consciousness of self-love and loving-kindness. Love is transformative.

It turns the one loved into one who loves. God is love and God is the lover. When we love others, they feel God's love. Love begets love. When we are loved, the world looks different, and we become the lovers we were created to be. Therefore, be lovers and watch the world change.

13. Let me sing for my beloved
    My love song.
    (Isaiah 5:1)

    "Let me sing for my beloved my love song." We all like a love song. If we don't, we can't listen to very much secular music. Isaiah writes that he is singing God's song of love to his people. It is easy to understand. Lovers sing love songs. Nevertheless, in this text God is singing a love song to us. All we need to do is sit still and listen to the love song that God sings in our hearts. When the love song becomes part of us, we can sing it to others.

14. "A generous heart is never lonesome." John O'Donohue

    I really like that phrase. Celtic Christians believed that blessings sent from the heart multiply and return to bless your own heart. "A generous heart is never lonesome. Loneliness in our age stems, in great part, from a failure in generosity. We compete with each other for goods, image and status."

    Generosity, however, is more than gift giving. People are given to us to cherish. When people are close to each other, they are in each other's soul-care. We secretly carry each other in our hearts, pray for each other, and cherish each other. It takes a generous heart to create that kind of space for another.

15. "Do not depend on the hope of results. You may have to face the fact that your work will be apparently

worthless and even achieve no result at all, if not perhaps results opposite to what you expect. As you get used to this idea, you start more and more to concentrate not on the results, but on the value, the rightness, the truth of the work itself. You gradually struggle less and less for an idea and more and more for specific people. In the end, it is the reality of personal relationship that saves everything." Thomas Merton

16. The logic of worldly success rests on a myth–the strange error that our achievements depend on the thoughts, opinions, and applause of others. A strange life it is to be living always in somebody else's imagination, as if that were the only place in which one could become real.

17. We are not at peace with others when we are not at peace with ourselves, and we are not at peace with ourselves when we are not at peace with God.

18. There is an old saying, "We teach what we want to learn." I also thinks there is a corollary; we preach what we need to hear. One of the things I've come to believe and have taught is; your are not the worst thing you've ever done. The foulest thing you've done does not define who you are. Let it go and God will redeem it and heal you of the memory of it. You are God's blessed child and God has loved you forever.

19. The writer of the Gospel of John proclaims that Jesus is the word of God. At the incarnation God "spoke" Jesus into existence. Similarly, God speaks you like a word. A word can never fully grasp the voice that expresses it. Instead, it becomes the echo of the speaker's voice. God speaks me like a word containing a partial thought of God. A word will never be able to comprehend the voice that utters it. The word is love. Be true to the love that

God utters through you. Be true to the love that you were meant to embody. Then you will be true to yourself.

20. Love is a special way of being alive.

There is no dichotomy between sacred and secular employment. Hence, instead of a line dividing the sacred and secular, I would like you to think in terms of a circle. Draw a circle around everything you do. Everything you do inside that circle, do it for the glory of God, and you are already living in a circle of the spiritual. All work is a spiritual enterprise, if you do it for the glory of God. Whatever is your work, if you do it for the glory of God—it is a spiritual work. Because your work is spiritual, your work is important to God. Do not ever think that what you do is useless. Your work is valuable and important in the sight of God. It is important because you do it for the glory of God and the benefit of humankind.

No job is greater or lesser in the eyes of God.
God does not compare.
God has no ruler to measure one against another.

21. Archbishop William Temple of Canterbury said in 1945, *"The church is one of few societies on earth that exists for the benefit of its non-members."*

He said this immediately after the World War II
when church buildings were bombed out, and
it would have been easy for church members to
neglect ministry and focus on their own needs.
A certain man noticed a listing of restaurants in the Atlanta Yellow Pages. One of the restaurants was called, *Church of God's Grill.* The peculiar name aroused his curiosity and he dialed the number. A man answered with a cheery, "Hello! Church of God's Grill!" He asked how the restaurant had been given such an unusual name, and

the man at the other end said: "Well, we had a little church mission down here, and we started selling chicken dinners after church on Sunday to help pay the bills. Well, people liked the chicken, and we did such a good business, that eventually we cut back on the church service. After a while, we just closed down the church altogether and kept on serving the chicken dinners. We kept the name we started with, and that's Church of God's Grill." George Macy. *The easiest thing in the world to do is to lose sight of the mission of the church.*
The following verses contain the clearest and most comprehensive command of our Lord. *Therefore go and make disciples of all nations, baptizing them in the name of the Father and of the Son and of the Holy Spirit and teaching them to obey everything I have commanded you.* (Matthew 28:19-20a)
This was the last command Jesus gave his disciples. We are the new disciples, and the commission is as much ours as theirs. As Archbishop Temple said, *"The church is one of few societies on earth that exists for the benefit of its non-members."*

22. To be grateful is to recognize the divine love in everything God gave us, and God has given us everything. Every breath we draw is a gift of love; every moment of existence is a grace. Gratitude therefore takes nothing for granted, is never unresponsive, and is constantly awakening to new wonder and to praise of the goodness of God. For the grateful person knows that God is good, not by hearsay but by experience. That makes all the difference.

23. God has a great secret to tell you:

You are all destined to become God's sons and daughters.
You are born with a divine promise.
YOU ARE GOD'S CHILD.
Once you have recognized God's great secret, you cannot avoid the call to see yourself and others differently.

We practice loving God by learning to love others.
We practice loving others by learning to love ourselves.

24. Animals live their true self. Thomas Merton (1968) calls them saints: they are as perfect as God has created them.

    A tree gives glory to God by being a tree. For in being what God means it to be it is obeying Him... The more a tree is like itself, the more it is like Him... The special clumsy beauty of this particular colt on this April day in this field under these clouds is a holiness consecrated to God by His own creative wisdom and it declares the glory of God. The pale flowers of the dogwood outside this window are saints. The little yellow flowers that nobody notices on the edge of that road are saints looking up into the face of God. Thomas Merton *New Seeds of Contemplation*

25. Cistercian Monk Thomas Merton wrote about seeing, truly SEEING the people in Louisville, Kentucky one day and being stunned with the realization of the blessing of the Incarnation, which meant that God was everywhere, in each of them, but "there was," he said, "no way of telling people that they are all walking around shining like the sun."
    The human predicament is that we are sleepwalking; unaware to what is happening around us. Pray for deeper vision and for the imagination and the ability to see that light of God that is within each and every person. It may cause us to look deeply because sometimes that light hides inside somewhere.

15

DID I REMEMBER TO TELL YOU ABOUT THE FRUIT OF THE SPRIT?

IN A FEW short sentences, St. Paul describes the joy of Christian living.

"The fruit of the Spirit is love, joy, peace, patience, kindness, goodness, faithfulness, gentleness and self-control." (Galatians 5:22)

He added, "Those who belong to Christ Jesus have crucified the sinful nature." Since we live by the Spirit, let us keep in step with the Spirit." (Galatians 5:14-25)

A Christian lives in step with the Holy Spirit. Being in step with the Holy Spirit, we harvest the ripened fruit of that relationship. The fruit of the Spirit has nine qualities. This is why it is the fruit – singular – of the Spirit, not the fruits of the Spirit. You do not choose these qualities like fruit in a market. "I'll have joy and peace, but I just can't handle self-control." They come as a package.

All nine are evidence of a person who walks stride by stride with the Spirit. They are all evidence of someone who belongs to Jesus.

Morning Devotion on the

Fruit of the Spirit

My Sacred Center AM
Written by Pastor Tom and Susan Coale

This morning I awaken to the Father, in whose arms I slept.
This morning I awaken to the Son in whose heart I am kept.
This morning I awaken to the Spirit in
whom all my joys are met.

This morning I am reminded that God
is with me wherever I go.

The fruit of the Spirit - love, joy, peace, patience, kindness,
goodness, faithfulness, gentleness, and self-control are
the fruit of God's life-giving presence (Gal. 5:22-23a).
Since I am God's beloved child, I know my Holy
Companion watches over me this day.

The Divine Lover accompanies me, and the Sacred
Helper guides me. I will see God everywhere - for
God, the Creator, is with me, and is ever before
me, welcoming me wherever I journey.
The Spirit shines through me, enabling me to see
Jesus deep in the spirit of each person I meet.

Jesus said, "Peace I leave with you."
Today, I will be peaceful.
The peace that Jesus gives "passes all understanding,"
and that peace cannot be taken away. My focus is
on Jesus who gives me peace and serenity.

Peace is a warm river flowing through my veins.
It quiets my thoughts and stills my heart.
Today the tranquil peace of Jesus flows through me. I will
bring peace to others and be a blessing to those I meet.

The Psalmist exults, "Joy comes in the morning."
Today, I choose to experience joy.
The sunrise bursts with the bliss of dawning light. Flowers
that closed at sunset open to greet the luminescent day.
Plants turn toward their source of life. The sun draws
them like iron filings to a magnet. God's Son, the source
of my joy, draws me to himself, and companions me this
day. As a gentle rain refreshes the earth, so will Jesus,
the Water of Life, wash joy over me all the day-long.
The deep knowledge that I am never alone fills me with joy.

God is more intimate than my breath and
nearer than my hands and feet.
The joy of God's presence sustains me.
Today I will be filled with hope.
I live with the assurance that God is always
present, active, and trustworthy.
Hope buoys me like a feather on a pond. There is no sinking.
Hope keeps me afloat. Hope is the food upon which I feed.
It draws me into the future and fills me with inner peace.
Hope is dependent solely on God's initiative.
Hope-filled confidence is a gift.
Hope surprises. Hope is sometimes subtle:
therefore, I will look intentionally for the hope-
filled assurance that God gives me.
God is hope. God resurrects hope. Hope is real
because resurrection is real. Easter comes every day
and my eyes behold hope in every situation.

The gift of the present moment is the presence of my
Holy Companion who transforms uncertainty and fear into
confident assurance. Today, I will be filled with hope.

The Spirit of Goodness and generosity will guide me today.
My generous heart is always filled with the joy of giving.
Goodness and generosity will give me courage to see
what others need and offer it without measure.
I will lavish praise on those I meet.
I will give from the well of my heart, the pure water of
meaning and purpose to those with whom I work. I will
seek to understand others, and exercise tolerance.
I will give the benefit of doubt when I am uncertain, and I
will be magnanimous with forgiveness for others and myself.
The Spirit of Goodness and Generosity guides me today.

Today, gentleness will abide in my soul. Like a precious
delicate flower receives a butterfly, so will I welcome others.
The peace and joy that dwell in the core of my
being will become visible in gentleness.
I will be a good listener and respond only when
I have something of value to say. Words will rise
from my deep center where God abides.
I am a vessel for God to use in bringing peace to others.
I will be gentle with myself as well, for gentleness
is the gift of a peaceful and merciful soul.
Today, gentleness radiates from me.

Today the love will guide my actions.
Jesus, who is deep in my soul, will birth
love out of me. I am love.
That is to say, I was born in love and I was born to love. My
name is love. My vocation is love. Birthed in this body, with this
personality, with this face, I am the only one who can love in my
own unique way. I am God's expression of love in the universe.

My love does not seek a reason, only an object. God is both the source of my love and the primary recipient of my love. Love pours out of me onto others, like an overflowing wellspring. As it flows, it grows and embraces others like a warm Irish mist. I will allow myself to receive love from others. Love flows from God through me, into others, and back to God, through me, into others and back to God, through me, into others, and back to God, and on and on. Love binds all of the fruit of the Spirit together into one, and gives them depth. Today, I am God's expression of love in the world. My entire day will be a prayer, because I am attentive to the still, small voice within me.

God loves me with a love that cannot be measured, save by the cross. God created me. God molded me in my mother's womb. God formed my face and gifted me with my own unique characteristics and personality. I am true to God's call when I am truly myself. I will ignore the false selves that others impose upon me and be the loving person God created me to be.

Today, I am in constant prayer.

Today is God's gift to me.

Today is my gift to God.

EVENING DEVOTION ON THE

FRUIT OF THE SPIRIT

My Sacred Center PM
Written by Pastor Tom and Susan Coale

This evening I thank the Father for creating the world I enjoyed today.
This evening I thank the Son for his loving presence, as my journeying companion.

This evening I thank the Spirit for guiding my footsteps
and embracing my heart with arms of peace.

The unity of God's creation and its infinite
beauty will stay with me this evening.
I approach this evening with a grateful heart
and a thankful mind, for my Holy Companion
blessed me with Divine Presence.
I celebrate the day as it was and is. The joy that
has been shared with me is a precious gift.
The people I met, welcomed, and spoke with, replenished
my life with meaning and purpose. Those interactions
were holy encounters because God was with them and
in them, and God's light shone through them.

Even in the most arduous and painful conversations, my
Sacred Companion was present. As I reflect on them, I behold
the Light of the World that illumined and surrounded me.
I have learned from both the joy and pain of being human.
I have grown in my understanding that all are
my brothers and sisters in Christ Jesus.
I know that this deepening understanding and desire
to do God's will is pleasing to the Creator.

As I reflect on my day, and ponder its meaning, I judge nothing
that occurred. I allow it to be just what it was. My only goal
is to recollect with love the events of the day. These loving
remembrances will bring me peace as bedtime draws near.

I recall the times I received the most love today.
I remember the people who loved me and how that
loving felt. That sense of being loved will linger with
me through the night. The love I received from others
today is but a dim shadow of God's love for me.

I am God's beloved child. God's love for me is wider
and deeper than I am able to comprehend. As I
rest, I will be cradled in God's loving arms.
The love of Jesus will bring healing to the hurts
of today and those of days long past.
The light of the Spirit will strengthen me and fill me
with hope as I prepare to enter the new day.

I am aware of the quiet joy and deep sense of peace that
Jesus, our Companioning Presence, has brought me today.
I have been enabled to be kind, patient, gentle,
generous, and loving beyond my own capabilities.
I am thankful, dear Jesus, that I was able to be an
instrument of your love and a catalyst of your peace.

A few years ago I read a wonderful little book entitled *Letters to
an Unborn Child*, written by David Ireland who, as he writes, is
dying from a crippling neurological disease. David writes these
letters to the unborn child still in the womb of his wife — a
child he may never see. He will be unable to take his child to
either ball games or ballet lessons. There will be no romps in
the park, no stories read on daddy's knee. Still, he wants that
child to know that dead or alive, "Daddy loves his little boy or
girl." Here are some of David Ireland's thoughts about his wife.

> Your mother is very special. Few men know what it's like
> to receive appreciation for taking their wives out to dinner
> when it entails what it does for us. It means that she has to
> dress me, shave me, brush my teeth, comb my hair; wheel
> me out of the house and down the steps, open the garage
> and put me in the car, take the pedals off the chair, stand
> me up, sit me in the seat of the car, twist me around so

that I'm comfortable, fold the wheelchair, put it in the car, go around to the other side of the car, start it up, back it out, get out of the car, pull the garage door down, get back into the car, and drive off to the restaurant. And then, it starts all over again: she gets out of the car, unfolds the wheelchair, opens the door, spins me around, stands me up, seats me in the wheelchair, pushes the pedals out, closes and locks the car, wheels me into the restaurant, then takes the pedals off the wheelchair so I won't be uncomfortable. We sit down to have dinner, and she feeds me throughout the entire meal. And when it's over she pays the bill, pushes the wheelchair out to the car again, and reverses the same routine. And when it's over — finished with real warmth she'll say, "Honey, thank you for taking me out to dinner." I never quite know what to answer.

This is an awesome story. It is a wonderful illustration of how the different aspects of fruit of the Spirit all work together. The woman in the story demonstrates all nine aspects of the fruit: love, joy, peace, patience, kindness, goodness, faithfulness, gentleness, and self-control. Wouldn't it be nice to be like her?

The answer is 'No." She undoubtedly is a wonderful person. I would surely like to have her as a friend. _NEVERTHELESS_, the way she demonstrates love to her husband may not be the same way you would. Nor should it be.

What I wish for you is that you begin to uncover how love, joy, peace, patience, kindness, goodness, faithfulness, gentleness, and self-control are made manifest in your life.

God's purpose for your life and mine is to make us more like Christ. The Holy Spirit is God's presence within you. The Spirit gives you the ability to become more like Jesus Christ and more like yourself. And what is Jesus Christ like?

On earth, his life embodied the nine fold fruit of the Spirit that Paul tells us about: Love, joy, peace, patience, kindness, goodness, faithfulness, gentleness, and self-control.
Luther said growth is always from the inside out. Aristotle maintained that if you do the good you become the good. Luther, and St. Paul before him, argued that before a person can change outwardly there needs to be a change from within. Only God can create that change. The fruit ripens from the inside out. Pastor and author Stuart Briscoe tells the story of a friend who often used an old fruit tree to escape from his second-story bedroom window, especially when his father was about to punish him.
One day the father announced that he was going to cut down the old tree because it had not borne fruit in many years. That night the boy and his friends purchased a bushel of apples and in the cover of darkness tied fruit to the unproductive branches. The next morning the father shouted to his wife, "Mary, I can't believe my eyes. The old fruit tree that was barren for ten years is covered with apples. It's a miracle, a miracle indeed, because it's a pear tree!"
We can no more make a dead tree grow fruit than we cultivate the fruit of the Spirit ourselves. The Spirit grows the fruit in us. When the nine traits of fruit of the Spirit all come together, it is a beautiful thing to behold.

1

DEVOTIONS ON THE THEME OF LOVE

Only love can teach love.

Love turns the one loved into one who loves.

The world changes when we treat it with love. We gentle it.

a. "Teacher, which commandment in the law is the greatest?" Jesus said to him, "You shall love the Lord your God, with all your heart, and with all your soul and with all your mind. This is the greatest and first commandment. And a second is like it, 'You shall love your neighbor as yourself.' On these two commandments hang all the law and the prophets." (Matthew 22:36-40)

God wants to shower the world with love. We hear the word 'love' and we think of Valentine's Day. That is not the kind of love that God desires. Love is hard work. It is more than good warm feelings. Love is what we do—how

we behave, not just what we feel. God calls us to love even
when we do not want to love. The test of our love is:
Can we act in love even when we feel contempt?
Can we act in love when we feel disdain?
Can we act in love when we feel rejected?
Can we act in love when we feel scorned?

b. This is my commandment–that you love one
another as I have loved you. No one has greater love
than this, to lay down one's life for one's friends.
(John 15:12-13)

This is a pretty stern instruction. Jesus commands us
to lay down our lives for our friends. It sounds as if
that means be ready at anytime, and all the time.
I have a close friend, whom I've known since college, who is
unambiguous on giving up his life for me. He would never do.
And, he says, he would never ask me to do it for him. This
has been his position for decades. He has given this a lot of
thought. "We're each given life as a gift," he explains. "It's
the most precious gift imaginable. It's our job to be the best
possible stewards of that gift – in terms of maintaining our
health and finding as much joy and fulfillment as possible."
Martin Luther King, Jr. took a very different
approach: "If a man hasn't discovered something
he would die for, he isn't fit to live."
I operate on the assumption that I would be willing to give
up my own life, in a heartbeat, for either my wife or our
two children. My love for them is powerful, unconditional,
and much like animal instinct. Knowing that makes my
life much more valuable in the time that I am alive.
When eight-year old Joey's little sister, Susan, underwent a
necessary operation, it turned out she had lost so much blood
that she needed an immediate transfusion. Susan had a very
rare blood type, but her brother Joey's blood type was the

same as his little sister's. "Will you give your sister some of your blood?" asked the doctor. Joey paused for a long time, then consented. The boy tried to be brave as the blood was being drawn from his veins, but the doctor noticed that he was growing paler and paler. When the draw was complete, Joey looked up at the doctor and timidly asked, "I was just wondering how long it will be before I die?" The doctor looked down at Joey and said, "Do you think people die when they give blood?" "Well, yes sir," serenely replied Joey. "And you were willing to die for your sister?' ' "Yes sir," he said quietly. I would like Joey to be my brother. I would like to be his brother.

c. Little children, I am with you only a little longer. You will look for me; and as I said to the Jews so now I say to you, "Where I am going, you cannot come." I give you a new commandment, that you love one another. Just as I have loved you, you also should love one another. By this everyone will know that you are my disciples, if you have love for one another.' (John 13:33-35)

Jesus' message is quite clear. The purpose of our life and the destination of our spiritual journey is the ability to love as Jesus loved. Jesus demonstrates love in every encounter and on every page of the Gospels. He loves the lovable, the unlovable, the wealthy, the poor, the healthy and the sick, you and me. No one was omitted from the love of Jesus: not the tax collector or the prostitute, not the demon-possessed or the Roman soldier, not even those who nailed him to that rough hewn cross. This kind of loving-kindness can only emerge from a deep and abiding faith in God. The Spirit birthed love out of Jesus. It is a love that does not seek an incentive to love, only someone to love. Love is merely what faith in action looks like. It is the natural outcome of being in communion with God. Love is born in us and out of us by a God who is personally involved in our spiritual health and wellbeing. To be a Christian is to make God's love apparent in our lives.

d. Above all, clothe yourselves with love, which binds everything together in perfect harmony.
(Colossians 3:14)

And we are put on earth a little space
That we might learn to bear the beams of love.
William Blake

I think Blake is right. We are here to bear and be "beams of love." We receive love and we bestow love. One of my greatest sorrows is to come across people who have not been loved. They pay for it in sadness, grief, and anger. Like infants who are not cradled in parental arms, they fail to thrive.

Personally, I have received more love than I deserve or could have earned. I cannot take credit for any of it. It is all gift. It is all grace. Moreover, when I awaken in the night I can feel a numinous presence in and around me. That presence is God. That presence is also the residual love people have shown me throughout my life.

The church sometimes attracts people who have never been loved. The church is the vehicle God has chosen to be God's loving presence in the world. Let us "learn to bear the beams of love."

e. The Lord appeared to me from afar,
"I have loved you with an everlasting love;
Therefore I have continued my faithfulness to you."
(Jeremiah 31:3)

O, how we long to hear those words, "I have loved you with an everlasting love." Like seeds sown in our hearts, these words produce the fruit of peace and joy.

One of the deepest longings in the human heart is to be loved for yourself alone. When we are touched by love, it reaches down into the deepest fiber of our being. It is difficult to overstate how much we really need love. Conversely, it is difficult to overstate how much the lack of love can harm a vulnerable heart.

After the Second World War, orphans were scattered all over Germany. One group of infants was sent to a convent. The sheer number of infants and babies overwhelmed the nuns there. To cope with the problem of feeding the infants they devised a system whereby the babies could eat while they were still in their cribs. It was not possible to hold each of them. Consequently, the babies seldom received a loving human touch from anyone.

The nuns, of course grew very close to the children. When they matured, the children left the convent. The nuns kept track of them. Many of them ended up in jail. Others could not keep a job or sustain a relationship. Nothing could make up for the lack of human touch they did not receive in infancy. Whom do you know that needs a loving touch? Give it. That simple act of love might change someone's life.

Lord, love us with an everlasting love. Lord, empower us to love each other with the love we have received from you.

f. I am my beloved's and my beloved is mine.
(Song of Solomon 6:3a)

The yearning to be loved is an eternal longing. It arises from a deep center that only love can touch. Love sustains us even in the bleakest times of our lives. Under the gaze and in the embrace of love, crippled hearts are transformed into long distance runners. When you are loved, you leap and run like a young colt who just found the joy of unfettered motion.

Being loved is like being found after having been lost. Love awakens us from sleep and transports us into a consciousness of self-love and loving-kindness. Love is transformative. *Love turns the one loved into one who loves.* God is love. God is the source of all love and God is our lover. When we love others, they feel God's love. When we are loved, the world looks different. When we are loved, we become the lovers we were created to be. Be lovers and watch the world change.

g. In the fourth century, Christians left the city for the desert to live the ascetical life of the hermit. These men and women are called the desert mothers and fathers and were the forerunners of the monastic movement. Many sayings and stories sprang up about their holiness that are still relevant today. The following is one such saying.

> God is a fire that warms and kindles
> the heart and inward parts.
> Hence, if we feel in our hearts the
> cold that comes from the
> devil - for the devil is cold - let us call on the Lord. He will
> come to warm our hearts with perfect
> love, not only for Him
> but also for our neighbor, and the
> cold of him who hates the
> good will flee before the heat of His countenance.

The world changes when we treat it with love. We gentle it. We bind up its wounds. Christians are not the judges of the world; we are its healers. Loving-kindness is a Godly act that transforms a sinner into a saint, a sin into a blessing, and an enemy into a friend.

h. There's a sweet saying that has been plucked from the chamber of that most prolific and famous author, anonymous, and has found its way into popular culture and right into my heart: Just when the caterpillar thought, "the world was over..." it became a butterfly.

It is not easy to change from a caterpillar into a butterfly.
It is exhausting work.
But the struggle is worth the effort.

I love the image this conjures up.
Transformation in nature or conversion of one's body and soul takes place after periods of hard work, pain, and discomfort. When healing does take place, it is, indeed, a metamorphosis.

Butterflies are amazingly beautiful creatures.
They take our breath away.
How many of us have found ourselves sitting outside in a warm sunlit spot catching a glimpse of a butterfly?

On a rare and joyful occasion, such a creature, for reasons unknown, may decide to settle somewhere on our body, tickling our knee or perching on our arm. When that happens, we stop breathing for a second. We do not move lest we lose this precious moment of connection. Too sacred to really understand, we gaze in wonder and awe at the loveliness of it all.

So we look for butterflies. Wherever they may be.

It takes a special gift to see butterflies
when the world is a lousy place.

Poverty has eyes that look back at us.
Squalor has feet that walk toward us.
Fear has arms that reach out to us.
Love has a heart that cannot remain idle in
the face of poverty, squalor, and fear.

In 2010 I visited this wonderful family. They live in El
Salvador and are members of our sister congregation there.
Their poverty breaks your heart.
Their living conditions are Spartan to say the least.
One room includes kitchen, dining and living room,
cordoned off by a blanket to hide the bedroom.

All their money goes to the essentials:
food, clothing, housing, etc.

Yet, when I left the two little girls gave
me a cherished stuffed animal.

My first reaction was to refuse the gift. How could
I? It gave them so much pleasure to give it.

These little butterflies were like an oasis
living in a desert of poverty.
There are butterflies all around us; we
just have to look for them.
It can be hard to do when everything appears dark and
menacing. However, that is when we need butterflies
the most. Seeing butterflies when your world is
crashing down around you is no easy task. Yet, in
the looking, in the trying, we are revealing the early
stages of hope and providing a hint of reassurance
that indeed there are butterflies out there.

As our spiritual growth progresses, seeing
butterflies becomes easier.

Maybe, just maybe we can be butterflies to others.
They certainly are needed. However,
we cannot do it on our own.

The ability to live the fruit of the Spirit comes
from acquiring a new set of eyes.

They are the eyes of the Holy Spirit.
These eyes are the fruit of a prayerful life.

They are divine eyes—holy eyes—sacred eyes.

These eyes have the ability to see joy
even when it is not obvious.

They do not come naturally.
We cannot wish for them.
We cannot obtain them by an act of the will.
We have to pray for these new eyes.
We have to ask the Lord to give us the
ability to see and be butterflies.

We get on our knees in humility and pray
to see the joy that surrounds us all.

We pray for the eyes of these two cherished children.
Pray that God will give you the ability to
see the world as God sees it.
I wish for you eyes to see the sacred in the world.
I wish you love, joy, peace, patience, kindness,
goodness, faithfulness, gentleness, and self-control.
The world needs it.
The world needs you.

2

DEVOTIONS ON THE THEME OF JOY

God runs to you with an eternal embrace and the kiss of intimacy.

Sadness, sorrow, and grief descend like a shroud,
but joy bubbles up from within.
Joy is always within. We merely access it.

a. As a mother comforts her child, so will
I comfort you. (Isaiah 66:13)

When I was six years old and living in New York City, a
car ran over my little puppy. It was Christmas time, and the
puppy was a present. Now he was gone. My Mom found
the dog. She dug a hole in the backyard, and wrapped the
dog in a blanket. She came to my room where I was playing,
and swooped me into her arms. She cradled me and rocked
me ever so tenderly. "Tommy, I have some very bad news
to tell you. Rex has died." I was crushed. I sobbed and

sobbed. Mom just sang to me and rocked me. We then
went into the backyard where we buried my little puppy.

Mom did not take away my pain, but she lessened it.
Mom did not sugarcoat the truth but she made it bearable.
Mom did not hide the death. She made me look at it.
Mom did not tell me to be a man. She cried with me.

That is what God did for the Israelites. That is what God does
for us. Out of the ash of sorrow rises the Phoenix of joy.

b. Let the Heavens be glad, and let the earth rejoice,
and let them say among the nations, 'The Lord is king!'
Let the sea roar, and all that fills it;
let the field exult, and everything in it.
Then shall the trees of the forest sing for joy
before the Lord, for he comes to judge the earth.
O give thanks to the Lord, for he is good;
for his steadfast love endures for ever. (1 Chronicles 16)

To be perfectly honest, 1 & 2 Chronicles are pretty boring
historical accounts of the kings of Israel and Judah.
Every once in a while, however, we find soaring psalms
like this text. "Then shall the trees of the forest sing for
joy." Have you ever heard a forest sing? You might think
me a little goofy, but I have. I have a cabin in the Virginia
Mountains. Occasionally, I will sit on the deck and listen.
Wind rustles through the leaves.
An old tree creaks as it sways to and fro.
A leaning tree is cradled by an evergreen and sings,
"Thanks," as they rub against each other.
Birds unabashedly sing for joy in the world's oldest love song.
Squirrels jump from branch to branch and from
tree to tree in a dance of exuberance.

Joy is all around us. If we can be still for a
few moments, the gladness of the earth will
surround us and instill that joy within us.

c. Our home is not so much a physical place
as it is where we love and receive love.

One of the greatest challenges in the Spiritual life is
to receive God's forgiveness. Something in us keeps us
clinging to our sins, and prevents us from letting God
erase our past and offer us a completely fresh beginning.

Forgiveness brings joy in Heaven. God delights in
restoring each of us to the full dignity of "Sonship" and
"daughterhood." Receiving forgiveness demands that we
allow God to be God: to heal, restore, and renew. As long
as we are unable to acknowledge total absolution, we remain
but hired hands. God calls us to be sons and daughters
with all the rights and privileges of that birthright.

God runs to you with an eternal embrace and the kiss of
intimacy. You are God's beloved child. Say it aloud until it
sinks in, "I am God's beloved child. I am God's beloved
child. I am God's beloved child." Amen. It shall be so.

d. The Parable of the Lost Sheep
Now all the tax collectors and sinners were coming
near to listen to him. And the Pharisees and the scribes
were grumbling and saying, "This fellow welcomes
sinners and eats with them.

So he told them this parable: 'Which one of you, having
a hundred sheep and losing one of them, does not leave
the ninety-nine in the wilderness and go after the one

that is lost until he finds it? When he has found it, he lays it on his shoulders and rejoices. And when he comes home, he calls together his friends and neighbors, saying to them, "Rejoice with me, for I have found my sheep that was lost." Just so, I tell you, there will be more joy in Heaven over one sinner who repents than over ninety-nine righteous people who need no repentance.

The Parable of the Lost Coin

'Or what woman having ten silver coins, if she loses one of them, does not light a lamp, sweep the house, and search carefully until she finds it? When she has found it, she calls together her friends and neighbors, saying, "Rejoice with me, for I have found the coin that I had lost." Just so, I tell you, there is joy in the presence of the angels of God over one sinner who repents.'
(Luke 15:1-10)

Every once in a while, I will come across a little lost kid. Sometimes, he is in a store. Sometimes, she is in a public place like a park. Not long ago I was skiing in a little resort in Virginia, when over the loudspeaker I heard, "Will the parents of Josh White please report to the ski school?" Sunday mornings at church have even produced a few lost children. Many times a little one will come and say to me, "I can't find my Mom." There is relief on the part of both when they are united.

Occasionally, a parent will come in and say, "My child is having drug problems. He has lost his way, and I don't know what to do."

At one time or another, most of us have lost our way. We become despondent or disconsolate. Sometimes we are crippled by guilt. Shakespeare wrote, "When sorrows come, they come not as single spies, but in battalions." Sometimes we are overcome. We cannot find the joy of life, and we do not know where to look. That is when we need to be found. The truth is; we cannot find ourselves without help. We may need the help of a friend or family member. We may need the help of a health care professional. Maybe we just need to confess our lostness. This is when God finds us. God holds the key to our happiness. God can unlock our shackles. God can open the door that leads to joy. When we "find" ourselves, there is great joy in Heaven.

e. "Quickly, bring out a robe—the best one—and put it on him; put a ring on his finger and sandals on his feet. And get the fatted calf and kill it, and let us eat and celebrate; for this son of mine was dead and is alive again; he was lost and is found!" And they began to celebrate. (Luke 15)

The story of the prodigal reminds us that love existed before the son rejected his father and existed even after the rejection had taken place. The author of First John, asserts, "God first loved us." (1 John 4:19) Prior to that statement, John boldly proclaims, "God is love." (1 John 4:8b)

The reward of coming home is joy: joy for the son and joy for the father. There is always joy in reunion, forgiveness, and reconciliation. There is joy because, "My son was lost and now is found." There is joy because, "I was lost and now am found." There is joy for both the one who finds and the one who was lost.

Joy is the mark of the Christian. In the parable, the father gives himself over to that joy and prepares a feast. Jesus repeatedly used the image of a banquet for the Kingdom of

God. Celebration belongs to God's Kingdom. Being found by God is festive. We feast on God and his love. But joy is a choice. It requires choosing light even when there is darkness. It demands choosing life even when we death surrounds us. It calls us to trust God even when circumstances indicate that it is counterintuitive. The reward for choosing joy is joy itself. To be home with God enriches our lives with celebratory joy.

f. A sorrow shared is half a sorrow; a joy shared is twice a joy. *(Unknown)* Happiness shared by one is half a happiness. A happiness shared by two is twice a happiness, whereas a sorrow shared by one is twice a sorrow and shared by two just half a sorrow. *(unattributed)*

A sorrow shared is but half a trouble, but a joy that's shared is a joy made double. *(Old Proverb)*

A sorrow shared is half the sorrow. A joy shared is twice the joy. *(Swedish proverb)*

The Dutch say, "A sorrow shared is a sorrow halved."

Shakespeare wrote, "a sorrow shared is a sorrow halved; a joy shared is a joy doubled."

There is joy in friendship. Christianity is about relationships: with God and with each other. We find joy in each other's joy and we support each other in sorrow. Jesus prays, "May they have my joy made complete in themselves." The deepest joy is the joy that comes from God. Only God is eternal and only eternal joy can come from God. We can give joy to each other, but it is always fleeting. We may be able to halve each other's sorrows, and double each other's joys, but the incalculable joy that comes from God survives the greatest sorrow. As we deepen our friendship with God, God deepens our joy.

3

DEVOTIONS ON THE THEME OF
PEACE

It is better to suffer violence than it is to cause it.

a. Grace to you and peace from God our Father
and the Lord Jesus Christ. (Philippians 1:20)

And the peace of God, which passes all
understanding, will keep your hearts and your
minds in Christ Jesus._(Philippians 4:7)

In the summer of 1968, my then fiancée, Faye, and I worked
at Green Lake Bible Camp in south central Minnesota. I
was a camp counselor and Faye was the camp cook. Green
Lake is an extraordinarily beautiful place, the camp has great
facilities, I enjoyed the kids, and loved the chapel, which
is a replica of a 12th century Norwegian Stave Church.

One August day we had a tornado warning. Such warnings were common. Minnesota can have some wild summer storms. The kids, however, were frightened. They had heard stories about the damage and death that such massive winds can bring. I decided to gather all the kids in a safe place where I could calm them down. The safest structure was the chapel. We hunkered down in the safest place in the chapel. It was a sanctuary of solace. I told the kids they were in the arms of God. We sang, we joked, kids held each other, and we prayed. A peace covered the kids like a warm blanket. It was blowing like crazy outside, but there was calm inside. It was a peace that defied logic. In fact, it was "a peace, which passes understanding."

If you have lived for any length of time, you have encountered a few storms in your life. Some have been weather storms like we encountered at camp. Some have been emotional storms. Like the kids in the storm, you can find peace in a sanctuary, in the arms of our Lord. Prayer connects you with your Inner Spirit of God. Your calm spiritual center may be compared to the peaceful eye at the center of a hurricane. Connecting daily with your Inner Spirit helps you to remain in that peaceful space throughout the day, thus anchoring you from being blown about by the winds of change and adversity.

b. Peace I leave with you; my peace I give to you. I do not give to you as the world gives. Do not let your hearts be troubled, and do not let them be afraid. (John 14:27)

> I've been through 2 hurricanes during my submarine days, and you'd be surprised at how deep the wave action can affect you. Of course, modern submarines can simply go to deep depths to avoid it. It's also standard policy for all ships and submarines to emergency sortie [get underway]

when a hurricane is imminent, as Navy vessels can
ride out the storm effectively at sea, whereas in port
the damage potential is extremely high. *(unknown)*

So it is with us. Storms can rage and roll around us, but deep in that center where God lives is a peace that can only come from God. The world does not bring peace. In fact, it often, brings trouble. Jesus comforted the disciples with these words, "Peace I leave with you; my peace I give to you. I do not give to you as the world gives. Do not let your hearts be troubled, and do not let them be afraid."

The God who created us can create a deep
peace that can help us weather any storm.

c. Salt is good; but if salt has lost its saltiness, how
can you season it? Have salt in yourselves, and
be at peace with one another.' (Mark 9:50)

Being at peace does not mean that there is not conflict or difficulty in relationships. "Wherever two or three are gathered" there is a difference of opinion. When I was a young pastor, conflict was an opportunity to compete. I wanted to demonstrate that my opinion was better than anyone else's was, and that I was the smartest one in the room. I was not interested in discovering truth or the best solution. I was interested in winning. Instead of being at peace with others, I generated discord. A pastor friend very clearly told me that I was being a jerk. He said that even if I win the struggle, I created so much disharmony that it negated anything good that might come from winning, even if my solution was the best solution. Because I am a slow learner, it took years before I was able to fully comprehend what he was telling me. I had lost my "saltiness." He taught me how to pray and meditate. He reminded me that God wants peace between people and that I was getting in God's way. I needed to give God the space, time, and opportunity to create peace within me. I pray that we all can become instruments of God's peace.

d. Do not let your hearts be troubled. Believe in God, believe also in me. In my Father's house, there are many dwelling-places. If it were not so, would I have told you that I go to prepare a place for you? And if I go and prepare a place for you, I will come again and will take you to myself, so that where I am, there you may be also. (John 14:1-4)

The secret of the soul is its deep longing for the divine. The longing is passionate and constant. We were created out of God and we long to be in God. In many ways, we are exiles in search of home. Our longing for God is an echo of God's longing for us. Only an abiding bond with God can quench this eternal and insatiable thirst. When we are in God, we have the sense of being at home.
Home is where we find a sense of belonging.
Home is where we are accepted for who we are.
Home is where our hearts find rest and our souls find peace.
Home is where we are called to be.
Home has been prepared for us.
Home is waiting for us. The bed is made and the room is ready.

e. As he came near and saw the city, he wept over it, saying, 'If you, even you, had only recognized on this day the things that make for peace! But now they are hidden from your eyes. (Luke 19:41-42

Carry no purse, no bag, no sandals; and salute no one on the road.
Whatever house you enter, first say, 'Peace be to this house!'
And if a *son of peace* is there, your peace shall rest upon him; but if not, it shall return to you. (Luke 10:6-4)

"Son of Peace". What a nice phrase. Jesus longs for us to be *Sons of Peace*. Those who are not *sons of peace* also desire peace. They speak of it, they rejoice in it whenever they can find it. They strive for it in many ways. We see this every day when we read of the efforts of national and world leaders to restore or keep peace in lands around the world. We see it when we read of those great national or world leaders who are accounted as worthy to receive the Nobel Peace Prize. This is not the peace of Jesus, however; it is *world peace* in one of its many varieties. It is a peace that is achieved only by struggling, striving, engaging in fierce negotiations, or by going to war. The peace of the world comes at a high price, it is preserved at a high price, and it is always uncertain and insecure. It is in diametric opposition to the peace of Jesus. The peace of Jesus is a simple gift; the peace of this world is won at great cost, great suffering, and bloodshed. The peace of Jesus was also won at great personal cost and suffering. The peace of Jesus is certain and secure, whereas world peace has no certainty from day to day.

Sons of Peace salt every age. There are always a few of them scattered about. Jesus and his disciples, of course, but other disciples after them have demonstrated that they are *Sons of Peace*. They are those who have suffered great tribulation for the cause of Jesus and his peace, even to the point of losing their lives. In the early years of the church, men and women such as Ignatius of Antioch, Perpetua, and Bishop Polycarp of Smyrna, shine out in history as cardinal examples of *Sons of Peace*.

1. After the arrest of Ignatius and while he was being transported to Rome, he found ways to strengthen and encourage the *Sons of Peace* in all the cities through which he travelled. He wrote ahead to the Church at Rome exhorting them not to work for his deliverance:

Now I begin to be a disciple. I care for nothing,
of visible or invisible things, so that I may but win
Christ. Let fire and the cross, let the companies
of wild beasts, let breaking of bones and tearing
of limbs, let the grinding of the whole body,
and all the malice of the devil, come upon
me; be it so, only may I win Christ Jesus!

Arriving in Rome and having been sentenced to die
by wild beasts, he heard them roaring and said,

I am the wheat of Christ. I am going to be ground with
the teeth of wild beasts that I may be found pure bread.

2. Perpetua was a Roman mother of a newborn infant, who
lived in Carthage, the provincial capital of North Africa.
The Romans arrested her when she was 21 or 22 years old.
In 202, Emperor Septimus Severus had issued an
edict forbidding conversion to either Judaism or
Christianity. The proconsul of Carthage applied the
decree with enthusiasm. Along with others, Perpetua
was arrested, convicted of civil disobedience, and
condemned to "fight with the beasts of the arena."

3. The aged Polycarp, urged by the Roman
proconsul to deny Christ saying, "Swear and
I will release you," Polycarp replied,

Eighty and six years have I served him, and
he never once wronged me; how then shall I
blaspheme my King, who hath saved me?

He was not nailed to the stake as usual, only tied when he
assured them that he would stand immovable in the flames.

4. Martin Luther King preached this sermon just a couple months before his assassination. He was a *Son of Peace* of extraordinaire.

> Yes, if you want to say that I was a drum major, say that I was a drum major for justice; say that I was a drum major for peace; I was a drum major for righteousness. And all of the other shallow things will not matter. I won't have any money to leave behind. I won't have the fine and luxurious things of life to leave behind. But I just want to leave a committed life behind.

Lord, make us *Sons and Daughters of Peace.* Amen

f. As God's chosen ones, holy and beloved, clothe yourselves with compassion, kindness, humility, meekness, and patience. Bear with one another and, if anyone has a complaint against another, forgive each other; just as the Lord has forgiven you, so you also must forgive. Above all, clothe yourselves with love, which binds everything together in perfect harmony. And let the *peace of Christ rule in your hearts,* to which indeed you were called in the one body. And be thankful. Let the word of Christ dwell in you richly; teach and admonish one another in all wisdom; and with gratitude in your hearts sing psalms, hymns, and spiritual songs to God. And whatever you do, in word or deed, do everything in the name of the Lord Jesus, giving thanks to God the Father through him. (Colossians 3:12-17)

There is a connection between our growth in holiness and our growth as people of peace. We were created as people of peace. Indeed, in the Garden of Eden there was no violence to or among the animals. The creation story in Genesis implies that we were created as vegetarians.

God said, "See, I have given you every plant yielding seed that is upon the face of all the earth, and every tree with seed in its fruit; you shall have them for food. And to every beast of the earth, and to every bird of the air, and to everything that creeps on the earth, everything that has the breath of life, I have given every green plant for food." And it was so. (Genesis 1:29-30)

The goal of the spiritual journey is to become who we truly are. The goal of the spiritual journey is to be transformed into the person God created each of us to be. This is what it means to be holy. The fruit of the spirit: love, joy, _peace_, patience, kindness, goodness, faithfulness, gentleness, and self-control can transform us into that person. However, what that fruit looks like in me may not be what it looks like in you. Each of us is unique. Each of us reveals peace in our own distinct way. What peace looks like in me may not be what it looks like in you. We do not have to imitate how others act. We just need to be who we were created to be. It is good enough.

g. And he answered them, "To you it has been given to know the secrets of the _kingdom of Heaven,_ but to them it has not been given. (Matthew 13:11)

Another parable he put before them, saying, "_The kingdom of Heaven may be compared_ to a man who sowed good seed in his field; (Matthew 13:24)

Another parable he put before them, saying, "_The kingdom of Heaven is like_ a grain of mustard seed which a man took and sowed in his field; (Matthew 13:31)

He told them another parable. "_The kingdom of Heaven is like_ leaven which a woman took and hid in three measures of flour, till it was all leavened." (Matthew 13:33)

"*The kingdom of Heaven is like* treasure hidden in a field, which a man found and covered up; then in his joy he goes and sells all that he has and buys that field. (Matthew 13:44)

"Again, *the kingdom of Heaven is like* a merchant in search of fine pearls, (Matthew 13:45)

"Again, *the kingdom of Heaven is like* a net which was thrown into the sea and gathered fish of every kind; (Matthew 13:47)

And he said to them, "Therefore every scribe who has been trained for *the kingdom of Heaven is like* a householder who brings out of his treasure what is new and what is old." (Matthew 13:52)

In both parable and discourse, Jesus repeatedly described the Kingdom of God. He encouraged his hearers to advance the work of the Kingdom and to participate in its effectiveness. He knew well that the way of the Kingdom stood in direct defiance of an antagonistic world.

Repeatedly, Jesus described the way of the Kingdom. "The Kingdom of God" or "The Kingdom of Heaven" is like a mustard seed, or the Kingdom of God is like yeast, or the Kingdom of God is like a treasure hidden in a field, or a pearl of great price, or like a great banquet, or like the "good" Samaritan, and on and on. He was not speaking about some future event; he was inviting people to walk the Kingdom's path and to participate in the Kingdom now. Jesus did not teach about himself nearly as much as he taught about the Kingdom of God. In the crucifixion and resurrection, Jesus is the clear archetype of the "way" of the Kingdom. Jesus did not choose to allow the world to kill him as a political strategy or because of some divine retribution, but to demonstrate that *it is better to suffer violence than it is to cause it*. The cross is the way Jesus elected to deal with evil. The resurrection is the way the Father responded to that evil. Prayerful presence to God gives us the ability and courage to live out our calling to walk in God's Kingdom here on this earth.

4

DEVOTIONS ON THE THEME OF PATIENCE

In God's Divine forgetfulness, God chooses to forget your sins.
"I will remember your sins no more."

God's "Sacred Memory" indicates that God has loved us
"with an everlasting love."

a. The late Irish writer and poet, John O'Donohue, asserts, "One of our deepest longings is to be seen." Have you ever watched a Little League baseball game? I still attend a game, occasionally. I love to see kids play ball. After the game many of the kids will ask, "Did you see me, Mommy?" When my golf game goes south, I will ask my wife to look at my swing. I cannot always tell what my swing looks like, even in a mirror. Similarly, there is no mirror for the soul. We can never truly observe ourselves. We need a Spiritual Friend. Such a friend's honesty can bring out the contours of our Spirit. A spiritual friend is the one who can truly see us. She can sow the seeds of love and peace into the good soil of our soul. It is beautiful to have such a friend in your life.

b. The signs of a true apostle were performed among you with utmost patience, signs and wonders and mighty works. (2 Corinthians 12:12)

Love is patient; love is kind; love is not envious or boastful or arrogant or rude. It does not insist on its own way; it is not irritable or resentful; it does not rejoice in wrongdoing, but rejoices in the truth. It bears all things, believes all things, hopes all things, and endures all things. (1 Corinthians 13)
You are capable of the love St. Paul describes, because you are the Sacred Echo of the God who created and formed you. You are the echo of a primal intimacy. Your lives are the echoes of the God who whispered love into your souls. The soul did not invent itself. It comes from the sacred realm. It comes from God and is the reverberation of God. Those capable of the highest love know that love arises from the heart of God, and descends into our own hearts. Our employment is to love and receive love. The greatest joy is to discover the hallowed love that resides within and share it with another.

c. I therefore, the prisoner in the Lord, beg you to lead a life worthy of the calling to which you have been called, with all humility and gentleness, with patience, bearing with one another in love, making every effort to maintain the unity of the Spirit in the bond of peace. There is one body and one Spirit, just as you were called to the one hope of your calling, one Lord, one faith, one baptism, one God and Father of all, who is above all and through all and in all. (Ephesians 4:1-6)

If there is one thing all the great religions have in common, it is the injunction to love each other and have patience with one another. The question we must answer for ourselves is, "Who is the 'other?'" Too often, the "others" are the only ones who love us. In the Sermon on the Mount, Jesus tells us to love even our enemies. In each of us resides a "Holy Remembrance." We remember how our Lord wants us to act. We remember we are forgiven. And we know that God remembers us. We are a Holy Remembrance for the world. We are sent here to learn to love and receive love. In St. Paul's words, "lead a life worthy of the calling to which you have been called, with all humility and gentleness, with patience, bearing with one another in love...."

d. Out of the depths I cry to you, O Lord.
  Lord, hear my voice!
Let your ears be attentive
  To the voice of my supplications!

If you, O Lord, should mark iniquities,
  Lord, who could stand?
But there is forgiveness with you,
  So that you may be revered.

I wait for the Lord, my soul waits,
  And in his word I hope;
My soul waits for the Lord
  More than those who watch for the morning,
  More than those who watch for the morning.

Hope in the Lord!
  For with the Lord there is steadfast love,
  And with him is great power to redeem.
It is he who will redeem Israel
  From all its iniquities.
(Psalm 130)

The writer of this Psalm exclaims. "Out of the depths have I cry to you."

We know that deep place. It is the secret cave of our spirit. We do not often access this place because worry, fear, guilt, and anxiety often reside there. Very seldom, do we give a glimpse of this deep place to another. It can be scary. The Psalmist declares, "In God alone is my soul at rest." If you want your deep places to find peace, quiet, and rest, allow God to walk in and among your worries and guilt. God walks gently, holding your hand as you go.

e. A word not made good by action is like an artist who makes pictures of water on walls, yet cannot quench his thirst with it. St. Isaac of Syria (7th century)

I realized a long time ago that children learn more by what they see than by what they are told. For instance, if a child is told that God loves him/her, but does not experience love at church, there is a disconnect between what is taught and what is experienced. That is true in a larger sense as well. If we profess to be disciples of Jesus but do not demonstrate Christ's love, what is the world to think about Christianity? Only love can teach love. God is patient with us. God will wait for us to grow. But growth can be as slow as the hour hand on a clock. If we stare at the hour hand, it does not move. Yet, if we wait for while and then look back at it, we notice that it is in a different place. It is similar with our growth in the Spirit. We may not perceive our progress, yet when we look back, we notice that we are in a different place. Be patient with yourself. Be gentle with yourself. Place yourself in God's hands. Through prayer and meditation, God will help you grow into the person you were called to be. Then your actions will match what you profess.

f. "I, even I, am the one who wipes out your transgressions for My own sake; and I will not remember your sins" (Isaiah 43:25; Heb. 8:12; 10:17).

God is forgetful. It is not a character flaw. It is not because God is senile. It is not because God forgets to do things. It is a **Divine forgetfulness**. It is born of God's patience. God chooses to forget your sins. *"I will remember your sins no more."* These are soothing words to our hearts. God forgives and forgets. We may forgive someone but forgetting is a challenge. In Holy forgetfulness, God remembers your sin no more. That means it is out of God's head. The Lord has no recollection of it. Your sin vanishes like a spring snow. You can live as a forgiven person because you are.

"Forget the former things; do not dwell on the past.
See, I am doing a new thing! Now it springs up; do
you not perceive it? I am making a way in the desert
and streams in the wasteland." (Isaiah 43:18-19)

"I, even I, am he who blots out your transgressions,
for my own sake, and remembers your
sins no more. (Isaiah 43:25)

g. While God's Divine Forgetfulness "remembers our sin no more," God's "Sacred Memory" indicates that God has loved us "with an everlasting love." God forgets our unfaithfulness but remembers God's own fidelity. God remembers to be slow to anger and quick to forgive. God remembers how you were "knit you together in your mother's womb."(Psalm 139) God remembers that you are a precious and cherished child. God has shown us the Divine Heart. It is full of love for you.

"I have loved you with an everlasting love;
Therefore I have continued my faithfulness to you."
(Jeremiah 31:3)

5

DEVOTIONS ON THE THEME OF
KINDNESS

God loves you more than the one who loves you most.

a. He who withholds kindness from a friend forsakes the fear of the Almighty. (Job 6:14)

I hate to admit it, but sometimes when I have been deeply hurt or rejected, I withhold a kindness purposely. I have the opportunity to be kind to the offender but do not act on it. It may be a small kindness like a smile, or letting him take my parking space. The hurt outweighs the desire to be kind. Later, when I have had time to rethink my position, I feel a little ashamed and petty. I also may feel a little embarrassed. I know what I should have done. I know how I should have acted. Now it is too late.

I also think that God may be a little disappointed in me. The book of Job says that to withhold a kindness forsakes God.

Pretty strong words, they are. As we grow in our relationship with God, so we mature in the faith and our ability to be kind.

> **b.** 'If you love those who love you,
> what credit is that to you? For
> even sinners love those who love them.
> If you do good to those who
> do good to you, what credit is that to
> you? For even sinners do the
> same. If you lend to those from whom
> you hope to receive, what
> credit is that to you? Even sinners
> lend to sinners, to receive as
> much again. But love your enemies,
> do good, and lend, expecting
> nothing in return. Your reward will be
> great, and you will be children
> of the Most High; for he is kind to the
> ungrateful and the wicked. Be merciful, just as
> your Father is merciful. (Luke 6:32-36)

Jesus certainly expects a lot. He tells us that God is "kind to the ungrateful and the wicked." Jesus then goes on to say, "Be merciful as your Father is merciful." I think if we are honest with ourselves, we both like this thought and hate it. We like the idea of a merciful God, but are not certain about how merciful we should be. When I was a kid, I watched Roy Rogers and other westerns on Saturday mornings. I loved it when Roy would jump off his horse, Trigger, and put a whipping on the outlaw. As far as I was concerned, there was no time for mercy.

Roy has been dead many years but the "good guys" still chase the "bad guys." We still root for good to

overcome evil. The question with which we all have
to grapple is, "What is the Father's way to overcome
evil?" How are kindness and mercy visible in your life?
How do you live it? The only way I know how to come
up with answers is through prayer. We simply ask,
"Lord what would you have me do in this situation?
How can I be an instrument of your love?"

c. Simon Peter, a servant and apostle of Jesus Christ,
To those who through the righteousness of our God and Savior
Jesus Christ have received a faith as precious as ours:
Grace and peace be yours in abundance through the knowledge
of God and of Jesus our Lord.
His divine power has given us everything we need for life and
godliness through our knowledge of him who called us by his
own glory and goodness. Through
these he has given us his very
great and precious promises, so that through them you may
participate in the divine nature and escape the corruption in
the world caused by evil desires.
For this very reason, make every effort to add to your faith
goodness; and to goodness, knowledge; and to knowledge,
self-control; and to self-control, perseverance; and to
perseverance, godliness; and to godliness, brotherly kindness;
and to brotherly kindness, love. For if you possess these
qualities in increasing measure, they will keep you from being
ineffective and unproductive in your
knowledge of our Lord Jesus Christ.
(2 Peter 1:1-8)

The letters of St. Peter are not read very often. They
do not have the sheer mass of, say the book of Romans
or the two letters to the Corinthians. What they lack in
size they make up for in depth. In essence, the author

of 2 Peter is saying; the more we know Jesus the more we understand kindness etc. The more we understand kindness, etc., the more we understand Jesus.

I do not know many Christians who feel they are kind enough, and I do not know many Christians who feel they know Jesus well enough.

What I do know is that Jesus knows you intimately and wants to be part of your life.

d. But the Father said to his servants, "Quick! Bring out the best robe and put it on him; put a ring on his finger and sandals on his feet. Bring the calf we have been fattening, and kill it; we celebrate by having a feast, because this son of mine was dead and has come back to life. He was lost and is found." And they began to celebrate. (Luke 15:22-24)

In these verses, from the parable of the Prodigal Son, we see the heart of the father and the heart of God the Father. God chooses to want us. In a way, God chooses to need us. As we are incomplete away from God, God is not satisfied to be separated or distanced from us. That is the reason for the incarnation. That is the reason for the gift of the Spirit at Pentecost. God wants to have an intimate relationship with us. That intimacy brings joy and it is celebrated with a feast. God wants to find us more than we want to be found. God wants to find us more than we want to find God.

God loves you more than the one who loves you most.

God says, "You are worth searching for."

The real question is not, "How will I love God?" but "How am I to let myself be loved by God?" And, finally the question is, "How am I to let myself be known by God?"

> **e.** But we appeal to you, brothers and sisters, to respect those who labor among you, and have charge of you in the Lord and admonish you; esteem them very highly in love because of their work. Be at peace among yourselves. And we urge you, beloved, to admonish the idlers, encourage the faint-hearted, help the weak, be patient with all of them. See that none of you repays evil for evil, but always seek to do good to one another and to all. Rejoice always, pray without ceasing, give thanks in all circumstances; for this is the will of God in Christ Jesus for you. Do not quench the Spirit. Do not despise the words of prophets, but test everything; hold fast to what is good; abstain from every form of evil.
>
> May the God of peace himself sanctify you entirely; and may your spirit and soul and body be kept sound and blameless at the coming of our Lord Jesus Christ. The one who calls you is faithful, and he will do this. (1 Thessalonians 5:12-24)

St. Paul is very clear in his teaching. In every one of his letters, he challenges the readers to be loving, kind, and faithful. To be less than kind can extinguish the flame of the Spirit of God. When Christians live out the call to be loving, kind, and faithful, the glow of the Spirit can light up the world. Let us set the world ablaze with our actions.

6

DEVOTIONS ON THE THEME OF
GOODNESS

Disciples represent more than themselves.
They represent Jesus.

Goodness goes beyond what ethical standards require.
Goodness is a quality that lies deep within us
and allows us to be kind and generous.
It describes a person's soul.

a. Allow me to do a little word study before we proceed into
our devotions around the theme of goodness. In Galatians,
St. Paul used a word that he coined: *agathosyne*. It appears only
four times in the New Testament, each time it is in one of
St. Paul's letters. It has no parallel in ancient Greek outside
Paul's writings. It is Paul's own word, so we should pay special
attention to it. Obviously, he did not think any other word
was sufficient to express his thoughts. It means an upright
spirit and a generous heart. Indeed, the New Revised Standard

Version translates the word as generosity. The other word used in the New Testament for goodness is *chrestotes*. It implies moral goodness. St. Paul invented the word *agathosyne* word because he wanted goodness to imply more than moral or ethical righteousness. To be good for Paul entails more than doing what is ethical or moral. Goodness goes beyond what ethical standards require. Goodness is a quality that lies deep within us and allows us to be kind and generous. It is superior to what is moral or ethical. It describes a person's soul, his essence, or her aura. I suspect you may know what I mean. You may say she is a "good person" meaning that there is some ineffable quality about her that makes you want to be in her presence. St. Paul describes that kind of "goodness" in this text. I think another synonym might be holiness.

b. I am the true vine, and my Father is the vine-grower. He removes every branch in me that bears no fruit. Every branch that bears fruit he prunes to make it bear more fruit. You have already been cleansed by the word that I have spoken to you. Abide in me as I abide in you. Just as the branch cannot bear fruit by itself unless it abides in the vine, neither can you unless you abide in me. I am the vine, you are the branches. Those who abide in me and I in them bear much fruit, because apart from me you can do nothing. (John 15:1-5 & 9)

Martin Luther wrote, "The greatest sorrow is feeling separate from God. The greatest joy is union with God." Instinctively, we know the truth of this statement. Before you were a glint in your father's eye or moved in your mother's womb, God knew you. Before your physical birth, your soul gestated in the Father's heart. Consequently, God knows you. Indeed, God is more intimate to you than you are to yourself. You do not

have to generate this union with God on your own. You do not
have to climb to the highest Heaven to attain it. God comes
to you. God draws near to you. God stoops down to you.

With open hearts, you can receive God, who
approaches you with outstretched arms.
God, who comes to you, will not desert you.
God, who comes to you, will lead you.
God, who comes to you, will cherish you.
God, in whom you abide, will harvest the succulent
fruit of joy and love, and your goodness will
draw others to the vine that is Christ.

O Lord, let me feel your abiding presence
and know you as I am known. Amen.

c. Spirituality is continual watchfulness to God's self-
disclosure through prayer, worship, and study. It is
discovering ways we can love God through service
to humankind. It is a holy life created by God.

Spirituality is transformation. It is growth in holiness. It
is evidenced by an ever-deepening love of God, self, and
neighbor. St. Paul describes it as a transformation of the
mind whereby the mind becomes capable of discerning
God's will (Romans 12:2). He reminds us that spirituality is
the formation of a new heart. "God's love has been poured
into our hearts" (Romans 5:5). He proclaims unflinchingly
that the spiritual person is "new creation" (Galatians 6:15).
He holds out the promise of a new life in which our old ways
die and Christ "is formed" and lives in us (Galatians 2:20 &
4:19). Ultimately, he declares a holy life is one that "lives by
the Spirit" and is "guided by the Spirit" (Galatians 5:25).

d. James and John, the sons of Zebedee, came forward to him (Jesus) and said to him, "Teacher, we want you to do for us whatever we ask of you." And he said to them, "What is it you want me to do for you?" And they said to him, "Grant us to sit, one at your right hand and one at your left, in your glory." But Jesus said to them, "You do not know what you are asking. Are you able to drink the cup that I drink, or to be baptized with the baptism that I am baptized with?" They reply, we are. "When the ten heard this [the request of James and John] they began to be angry with James and John. So Jesus called them and said to them, "You know that among the Gentiles those whom they recognize as their rulers lord it over them, and their great ones are tyrants over them. But it is not so among you; but whoever wishes to become great among you must be your servant, and whoever wishes to be first among you must be slave of all. For the Son of Man came not to be served but to serve, and to give his life as a ransom for many." (Mark 10:35-45)

It is so easy to misunderstand what discipleship means. It is easy to misconstrue what greatness is. James and John were looking for places of honor. They were not prepared for what sitting in those places of honor entailed. In this lesson, Jesus redefines greatness. Greatness is not about power and control. It is about drinking from the cup of Jesus. The cup from which Jesus drank was the cup of suffering love.

In so doing Jesus not only reversed the "pecking order" he abolished it. The authority about which Jesus spoke was not authority to control but an authority of function. His mandate is radical. There is a difference between "choosing to serve" and "choosing to be a slave." A servant still has a choice whether or not to serve. A slave does not.

In choosing to serve, you are still in control. You can say, "No!" You control when you want to serve and how you want to serve. When you become a slave, you give up the right to be in charge. When you finally realize that God has the right to direct your life, you are ready to give away your desire to control and you are ready to become a disciple.

There is great freedom in becoming a slave. You can serve without the need for recognition or even the desire for thanks. The reward for serving is the work itself. Then service is not some duty we "have to perform," but an opportunity to do the Holy Work of a disciple.

e. Three times, I appealed to the Lord about this, that it would leave me, but he said to me, "My grace is sufficient for you, for power is made perfect in weakness." So, I will boast all the more gladly of my weaknesses, so that the power of Christ may dwell in me. (2 Corinthians 12:8-9)

From September 1969 until his death in April 1970, Pastor Ed Goetz was one of my intern supervisors. During that time Ed—or Dr. Goetz, as I called him–showed me the pastoral ropes. He spoke at length about prayer and devotions. His favorite text was the one quoted above, "My grace is sufficient for you." Early in 1970, Dr. Goetz's cancer recurred. The outlook was bleak, but Dr. Goetz did not change much. He still laughed and enjoyed life. He still loved and cherished time with his wife Dorothy. He still had time to instruct me in the art of living and dying in the faith.

I asked him once, "Don't you ever get sad? Don't you ever get angry?" He replied, "Yes, of course. And I weep sometimes. But God's grace is sufficient for me."

I watched him die slowly over the next few months. God's grace was indeed sufficient. He died filled with anticipation of the resurrection.

Before he became ill, he told me that one of the fruits of a life of prayer is "the ability to see God more easily"-to see God in the morning sun and in the midst of suffering and death. It is being able to see the Christ in others and the Christ in yourself. It is to know that God's grace is sufficient to go with us wherever the journey takes us.

The gift of prayer is to be seized by God's grace and sustained by the presence of the Holy Spirit.

Thanks Dr. Goetz, I haven't forgotten.

f. Train yourself to be godly. For physical training is of some value, but godliness has value for all things, holding promise for both the present life and the life to come. (1 Timothy 4:7b,8).

St. Paul tells us that to be a disciple we need inner training in "godliness." It is not, however, our work that changes us interiorly, it is God's work. We cannot "make ourselves godly!" Only God can do that. After all, it makes sense. We are not godly or holy by nature. We can only become godly or holy if God, the Holy one bestows the gift. St. Paul steadfastly maintains that holiness and righteousness are gifts of God. The spiritual disciplines of prayer, confession, study, fasting, meditation, and service put us on the path to inner transformation. Furthermore, it is essential to remember that the path itself does not lead to this transformation. The spiritual disciplines of prayer, worship, and daily devotions put us in a place where God can work the change in us.

This inner transformation generates love, joy, peace, patience, kindness, hope, etc. It also creates disciples. Regardless of our occupation, God calls us all to be disciples. Discipleship is both an honor and a responsibility. It is an honor to be called by our Creator and Redeemer. It is a responsibility because disciples always represent more than themselves. Disciples represent Jesus. It is also dangerous work, because the work of God's people is so often counter cultural and the world will neither understand it nor respect it.

g. He also said, 'The kingdom of God is as if someone would scatter seed on the ground, and would sleep and rise night and day, and the seed would sprout and grow, he does not know how. The earth produces of itself, first the stalk, then the head, then the full grain in the head. But when the grain is ripe, at once he goes in with his sickle, because the harvest has come.' (Mark 4:26-29) If you want to see goodness in action, visit our sister congregation in El Salvador. One such family has a Father who works three jobs and a mother who is at home with her two children, Maria Jose and Flora. I spoke of them in another chapter. They live in a little barrio called Cabañitas about half an hour from San Salvador. Trust me when I say they are very poor, at least if we use money as a measure. In other ways, this family is wealthy. They know about *agathosyne:* Paul's word for goodness, generosity, and an upright spirit, with a dash of holiness to sweeten the soul.

They live in a tiny little home with barely enough room for them. They live in a neighborhood that is controlled by gangs and is dangerous. You would never know it though from their disposition.

After my visit with them where we shared a meal, the oldest daughter brought out a treasure. It was a stuffed animal. After

I held it and admired it, she motioned that she wanted me to keep it. My first reaction was to decline her kind offer, but I did not. How dare I turn down such a gift of the heart? It gave her such joy to give it. I hugged and kissed her in gratitude for the precious gift and told her I would give it a place of honor in my home. She lit up like a Christmas tree. Just then, the youngest gave me a little rubber animal and jumped into my arms.

If you want to know what goodness is—you need to look no further than this family. If you want to understand what generosity looks like, look no further than these to precious little girls.

I recall an incident from the Gospels. Jesus and the disciples were at the Temple. Wealthy men came by and placed large sums of money in the offering basket. A widow put in one penny. Jesus turned to the disciple and remarked, "She put in the greatest gift. The others gave from their great wealth. She gave from her poverty—everything she had to live on."

h. "Let not your hearts be troubled…I go to prepare a place for you." This announcement is not just some fabricated fanciful wish-dream, but a solemn promise, an edict uttered by a sovereign, and an oath pledged by the Creator of the universe. To those who are dying, these are words of comfort, and consolation. In these treasured words, Jesus reminds those who grieve a loss, that their loved ones are resting on the lap of God in a room especially prepared for them.

When one of our members, Ruby Supcoe, was dying, I told her that God has a room all picked out for her. The bed is made, and the door is open. Anytime she wanted to move in, God would be ready for her. Ruby was not always "with it" those last months, but that day she was. With her drawn face, she gave a big smile and asked, "Really?" "Oh yes," I replied. "Oh yes indeed." With that she closed her eyes and slept in the promise of those words. Jesus speaks to our deepest longings and calms our darkest fears and announces God's gift of eternal life for us all. In the midst of our most personal struggles we may sometimes wonder, "Is faith in God worth it?" This text asserts a bold—yes.

The Father has created a dwelling place for each of us in Heaven. The kingdom for which the disciples clamored was established. In addition, Jesus declares, "If you want to know the heart of the Father, gaze at my heart. They are one and the same."

The world is about death. God is about life. The "*YES*" of our Beloved God counters the "*NO*" of the world. The eternal "Yes" of resurrection demolishes the "No" of the power of death. To be a disciple is to say "Yes" to the Kingdom—"Yes" to life with Christ and "Yes" to faithful discipleship. The Son in whom the Father abides has revealed the truth of who God is. That same truth can reside in us. Cherish it as a mother treasures her child. Teach it as though it were the most important thing in your life.

7

DEVOTIONS ON THE THEME OF FAITHFULNESS

The spiritual disciplines of prayer, confession, study, fasting, meditation, and service put us on the path to inner transformation.

a. The fruit of the Spirit get less and less showy as we go on. Faithfulness means continuing quietly with our given job in the situation where we have been placed; not yielding to the restless desire for change.

It means tending the lamp quietly for God without wondering how much longer you have to do it. It means keeping everything in your charge in good order for love's sake, polishing the silver, scrubbing the glassware even though you know the Master will not be looking round the pantry next weekend. If your life is really part of the apparatus of the Spirit that is the sort of life it must be. You have got to be the sort of cat who can be left alone with the canary; the sort of dog who follows, hungry and thirsty but tail up to the end of the day.

"Faithfulness and Goodness—they are doggy qualities. Fancy that as a Fruit of the Spirit! But then the Spirit is Love, and doggy love is a very good sort of love, humble and selfless and enduring." Evelyn Underhill (1875-1941) *The Fruits of the Spirit.*

b. I really like the word faithful. For me it conjures up many memories. I think of my Dad who would come home worn out only to hear his son ask, "Hey Dad, wanna have a catch?" "Sure, son. Let me get changed." It was not until later I knew how tired he really was.

c. When the Sabbath was over, Mary Magdalene, and Mary the mother of James, and Salome bought spices, so that they might go and anoint him. And very early on the first day of the week, when the sun had risen, they went to the tomb. They had been saying to one another, "Who will roll away the stone for us from the entrance to the tomb?" When they looked up, they saw that the stone, which was very large, had already been rolled back. As they entered the tomb, they saw a young man, dressed in a white robe, sitting on the right side; and they were alarmed. But he said to them, "Do not be alarmed; you are looking for Jesus of Nazareth, who was crucified. He has been raised; he is not here. Look, there is the place they laid him. But go, tell his disciples and Peter that he is going ahead of you to Galilee; there you will see him, just as he told you." So they went out and fled from the tomb, for terror and amazement had seized them; and they said nothing to anyone, for they were afraid. (Mark 16:1-8)

The women who followed Jesus were faithful beyond measure. They followed him to the cross, stayed with him while he was dying, watched him writhe in pain, stood helpless and distraught while life ebbed from him, lowered him from the cross, brought him to the tomb, and now in their last full measure of devotion prepared to anoint him in death.

If you want to know what faithful devotion looks like you don't have to look any further than these very beloved women.

Their loyalty brought unexpected dividends. They were the first followers of Jesus to discover that Jesus was faithful beyond their wildest hopes. They discovered that not even death could bury the promise of Jesus that he would always be with them. Not even the cross could crucify love. No tomb could encase hope.

The resurrection of Jesus was a resurrection of the hopes and dreams of his followers. It was vindication of their faith in the eternal presence of Jesus. In the resurrection, Jesus reasserted the promise; "Lo I am with you always." It is clear that God is faithfully present. We are not alone.

The post-resurrection Christian knows that
death is not an eternal abyss, but a bridge to
a more perfect relationship with God.
The post-resurrection Christian knows concretely
that the presence of God is eternal—unending.
The post-resurrection Christian knows that the promises of Jesus are unconditional. Death does not invalidate the promise of presence, for even in death the promises are true and valid. Jesus is on the other side of death—yet he is alive.

d. Now before the festival of the Passover...Jesus knowing that the Father had given all things into his hands, and that he had come from God and was going to God, got up from the table, took off his outer robe, and tied a towel around himself. Then he poured water into a basin and began to wash the disciples' feet and to wipe them with the towel that was tied around him.

"Therefore, if I, your Lord and Teacher, have washed
your feet, you also ought to wash one another's feet.
For I have set you an example, that you should do
as I have done to you." John 13:3-5 &14-15

There sat the disciples. Their feet caked with mud and dirt
from Jerusalem's roads and fields. No one said anything.
They all must have been thinking the same thing: "Who is
going to wash our feet?" One of the dirtiest jobs in antiquity
was to wash another's feet. It was the job of a servant.
The first to move is Jesus. He got up, poured water into
a basin, and washed the feet of his disciples. It must have
been almost too much for the disciples to bear. In fact, it
was for Peter. He recoiled in distress that the Lord should
wash his feet. We all understand how he must have felt.

As he is lovingly cleans the caked mud from their feet, Jesus
tells the disciples to do this for one another. Jesus calls them
to get their hands dirty with the work of the kingdom.

In our hearts, we want to do something grand,
something important. Jesus calls us to menial work,
servant's work, mundane work, and trivial work.

The spiritual authority of Jesus was not found
in control, manipulation, or power, but in a
towel. "I have set you an example…"

e. When they had finished breakfast, Jesus said to Simon Peter,
"Simon son of John, do you love me more than these?" He
said to him, "Yes, Lord; you know that I love you." Jesus said to
him, "Feed my lambs." A second time he said to him, "Simon
son of John, do you love me?" He said to him, "Yes, Lord; you
know that I love you." Jesus said to him, "Tend my sheep." He
said to him the third time, "Simon son of John, do you love

me?" Peter felt hurt because he said to him the third time, "Do you love me?" And he said to him, "Lord, you know everything; you know that I love you." Jesus said to him, "Feed my sheep." (John 21:15-17)

These are some of the last commands of Jesus before his ascension into Heaven. For that reason, they are obviously important words. Following them is essential to faithful Christian discipleship.

Jesus simply is telling us, "If you want to be a disciple of mine, learn to love each other." He says it three times because we are slow learners. Love is not easy. It is hard, in fact. Earlier in this Gospel Jesus proclaims:

> Love each other as I have loved you.
> WBy this love you have every one will know
> that you are my disciples.

The mark of Christian discipleship is love. We should carry it around like a badge of honor. Our lives of love should be easy to see. After all, the love of Jesus is inscribed in our hearts and written on the lines of our lives.

How can you tend Jesus' sheep today?
What lambs need your love?
To be a faithful disciple is to find your neighbor.

> 1. Hungry sheep in search of pasture
> Lonely sheep in search of home.
> Blessed sheep who love the master.
> Holy sheep to call your own
> Chorus:
> Do you love me?
> Say you love me?
> Do you love me?

Love me true?
If you love me
Really love me.
Feed the sheep
I give to you.
2. Follow me I am your future
Lead my sheep into the light.
Tend my lambs with caring nurture.
Feed my sheep the bread of life. Chorus:

3. On this day we come to worship
We receive a shepherd's call.
Bowing down in adoration.
Serving God through one and all. Chorus:

f. Years ago I came across these principles. I have changed much of it but most of comes from a source I fail to remember. My apologies to the author.

ELEVEN PRINCIPLES OF SPIRITUAL LEADERSHIP

Essence of the Servant-Leader

Discipline
- Is faithful in daily devotions
- Has Capacity to lead and follow
- Has Commitment to loving service
- Has Perseverance
- Loves God by serving others
- Service to others is grounded by faithfulness in prayer

Vision
- A. Is keeper of the vision; vision is the ability to catch a glimpse of the dreams of God.
- B. Encourages foresight as well as insight into what is wrong
- C. Injects hope and optimism into chaos,
- D. Inspires and transmits vision to others while inviting others to share the vision.

Listening
- Listens with the ear of the heart
- Listens to understand not to judge
- Listens often and long

Courage
- Does not shy away from difficult situations
- Is able to face human inertia and opposition
- Has absolute trust in God
- Is able to admit mistakes

Decision
- Is able to make difficult choices
- Can compromise and collaborate
- Takes responsibility for decisions and does not look back
- Listens for the "Voice of the Spirit" through prayer and meditation

Humility
- A. Takes hidden path of sacrificial service– has the attitude of S servant-leader.
- B. Allows others to succeed
- C. Grows through the grace of prayer and humility
- D. Admits frailty and vulnerability
- E. Does not expect others to do what you are not willing to do
- F. Is joyful at another's success

Integrity
- Is open, without guile
- Is sincere and keeps promises
- Is patient with self and others
- Is loyal in service and honest in speech

Humor
- Uses humor to lighten up tension and difficult situations
- Sees things in perspective and can laugh at self
- Has a keen sense of humor combined with sense of God's grace
- Knows the difference between humor and sarcasm

Inspirational Power
- Is a light for others
- Inspires others to service and sacrifice

- Realizes that it is the Spirit that infuses initiative, enterprise
- Translates vision into activity
- Apprehends that it is the Spirit of God that brings success
- Is in constant prayer for the congregation, staff, and leaders

Collaboration

- Partners with the Holy Spirit in building up the community of God
- Shares leadership with others
- Lays aside hidden agendas and hidden motives

Trust

- Trusts God to work in his/her life
- Trusts others
- Trusts the actions of the church council and ministry teams
- Is able to give both responsibility and authority
- Trusts the congregation

8

DEVOTIONS ON THE THEME OF GENTLENESS

Gentleness is not passive.
It has the selflessness to be humble and meek,
and the strength to confront evil without arrogance or pride.

a. As God's chosen ones, holy and beloved, clothe yourselves with compassion, kindness, humility, meekness, and patience. Bear with one another and, if anyone has a complaint against another, forgive each other; just as the Lord has forgiven you, so you also must forgive. Above all, clothe yourselves with love, which binds everything together in perfect harmony. (Colossians 3:12-14)

St. Paul used the Greek word *praotes* for gentleness. Biblical scholar, William Barclay, called *praotes* the most untranslatable word in the New Testament. It overflows with meanings. Plato considered it the "cement of society." Aristotle defined it as the mean between never becoming angry and becoming too angry. On the one hand, it is polite, considerate, courteous, and kind. On the other, it is indignant at the wrongs and sufferings of others. In the Old Testament, gentleness describes our attitude toward God. In the New Testament it is used in the manner that we treat each other.

Gentleness is not passive. It has the selflessness
to be humble and meek, and the strength to
confront evil without arrogance or pride.

b. Now there was a man of the Pharisees, named Nicodemus, a ruler of the Jews. This man came to Jesus by night and said to him, "Rabbi, we know that you are a teacher come from God; for no one can do these signs that you do, unless God is with him." Jesus answered him, "Truly, truly, I say to you, unless one is born anew, he cannot see the kingdom of God." Nicodemus said to him, "How can man be born when he is old? Can he enter a second time into his mother's womb and be born?" (John 3:3-6)

Nicodemus was a "ruler of the Jews," a Pharisee, a leader, a member of the powerful elite of the religious establishment of his day. He came to Jesus apparently in the darkness. He asked a question and received the answer that he "must be born anew". The old translation is "be born again." It is, however, better translated "be born from above." Being born once would seem to be enough. It is a shock in many respects. It is a movement in many respects, none of them easy:

> From the womb of safety to vulnerability
> From the womb of protection to risk
> From the womb of quiet to noise
> From the womb of union to separation
> From the womb of darkness to light

The process is filled with fragility and fear, frequently with pain. Being born the first time is not easy. Jesus tells Nicodemus he must be born another time. Being born a second time requires us to look at the world differently and leave behind some long-held beliefs and concepts about the world. Being born "from above" requires us to see the world through the eyes of God who lives "above."

> **c.** I am not writing this to make you ashamed, but to admonish you as my beloved children. For though you might have ten thousand guardians in Christ, you do not have many fathers. Indeed, in Christ Jesus I became your father through the gospel. I appeal to you, then, be imitators of me. For this reason I sent you Timothy, who is my beloved and faithful child in the Lord, to remind you of my ways in Christ Jesus, as I teach them everywhere in every church. But some of you, thinking that I am not coming to you, have become arrogant. But I will come to you soon, if the Lord wills, and I will find out not the talk of these arrogant people but their power. For the kingdom of God depends not on talk but on power. What would you prefer? *Am I to come to you with a stick, or with love in a spirit of gentleness?* (1 Corinthians 4:14-21)

The world knows about sticks. It responds that way to those it dislikes. "Speak softly but carry a big stick," admonished Teddy Roosevelt. We understand "big stick" ideology. St. Paul contrasts the big stick with gentleness. But, don't mistake gentleness with weakness. Martin Luther King Jr. stood for justice, but did it with the gentleness of a saint. His non-violent response to those with clubs and fire hoses inspired a nation, and brought about a change in America's Jim Crow laws. In a letter written from a Birmingham jail, King wrote:

Oppressed people cannot remain oppressed forever. The yearning for freedom eventually manifests itself. I have tried to say that this normal and healthy discontent can be channeled into the creative outlet of nonviolent direct action. And now this approach is being termed extremist. But though I was initially disappointed at being categorized as an extremist, as I continued to think about the matter I gradually gained a measure of satisfaction from the label. Was not Jesus an extremist for love: "Love your enemies, bless them that curse you, do good to them that hate you, and pray for them which despitefully use you, and persecute you." Was not Amos an extremist for justice: "Let justice roll down like waters and righteousness like an ever flowing stream." Was not Paul an extremist for the Christian gospel: "I bear in my body the marks of the Lord Jesus." Was not Martin Luther an extremist: "Here I stand; I cannot do otherwise, so help me God." And John Bunyan: "I will stay in jail to the end of my days before I make a butchery of my conscience." And Abraham Lincoln: "This nation cannot survive half slave and half free." And Thomas Jefferson: "We hold these truths to be self evident, that all men are created equal . . ." So the question is not whether we will be extremists, but what kind of extremists we will be. Will we be extremists for hate or for love? Will we be extremists for the preservation of injustice or for the extension of justice? In that dramatic scene on Calvary's hill three men were crucified. We must never forget that all three were crucified for the same crime–the crime of extremism. Two were extremists for immorality, and thus fell below their environment. The other, Jesus Christ, was an extremist for love, truth and goodness, and thereby rose above his environment. Perhaps the South, the nation and the world are in dire need of creative extremists.

d. Rejoice greatly, O Daughter of Zion! Shout, Daughter of Jerusalem! See, your king comes to you, righteous

and having salvation, gentle and riding on a donkey,
on a colt, the foal of a donkey. (Zechariah 9:9)

A shoot shall come out from the stock of Jesse,
    and a branch shall grow out of his roots.
The spirit of the Lord shall rest on him,
    the spirit of wisdom and understanding,
    the spirit of counsel and might,
    the spirit of knowledge and the fear of the Lord.
His delight shall be in the fear of the Lord.

He shall not judge by what his eyes see,
    or decide by what his ears hear;
but with righteousness he shall judge the poor,
    and decide with equity for the meek of the earth;
he shall strike the earth with the rod of his mouth,
    and with the breath of his lips he shall kill the wicked.
    Righteousness shall be the belt around his waist,
    and faithfulness the belt around his loins.
The wolf shall live with the lamb,
    the leopard shall lie down with the kid,
the calf and the lion and the fatling together,
    and a little child shall lead them.
The cow and the bear shall graze,
    their young shall lie down together;
    and the lion shall eat straw like the ox.
The nursing child shall play over the hole of the asp,
    and the weaned child shall put its hand on the adder's den.
They will not hurt or destroy
    on all my holy mountain;
for the earth will be full of the knowledge of the Lord
    as the waters cover the sea. (Isaiah 11:1-9)

This is the great text of the "peaceable kingdom."
Christians think of Jesus when we read this text. It is

the kingdom of creation, and it is the kingdom that
will be established when Christ comes again. Dietrich
Bonhoeffer, who was executed for his stance against
Hitler, wrote in his seminal work, *The Cost of Discipleship:*

> *"Blessed are the peacemakers: for they shall be called the children of
> God."* The followers of Jesus have been called to peace.
> When he called them they found their peace, for he is
> their peace. But now they are told that they must not only
> *have* peace but *make* it. And to that end they renounce
> all violence and tumult. In the cause of Christ nothing
> is to be gained by such methods. His kingdom is one of
> peace, and the mutual greeting of his flock is a greeting
> of peace. His disciples keep the peace by choosing to
> endure suffering themselves rather than inflict it on
> others. They maintain fellowship where others would
> break it off. They renounce all self-assertion, and quietly
> suffer in the face of hatred and wrong. In so doing they
> overcome evil with good, and establish the peace of God
> in the midst of a world of war and hate. But nowhere
> will that peace be more manifest than where they meet
> the wicked in peace and are ready to suffer at their hands.
> The peacemakers will carry the cross with their Lord,
> for it was on the cross that peace was made. Now that
> they are partners in Christ's work of reconciliation, they
> are called the sons of God, as he is the Son of God.

e. Every so often, I get to know people whose lives are a
mess. By a mess, I mean that the problems they have are so
complex, so integrated with another's, that it is like a huge
ball of string that has been knotted repeatedly so that no
matter where you start to untangle it, you will be stuck!
Sometimes these messes are financial. Sometimes they have to
do with work, sometimes with faith. Most often, they have to
do with messed-up relationships. Many times all of these things

build upon each other until you are in the tangled in a mess with seemingly no way out. In the fourth chapter of John, Jesus met a woman from Samaria whose life was a mess. She seems to have made some rather poor decisions about her love life–to get through five husbands takes some doing–whereas divorce was allowed for Jews and Samaritans, that number of divorces, would, then as now, give rise to some comments. She was also living with someone to whom she was not married - again very unusual in that age. His gentleness toward her is truly inspiring. Jesus did not arrogantly reprimand her but drew her into his heart. Jesus managed to see past the mess of the woman's chaos and see her inner thirst for the Water of Life.

Churches often encounter people whose lives are in disarray. We need to meet them tenderly, love them gently, teach them fully, and comfort them completely.

9

DEVOTIONS ON THE THEME OF SELF CONTROL

Into your hands O Lord, I commend my spirit.

a. Self-control is really Spirit-control. As Jesus began his walk
to the cross he had to answer two questions, "Am I to follow
my own wants and desires? Or will I be led by the spirit?"
The questions are the same for each of us.
These devotions follow Jesus as the Spirit leads him
to the cross and ultimately the empty tomb.

b. "Those who do not speak for the Jews have no right to sing
hymns." Pastor Dietrich Bonhoeffer in Nazi Germany, 1943

When I was a seminarian, a saintly old professor, who had
been in a Nazi concentration camp, told me, "If you have not
prayed for the suffering people of the world you will never
understand the suffering of Jesus." Initially, his words had
little impact. Nevertheless, like so many maxims, the phrase

stayed with me. My life, like so many in the United States, has known little suffering. One-third of the world goes to bed hungry. Countless millions live in shacks or sleep on the world's streets. There are Christians who suffer persecution for the faith and lay their lives on the line every day. We who have both the means and voice need to speak for them. To profess Christ as Lord is to stand for justice among all peoples. We can be the voices of those whose voice is never heard.

c. Then Pilate took Jesus and had him flogged. And the soldiers wove a crown of thorns and put it on his head, and they dressed him in a purple robe. They kept coming up to him, saying, "Hail, King of the Jews!" and striking him on the face. Pilate went out again and said to them, "Look, I am bringing him out to you to let you know that I find no case against him." So Jesus came out, wearing the crown of thorns and the purple robe. Pilate said to them, "Here is the man!" When the chief priests and the police saw him, they shouted, "Crucify him! Crucify him!" Pilate said to them, "Take him yourselves and crucify him; I find no case against him." The Jews answered him, "We have a law, and according to that law he ought to die because he has claimed to be the Son of God."

Now when Pilate heard this, he was more afraid than ever. He entered his headquarters again and asked Jesus, "Where are you from?" But Jesus gave him no answer. Pilate therefore said to him, "Do you refuse to speak to me? Do you not know that I have power to release you, and power to crucify you?" Jesus answered him, "You would have no power over me unless it had been given you from above; therefore the one who handed me over to you is guilty of a greater sin." From then on Pilate tried to release him, but the Jews cried out, "If you release this man, you are no friend of the emperor. Everyone who claims to be a king sets himself against the emperor." (John 19:1-12)

How are we to understand the actions of Jesus in front of Pilate? Pilate never pronounced Jesus guilty of anything, yet he had him flogged. He undoubtedly thought Jesus would be compliant and beg for mercy. Pilate's wife had a dream about Jesus and in essence said, "Watch out for this Jesus." Pilate tried to release Jesus but acquiesced to the wishes of the crowd.

In the midst of all this intrigue, Jesus and Pilate have this fascinating discussion about power and authority. Pilate says, "I have the power to release you." Evidently, he did not. He wanted to pardon Jesus, but was fearful to go against the wishes of the mob. Jesus on the other hand was true to himself. He had told the disciples, "Greater love has no one than to lay down one's life for friends." He was prepared to do just that. His interior strength, courage, self-control, and calling helped him live out his creed. Jesus had the power over his own destiny, not Pilate.

It takes a special kind of love to die for someone else.
It takes a special kind of courage to stand firm
against the greatest empire on earth.
It takes a special kind of faith to entrust
yourself into God's hands.
It takes a special kind of man to go willingly to the cross.
It takes a special kind of God to suffer for you.
It takes a special kind of power to bring life
out of death and light out of darkness.
It takes Jesus.

d. He came out and went, as was his custom, to the Mount of Olives; and the disciples followed him. When

he reached the place, he said to them, "Pray that you
may not come into the time of trial." Then he withdrew
from them about a stone's throw, knelt down, and prayed,
"Father, if you are willing, remove this cup from me;
yet, not my will but yours be done." Then an angel from
Heaven appeared to him and gave him strength. In his
anguish, he prayed more earnestly, and his sweat became
like great drops of blood falling down on the ground.
When he got up from prayer, he came to the
disciples and found them sleeping because of grief,
and he said to them, "Why are you sleeping?
Get up and pray that you may not come into the time of trial."
(Luke 23:39-46)

We all have had our own Gethsemane and Mount of Olives
moments. We understand fear. We are not unfamiliar with
dread. We all travel outside of our comfort zone from time
to time. Many times, cherished friends will accompany us,
but they may not have the staying power to hold the cup
while we drink. They too might fall asleep in the garden.
We may be asked to go it alone. I saw a movie once entitled,
"*Though none will go with me, yet will I go.*" None went with
Jesus, but he conquered his fear and went anyway.

Lord, when I am overwhelmed and throw myself face down
on the ground in a prayer that sweats drops of blood, be
there, O my beloved, to raise me up into your arms of grace.

You, O Lord are ever before me and ever behind
me. You encircle me with your divine presence.
When my hands are too weak to grasp the cup, steady them.
When the cup is too bitter to drink, give me strength.
Furthermore, if I fall, hold me in your sturdy and steady arms.
And if I stumble on the journey, carry me. Amen.

e. Simon Peter and another disciple followed Jesus. Since that disciple was known to the high priest, he went with Jesus into the courtyard of the high priest, but Peter was standing outside at the gate. So the other disciple, who was known to the high priest, went out, spoke to the woman who guarded the gate, and brought Peter in. The woman said to Peter, "You are not also one of this man's disciples, are you?" He said, "I am not." Now the slaves and the police had made a charcoal fire because it was cold, and they were standing round it and warming themselves. Peter also was standing with them and warming himself. They asked him, "You are not also one of his disciples, are you?" He denied it and said, "I am not." One of the slaves of the high priest, a relative of the man whose ear Peter had cut off, asked, "Did I not see you in the garden with him?" Again Peter denied it, and at that moment the cock crowed. (John 18:15-18 & 25-27)

I can remember when I was a young lad, hearing stories of brave souls who died simply because they were Christian. In 1960 and 1961, when I lived in Berlin, Germany, my family met men and women from the East Zone, who were literally persecuted for their faith. I would lie awake in bed at night and fantasize about being valiant and obedient in the face of those who wanted me to deny my faith in Jesus. In my youthful imagination, I was always courageous and bold. The truth is we never really can predict how we will react in those circumstances until we face them.

The members of our sister congregation in Krajne, Slovakia understood persecution under the communists. Pastor Novemetsky was beaten when, as a soldier, he decided to attend seminary and become a pastor. Other members risked everything to attend Sunday morning worship.

The decision to live our faith confronts us every day: When someone tells a racist joke and our tongue stays silent. When we know what we should do yet fail to do it. When we fail to love and forgive another who has wronged us. When our employer asks us to do something unethical and we remain silent.

There are literally dozens of times each day when we have the occasion to live out our faith. It is, however, risky business. Someone may think we are "religious fanatics" or "holier than thou." Sometimes we are brave and obedient and take the risk and sometimes we cringe and hide. All of us understand Peter. We all feel for him as the cock crows, for all of us have heard it. We all know that we are Peter fleshed out in different skin.

> **f.** Luke's account of the Crucifixion gives us the supreme glimpse into the heart of Jesus. The three sentences that Jesus speaks from the cross are unique in Luke. Jesus is not concerned about himself. He is concerned about others. He prays for those who nailed him on the cross. "Father forgive them for they know not what they do." He comforts one of the thieves hanging next to him. "Today, you will be with me in paradise." Finally at the time of his death he speaks those heartfelt words, "Father, into your hands I commend my spirit." Christians have ended their day with those words for two thousand years. In the service of Compline (evening prayer), we chant those same words, "Into your hands O Lord, I commend my spirit." Sometimes people will ask me, "How can I best help my friend [brother, daughter, etc.] come to faith?" I tell them to do what Jesus did. Commend them into the hands of our Father. There is no better place to put them.

MAY YOU REST IN GOD'S EMBRACE

1. I pray you find peace when all around you is swirling.
   A peace the world cannot give when
   winds about you are whirling.
   When all is said done may you rest in Gods embrace.
   When all is said done I wish you peace.

2. I wish you comfort when darkness overcomes you.
   I pray there are arms to hold and comfort you.
   When all is said done may you rest in God's embrace.
   When all is said done I wish you peace.

3. The Lord bless you and keep you; the Lord
   make His face shine upon you.
   The Lord look kindly on you and grant you peace.
   When all is said done may you rest in God's embrace
   When all is said done I wish you peace.

4. I pray you find peace. I pray you find hope.
   I pray you find strength in our risen Lord.
   When all is said done may you rest in God's embrace.
   When all is said done I wish you peace.

Made in the USA
San Bernardino, CA
17 April 2014